Conversations about Painting with Rudolf Steiner

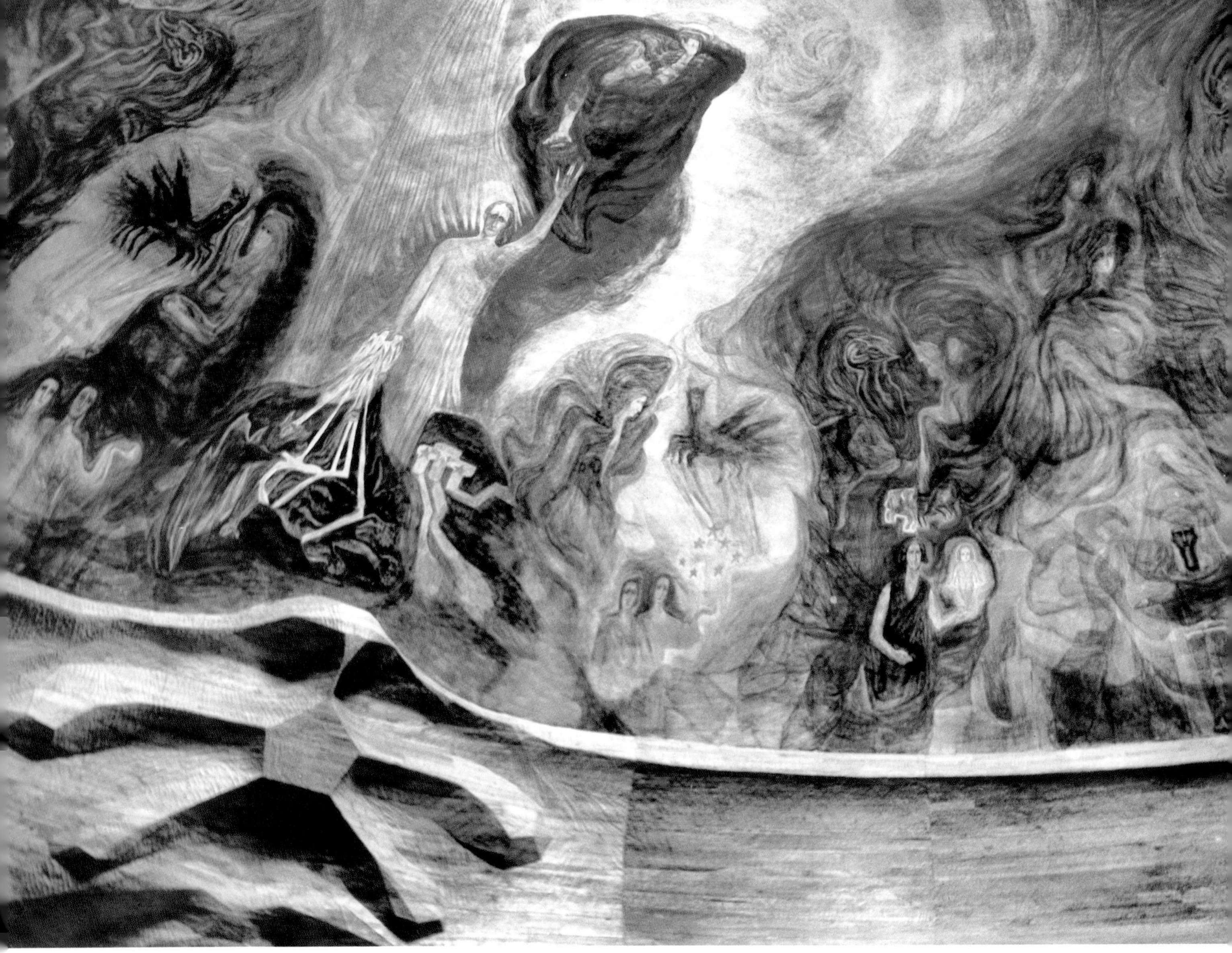

Partial view of the painting in the small cupola of the first Goetheanum (toward the southeast).
Dokumentation am Goetheanum-Bildarchiv.

Conversations about Painting with Rudolf Steiner

Recollections of Five Pioneers of the New Art Impulse

Maria Strakosch-Giesler

Hilde Boos-Hamburger

Henni Geck

Margarita Voloschin

Assya Turgenieff

Translated and Edited
by Peter Stebbing

STEINERBOOKS
2008

Published by SteinerBooks
610 Main Street, Great Barrington, MA 01230

ISBN: 978-0-088010-590-3
Library of Congress Cataloging-in-Publication Data
Conversations about painting with Rudolf Steiner : recollections of five pioneers of the new art impulse / Maria Strakosch-Giesler ... [et al.] ; translated and edited by Peter Stebbing.

p. cm.

Includes bibliographical references.

ISBN 978-0-88010-590-3

1. Steiner, Rudolf, 1861-1925. 2. Anthroposophy. 3. Art. 4. Architecture. 5. Painting. I. Steiner, Rudolf, 1861-1925. II. Strakosch-Giesler, Maria, 1877-1970. III. Stebbing, Peter.

BP595.S895C66 2008

299'.935--dc22

2008013923

Quotations from written works and lectures of Rudolf Steiner are printed by permission of the Rudolf Steiner Nachlassverwaltung, CH-4143 Dornach.

Black-and-white photographs and color reproductions, courtesy of the Goetheanum Archive (Dornach), the Rudolf Steiner Archive (Dornach), and the Verlag am Goetheanum.

Biographical texts, courtesy of the individual authors.

Cover illustration:
The interior model of the first Goetheanum by Rudolf Steiner. 1913.
Scale 1:20. (Detail showing the large cupola). Goetheanum Art Collection (Dornach).
Copyright holder: Rudolf Steiner Nachlassverwaltung (Dornach). Restored 2005.

CONTENTS

ILLUSTRATIONS

FOREWORD

With the construction of the first Goetheanum between 1913 and 1920, a completely new style in architecture, sculpture and painting was inaugurated by Rudolf Steiner. Here the new painting impulse became fully apparent for the first time when Rudolf Steiner himself painted the southern half of the small cupola at the request of the team of painters working with him. This unique and comprehensive work of art was destroyed by arson only ten years after being built.

The primary aim of this book is to further the understanding and appreciation of Rudolf Steiner's painting impulse. This was not given to the world in any abstract form, but arose as the result of actual questions and requests put to Rudolf Steiner by a diverse group of artists in the early part of the twentieth century.

Each of the five artists included here contributes a vital aspect, and can be counted among the most important ones to have worked with Rudolf Steiner. But there were others no less significant in their individual accomplishments, such as Baron Arild Rosenkrantz and Hermann Linde, for instance, both of whom played a leading role in the painting of the cupolas of the first Goetheanum. Yet they do not add in the same way to what may be called our practical understanding of the full scope of Rudolf Steiner's painting impulse.

Such an understanding is best achieved by looking at how these five pioneer artists of the anthroposophical movement especially reflect Rudolf Steiner's original intention. Taken together, they convey an impression of the new painting impulse in its true grandeur. In this sense, the value of this book may be said to far exceed its importance as historical documentation.

Without adequate insight into what was originally intended, it hardly seems possible that later contributions to the elaboration and further development of Rudolf Steiner's art impulse will receive their due. One aim of this book is therefore to lay the foundation for future comprehension of this new direction in art.

Of the five main artists who recount their experiences here, Maria Strakosch-Giesler was most of all associated with leading contemporary personalities in the art world and gained the most acceptance and outward success. Yet she probably faced the greatest struggle in terms of fully "reminting" her natural capacities to serve the new aspirations.

The title of this volume, *Conversations about Painting with Rudolf Steiner,* derives from Hilde Boos-Hamburger's little book called, in German, *Aus Gesprächen mit Rudolf Steiner über*

Malerei. It sheds a significant and unique light from many angles on Rudolf Steiner's new art of painting and is included here *in toto.* She does not approach her subject as an academic. Rather, as with Maria Strakosch-Giesler, her style has the characteristic immediacy and freshness of an eyewitness account. Hilde Boos-Hamburger mainly describes experiences, some of them ground-breaking, in which she was herself directly or indirectly involved. It was her lifelong aim to communicate essential aspects of the new way of painting that she had come to recognize. In the translator's opinion, she succeeds admirably in this. Yet there is a curious omission – in spite of her inclusive approach – in that she does not refer here even once to the all-important twenty-three training sketches for painters given by Rudolf Steiner to Henni Geck.

The translator first conceived the idea of transposing Hilde Boos-Hamburger's recollections into English some thirty years ago. In following through so late on his intention, he trusts that this book as a whole will meet an objective need and make up for the delay.

Perhaps partly because she put so little in writing, Henni Geck remains hardly known fifty years after her death. Yet she is undoubtedly the indispensable central figure in the inauguration and initial development of Rudolf Steiner's painting impulse. Her dedication and self-effacement may well have been crucial in eliciting the wealth of sketch-motifs we now have in response to her original question to Rudolf Steiner. Beyond the brief, yet substantial, statement of Henni Geck given in these pages, she wrote almost nothing down. We therefore add reports (with some unavoidable repetition) of several of her former students.

In a vivid description of her experiences in carving and then painting in the first Goetheanum, Margarita Voloschin (nee Sabaschnikova) makes clear the radical transformation required of the pioneering artists around Rudolf Steiner. The underlying principles of the new art (all too easily forgotten today) come out in her frequently lapidary, soaring prose. Her autobiography, *Die Grüne Schlange* (The Green Snake), should especially be mentioned: originally published in 1954, this book documents the extraordinary first half of her life and belongs among the classic works of literature. A translation into English is long overdue. (The title comes from Goethe's fairy tale "The Green Snake and the Beautiful Lily.")

Though not a painter, Assya Turgenieff worked in the related new art of light-and-dark drawing, and was responsible for carrying out, by means of a specially developed technique, the engraving of the colored glass windows of the second Goetheanum. A remarkable correspondence emerges between the artistic method she describes for the art of "light and dark" and that of painting.

Art need not remain remote from everyday life, as Daniel van Bemmelen's report of a drawing class with Rudolf Steiner brings out. It can be seen how the new art impulse has the potential to directly enliven education, and ultimately, through applied art, to transform the objects that surround us.

Peter Stebbing
Arlesheim, Switzerland
January 2008

The motif, which until now has been the starting point in painting, must become the result in the painting of the future!

– Rudolf Steiner

MARIA STRAKOSCH-GIESLER

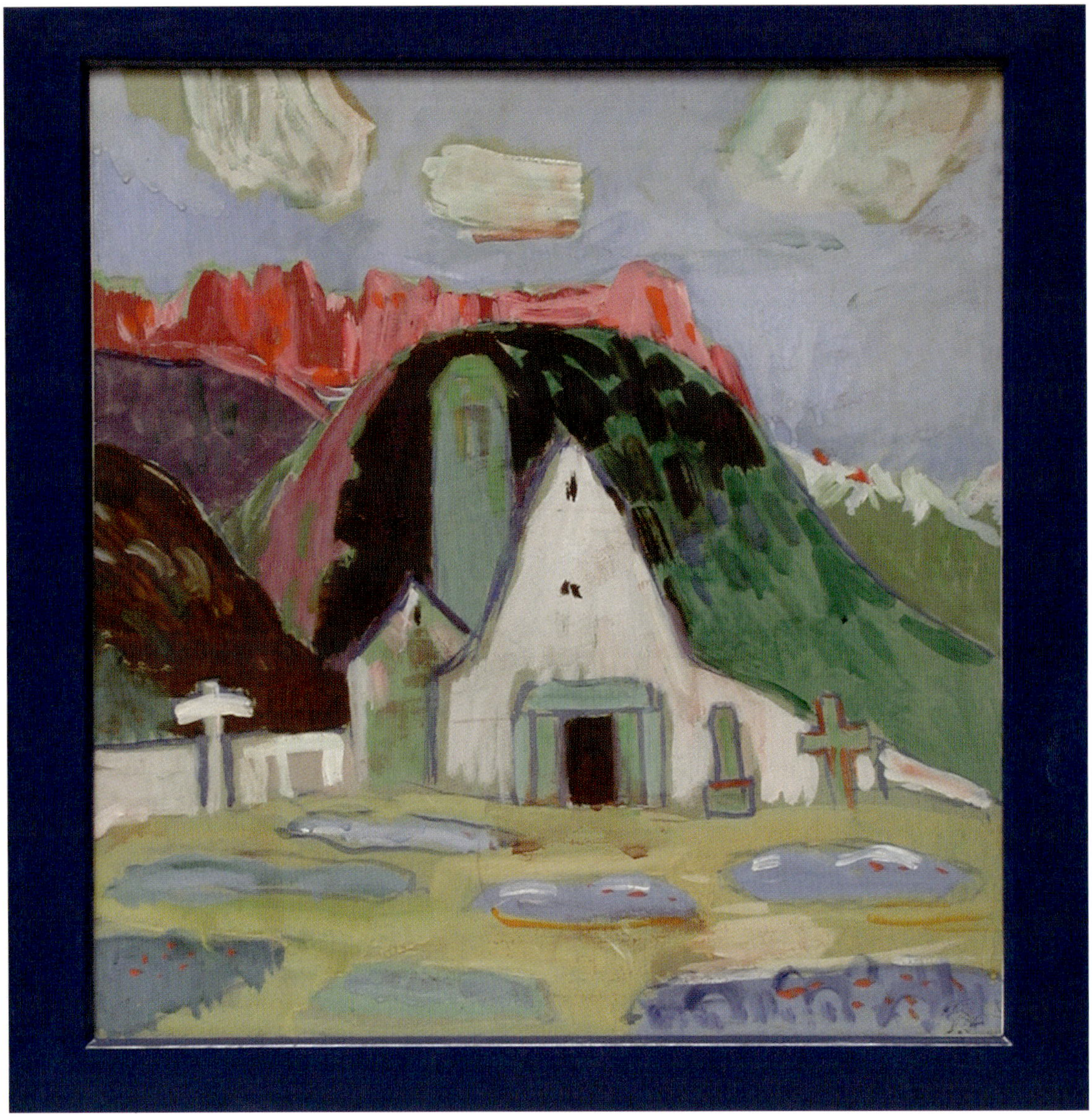

Village Church above Meran by Maria Strakosch-Giesler 1909.
Tempera on pasteboard. 57.5 x 53.5 cm. Goetheanum Art Collection (Dornach).

A variation of the "impression" referred to by the author on p. 6.

INDICATIONS GIVEN BY RUDOLF STEINER TO A PAINTER

Maria Strakosch-Giesler

On the occasion of the Theosophical Congress in Budapest in 1909, I was able to show Rudolf Steiner my paintings for the first time. Before that I had been a pupil of Kandinsky and had already searched to the best of my ability for a means of expression, a language arising out of color – but in vain.

In April 1908 we[1] first met Rudolf Steiner in Berlin, after a lecture he gave in the *Architektenhaus*. A few days later I received meditations from him concerning colors, which gave me the possibility of experiencing a completely different aspect of painting than I had known hitherto. Previously I had not progressed beyond studying nature. At that time Impressionism was prevalent, and Kandinsky himself struggled for a way to surpass it. I still remember quite well, how impossible it seemed to me, to get beyond what the senses perceive.

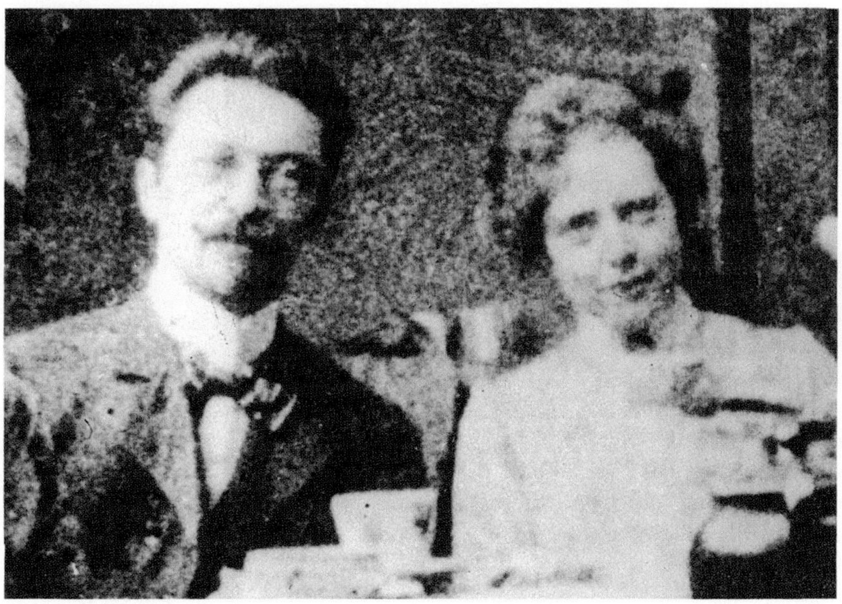

Wassily Kandinsky and Maria Giesler (1902/03)

[1] I.e., the author and her husband, Alexander Strakosch (1879–1958).

However, I diligently practiced at that time the meditations given to me, without having any notion as to what would come of it.

In the spring of 1909, I had been in southern Tirol in a small village with a church situated high above Meran. The cemetery on the mountainside surrounded the picturesque little white church. The snowy peaks towered up into the silent blue-gray of the sky. I sat toward evening and painted the church, which stood amid its white crosses. I could hear the muffled gurgling of a nearby spring. A shiver ran down my spine. I had to lay my study to one side, since the picture had transformed itself completely in front of my eyes: the previously white church loomed a deathly green into the sky; the tower-window had acquired an eerie expression, and a cold, mysterious violet looked out from it. The sky had changed to a dark blood-red, into which the snow-peaks now towered in a pallid bone-white tone. Behind and above the cemetery there lay a strange wan-violet and yellow-ochre "something."

Later I painted the impression at home and now knew how colors can begin to take on a life of their own.

In Budapest I was thus able to show these and many other studies to Dr. Steiner. He encouraged me to continue painting and made me aware that I should now pay attention to the shapes of the mountains and how they had certain characteristic forms.

Later, when we were with him in Veldes in Krain, he said of the Schlossberg, a mountain on Lake Veldes: "Have you noticed that it calls forth the imagination of a lion?"

I now returned from Budapest to Trieste, where we lived at that time. The whole world now had a different appearance; colors wanted to say meaningful things.

I liked best of all to observe the twilight. When shadows already covered the ground, the colors acquired an eerie life. Reflections from the lights on the shore darted on the waves and gave the play of colors the semblance of will-o'-the-wisps. If one's glance passed over the houses with their grotesquely-shaped chimneys or over the arched contours of the mountains to the sky above, little shining golden-yellow clouds swam there like blessed spirits, amid the most peaceful cyan-blue.

All this splendor I only painted at home, as a composition. What emerged was so completely different from the prevailing Impressionism, that no one could make anything of these paintings. They were tempera pictures in quite strong colors.

I did feel myself somewhat like a godforsaken sinner for painting like that.

It then turned out that I was able to travel to Munich in the year 1910 for the performance of the Mystery Plays and the lecture cycle. I took a bundle of paintings with me and was able to show these to Dr. Steiner and *Fräulein* von Sivers (*Frau* Dr. Steiner). Anxiously I unpacked them. *Fräulein* von Sivers said: "Those are fairy tales!" *Herr* Dr. Steiner said, in response to my question as to how one could properly integrate the form of the human being into a landscape: "Start from the plant kingdom and tell yourself: plants are light. Include water and clouds in this kingdom. As regards the mineral kingdom, tell yourself: it has remained behind the light in evolution; and as regards the animal kingdom as well as the human kingdom, tell yourself: they have hurried ahead of the light. And in this way you can let them flit through the landscape."

In the year 1911 it happened that *Herr* Dr. Steiner went for a time to Portorose in the vicinity of Trieste. During this time in which we were able to see Dr. Steiner frequently, the sea with its shoreline became for me ever more splendid and the colors appeared more and more as though imbued with being. Something elemental came to life in them.

I attempted to paint it, and when I showed these attempts to Dr. Steiner, he understood what I stammeringly intended there. From the many pieces of work he selected seven pictures and said: "These we shall show to the theosophists in Munich." This then actually took place at the time of the 1911 lecture cycle in Munich. Dr. Steiner himself determined how the pictures were to be framed, indicating a somewhat dark-blue frame, quite wide, raised toward the outside and becoming flatter toward the picture inside. He said the color of the frame would always have to repeat a color in the picture.

I was astonished to see how the pictures now looked, how harmoniously the strong colors, placed next to each other without many in-between tones, were held together by means of the blue.

Then Dr. Steiner had a golden-yellow burlap stretched over the wall and the pictures hung in a particular sequence. One picture was hung quite high up in the middle of the wall, with three pictures to the left inclining in stages toward the middle one, and the remaining three on the other side inclining in stages down again from the middle.

This arrangement rather surprised me; but then all at once I understood something. And Rudolf Steiner then told me that in painting out of the color it can be a matter of a series of pictures, and that I should try painting the same motif out of the color seven times.

Thus I now stood once again before a great riddle.

Rudolf Steiner held a matinee lecture on those seven pictures, in which he referred for the first time to the necessity of using another medium than the commercially available tube-colors.

From then on I made many technical experiments: woodcuts, wood-engravings, etc., until the plant colors were developed and brought out.

Gradually my attempts at painting a series of pictures took on more definite form. The colors of the rainbow, as something capable of metamorphosing, acquired life for me. One day I grasped it!

A motif transforms its shape, according to whether it appears in black, rose-red, blue, green, yellow, red, or sun-white.

I stood as though before a tremendous process at the end of which, as the completion of a long path, the seven Apocalyptic Seals shone forth. I worked on a series of seven small woodcuts in the form of landscapes with human figures, and then on seven wood-engravings with a stronger figurative emphasis. They were only small motifs that my soul could apprehend, and yet I experienced incredible things in doing them – death and resurrection, extending almost to the physical.

When the wood-engravings were finished after a length of time, I was able to show them to Dr. Steiner. In a kindly manner, he said: "With these pieces of work one can perhaps penetrate 2 cm (.8 inches) below the surface. – Take a look at my Mystery Dramas, I have written them in such a way that one can never get to the bottom. You must also try to work like that, so that one doesn't so soon get to the bottom of it."

Later, when I once became very despondent as a result of difficult circumstances, he said: "One does not need to lose heart, if one has done work like that." And to this day this kind word has given me courage.

In 1918 *Herr* Dr. Steiner came to Vienna and held, at the request of some friends, a lecture to which mainly Viennese artists were invited, on the theme: "The Sensible-Supersensible –Spiritual Knowledge and Artistic Creation" (in GA 272).

At that time it was possible for me to show Rudolf Steiner some sketches for larger pictures. They arose from a process of coming in touch with the world of colors, deepened by occupation with the Mystery Dramas. The basis was especially the Egyptian scene (fourth Mystery Drama), in which the representatives of the several elements speak. What is contained in the words of this scene can bring powerfully before the soul the heavy weight of earth, the lightness of air, the sacrificial strength of fire, and the awakening cosmic sounding of water. – In this way, what had been dully felt as the life of the elements in color was brought to clarity: earth, air, fire, water worked together. In the sketch concerned with the element of fire I had shown fire as red. Dr. Steiner said: "A flame cannot be painted. Make the red flatter (more two-dimensional) and let it take on forms." As far as I remember, he also said on this occasion: "Blue is the form-giving element; with red one cannot give form. If one attempts it and lays the red on in superimposed layers, then it is as though one had painted veins."

As a result of the Mystery Drama performances, it came about that some of us were permitted to help in one way or another with the sets. The world of color was then sometimes wonderfully revealed to us. The costumes in particular made a deep impression on me, when their colors and forms appeared in the lighting indicated by Rudolf Steiner, with its harmonizing and expressive qualities.

Later on, we were led further into the activity of color with the lectures "Ways to a New Style in Architecture," which were held in the Carpentry Workshop as preparation for the work on the Goetheanum building. *Frau* Dr. Steiner later brought these lectures out in a book. How amazed we were by the studies on large plywood panels already carried out by a number of artists, based on sketches by Dr. Steiner, as preparatory work for painting the two cupolas of the Goetheanum. The painting was done from paint-dishes using plant colors on a specially prepared ground. The colors that emerged from this seemed miraculous to us. A painter told me that Dr. Steiner had said to him, in painting he should let the colors as though weave themselves together in the light.

I only saw these preparations; then I had to leave Dornach and only came back there in 1920 when the Goetheanum was opened with a color- and light-flooded eurythmy performance of the "Twelve Moods." Above the stage arched the cupola painted by Rudolf Steiner himself. Again and again I was able to immerse myself in these figures that formed themselves out of the colors. Dr. Steiner once said to me, when I showed him a series of seven pictures I had painted: "Now paint that all in one picture." I had not managed to do it. But now I saw it here in front of me in the paintings of the small cupola: Below lay Ahriman, in black, gray-brown and dark violet tones. Above him, fettering him in rays of light, stood the Christ figure in sun-white radiance. On each side were two angels, one blue and one yellow-orange. Red flamed forth from his heart and his left hand pointed to the red of Lucifer, who was enclosed by a most beautiful bluish-green tone above and seemed to incline toward the moon.

At that time, in repeatedly contemplating this cupola painting, a great feeling of peace came over me. As long as this painting is there for us to see, I thought, with its healing effect, everything would have to turn again and again toward the good and noble. And now it has been destroyed by fire! And we can only carry it in our hearts, knowing that the way the spiritual world works into our earthly world had been there for us to see with physical eyes.

Often as I sat absorbed in front of the painting of the small cupola, people asked that I point out to them how to enter into it more fully. The thought occurred to me, that I could best do so, if I were able to show such questioners how to paint. Later I asked Dr. Steiner whether he could show me something, as he had done with eurythmy, by which one could introduce others to painting. He said: "Paint a self-portrait, the whole figure, and make everything you see dark, for example, hands, arms, feet, legs; and everything that you do not see, you can leave white. What you barely see, you can make yellow; for example, the tip of your nose. What you can see still more of, you can make green, etc. But you must do it twenty times. By this means you can come to the consciousness preceding birth."[2]

Leaving everything else aside, and as though making a new beginning, I went to work on this task – so new and unique did this indication appear to me. Peculiar figures emerged. While working, I felt a definite restorative effect. A quite new relationship to the body entered in. And yet I was very uncertain as to whether I had understood Dr. Steiner correctly. However, when I showed him the work I had done, he told me new things, leading further on the basis of the previous attempts, namely, how I should now also include the background to the figures.

Since then I have made many studies on the basis of this indication, as well as other studies.

If one looks back into the cultures of the past, it becomes ever clearer that only in achieving a new artistic conception of the human form can we come to a new way of painting today. In occupying myself with the human form as Dr. Steiner had indicated with these few words, something arose for me that I can only describe as like "standing with one's own self within the color."

In the background, the forces can become effective by means of color that form the human being. In the limbs below are the dark colors belonging to the earth's depths, above in connection with the head are the light, floating ones. They strive from above downwards and from below upwards; darkness from below, light from above. – The actual colored world lives, however, in the rhythmic system, and transforms itself in gradations as in the rainbow, surging from light to dark and from dark to light.

---

[2] Striking to anyone familiar with Rudolf Steiner's pastel sketch entitled *The Threefold Human Being* is the correspondence between this sketch-motif (made on June 12, 1923) and the exercise given here by Rudolf Steiner to Maria Strakosch-Giesler in 1921. – See the reproduction of Rudolf Steiner's sketch on p. 115. (*Transl.*).

The one who disclosed these sacred worlds to us and who conjured forth an archetype of painting before us in the small cupola, which should have been for the salvation and consolation of past and future generations, his hand now rests.

Yet in our souls what we saw there in the cupola must ever and again rise from the ashes: Christ the victorious Helper.

Translated from *Die erlöste Sphinx* (The Sphinx Redeemed) by Maria Strakosch-Giesler. Novalis-Verlag, Freiburg im Breisgau 1955.

A COLOR MEDITATION GIVEN BY RUDOLF STEINER

(1)
In der *Finsternis* finde ich Gottes-Sein
2
Im *Rosenrot* fühl ich des Lebens Quell
3
Im *Ätherblau* ruht des Geistes Sehnsucht
4
Im *Lebensgrün* atmet alles Lebens Atem
5
In *Goldesgelb* leuchtet des Denkens Klarheit
6
In *Feuers Rot* wurzelt des Willens Stärke
7
Im *Sonnenweiss* offenbart sich meines Wesens Kern

*

(1)
In *darkness* I find the existence of God
2
In *rose-red* I feel the source of life
3
In *aether-blue* reposes the spirit's longing
4
In *life's green* breathes the breath of all life
5
In *gold's yellow* shines the clarity of thinking
6
In *fire's red* the strength of will is rooted
7
In *sun-white* my being's kernel manifests itself

The above notebook entry by Rudolf Steiner from the year 1908 (Archive No. 337) is included here for its relation to Maria Strakosch-Giesler's report.

THE HUMAN FORM AND COLOR

Maria-Strakosch-Giesler

A demand of our time is that the human being once again be recognized as a microcosm, formed out of the macrocosm. In affirming the macrocosmic origin in every particular of the human form, we find the cosmic powers which brought it forth. With the help of color it is possible to represent the human being in accordance with these creative powers. A requirement is that we come gradually to recognize color as having its true being in the cosmos, in the zodiac, in the planetary spheres.

[Here the author refers once more to the task set her by Rudolf Steiner of painting a self-portrait by other means than by looking in a mirror. This is already given in the previous report. – See page 10.]

Many years of work have shown that by means of this indication of Rudolf Steiner's, it is possible for the painter also to collaborate on the most stupendous spiritual task of our time, the reuniting of human consciousness with cosmic consciousness. It can scarcely be imagined with what inner enthusiasm a person approaches such a task, long yearned for. However, the difficulty connected with transforming a consciousness that has not as yet overcome the all-too strong attachment of the soul to the body (as with all modern human beings) can perhaps be understood. These difficulties can take on an unforeseen dimension, till at last a new world begins to glimmer in one's consciousness. And yet, in all the arts anthroposophy demands, if taken seriously, the striving for this new consciousness – in the field of painting as well. In the circles connected with the Free Waldorf School in Stuttgart there was interest in these endeavors.[3] This new conception of the human being as a spirit being was sought there, because in the educational work with children the central importance of the problem was experienced. Still, it can fill one with painful astonishment, how little interest in such a quest in Rudolf Steiner's sense is to be found in other places, where strictly speaking it might have been expected.

If one contemplates the works of sculpture and painting that have arisen in the course of the ages with regard to their significance as documents of history, one can recognize that

---

[3] Maria Strakosch-Giesler founded a painting school in Stuttgart in 1921 which she continued until 1937. It was called Painting School for Rudolf Steiner's Color Theory (Malschule für Rudolf Steiners Farbenlehre).

the chief characteristic of a cultural epoch is always the manner of conceiving the human form – as has already been pointed out.

In the manner in which the ancient Egyptians portrayed the human figure, we can appreciate how immense cosmic forces streaming in from outside form it, while with the Greeks the focal point of the forces is centered in human beings themselves, and for the first time they could let these forces ray out from within. What tremendous transformations and revolutions must have occurred in order to bring about this new conception of the human figure? Today a new culture is also preparing itself with a new idea of the human being. We live in the midst of a decisive battle as to whether this approach to the human being as a cosmic-spiritual entity will prevail, or whether the world will hold on to the depleted life-forms of the past and sink into chaos and darkness.

Going back to what Rudolf Steiner said about representing the human figure, we may note the following: First of all it is a matter of what one sees most easily of one's own form. Here it is above all a question of the limbs, and they are to be painted dark. In penetrating the darkness shaped in the form of the limbs, something of the earth's materiality comes to meet us, which is taken hold of by the will-nature of the human being. On the other hand, what the human being has only a slight notion of is to be painted in light tones. This lightness, tinged for example yellowish, has a shining, relatively unformed character, and unites itself more directly with the surface, while the darkness lets the limbs be more graphically formed and delimited. What one can see least of is above all the head, of which one sees only a few parts of the face. The back of the head, as well as our back, are not visible for us. Spinal cord and brain, in which consciousness and thinking above all take place, are included in this area to be represented as light. In the rhythmic system visible and invisible are woven together and yield an animated picture of feeling. It thus becomes evident that the light rays in from behind into what is dark.

In this connection it is of central importance to become clear as to how these three members of the human being stand in relation to the element of spirit. As an outcome of his spiritual research, Rudolf Steiner expresses this in the following words:

> Consider the following: If we look at the head in the way we carry it as human beings, then as regards its outer formation, it most of all reveals the spirit. The head is most of all an image of the spirit, most of all a manifestation of the spirit; the spirit has here entered farthest into matter. In this way it has, however, left the least behind in the spirit itself. Since the human being has expended so much work on the head, so as

> to reveal the external corporality spiritualized, little is left in the spirit. While in the lower parts of the human corporality, that which has formed itself outwardly is least of all spiritualized, least of all worked out spiritually; in regard to these lower parts the most has remained behind in the spiritual. The head as head conforms least of all to what is spiritual, because it has the most spirit in it; the lower body corresponds most of all to spirit, which does not live in the corporality. There the "I" lives during sleep.
>
> Think of this wonderful adjustment: while the human being has a lower nature in regard to his corporality and the "I" immerses itself in this lower nature upon awakening, this lower nature is only lower nature because the spirit has worked least of all, because the spirit has held back so much in the spiritual realm. But within what it has held back, there the "I" is during sleep. Thus the "I" is already today together with that which the human being will develop, will help to realize, only in the future, what is today only little, I should like to say, only first indicated, still but little developed in the corporality of the human being. Hence if the "I" becomes aware of the state in which it finds itself during sleep, if it becomes in truth conscious of this state, then it can say to itself: During sleep I am in that which is my most sacred human predisposition, and in emerging from sleep, on awakening, I go from the world of my most sacred tendencies over into what is only a weak indication of this most sacred tendency.[4]

If one takes up such a finding into one's painting activity, one is led to a wealth of experiences. Here one can almost speak of an investigative consciousness. One experience has to do with the weaving life of color in its interplay with light and dark. Here we shall go into this a little more closely.

By means of the raying in of the light from behind into the darkness, we encounter something of the mineral forces in the physical body of the human being. In the richly toned metamorphosis of the darkness of the limbs into the light of the head, one can sense something like a transformation from the dark leaf of the plant to the light-filled blossom. In the plant lives the etheric, while the astral rays into the blossom from outside. However,

---

[4] Rudolf Steiner: *Bausteine zu einer Erkenntnis des Mysteriums von Golgotha.* Lecture 1, p. 102 (GA 175). Rudolf Steiner Verlag, Dornach. This lecture of February 20, 1917, is contained in *Cosmic and Human Metamorphoses,* Garber Communications 1989.

that which is animal-related in the astral comes to meet us in observing the darkness of the lower part of the human body as compared with the lightness of the upper part of the body. Here something of the being of the centaur takes hold of one.

In the entire figure of the human being, that which is actually most human presents itself to the painter most movingly in the region of the thorax in its interweaving of colors and forms. Added to that is how the head region and the limbs (the representatives of the nervous system and the metabolic system) unite themselves with the middle region, the rhythmic system, to become the tripartite human being. Here we touch upon the deepest mystery of the human being. However, it can only be grasped by a consciousness that experiences reality in pictorial form: imaginative consciousness.

RECOLLECTIONS OF TWO LECTURES BY RUDOLF STEINER ON PAINTING

Held during the Youth Course Stuttgart, October 3–15, 1922

Maria Strakosch-Giesler

When in the year 1922 Rudolf Steiner held the Youth Course in Stuttgart – from October 3 through 15 – he also spoke about painting in two special lectures. There were many young people who came to participate in this Youth Course who wanted to take up a profession and sought advice in this regard. Some of them were interested in pedagogy in general. Rudolf Steiner took this fact into account in his remarks, giving a number of indications in the field of pedagogy. Today (1955) we have quite a few personalities among Waldorf teachers and directors of curative institutions who took part at that time in the Youth Course. It was Rudolf Steiner's task to awaken the sense for the artistic in his hearers. Thus painting and the color-world were given a certain priority.

Rudolf Steiner not only gave the most valuable indications in two lectures, but also took brush in hand and demonstrated a number of painting exercises.

At that time *Der Kommende Tag AG* (The Coming Day Inc., a joint venture for promoting spiritual and economic values) supported a "Natural Scientific Research Institute" in Stuttgart. In one of the laboratories, plant colors were produced by a chemist who entered into the suggestions of Rudolf Steiner with understanding; and these were already developed to the point of being usable to a certain extent. Not long afterwards, *Der Kommende Tag* was forced for economic reasons to suspend the extensive activities of this research institute.

When Rudolf Steiner now held his lectures on painting during the Youth Course, he requested the plant colors as a painting medium, since he wanted at the same time to test how usable they had become for painting. Since I was involved in these experiments in painting and in some of the manual preparation of the plant colors, it was incumbent on me to prepare the material for Rudolf Steiner.

First Lecture of October 13, 1922

The first lecture on painting was arranged so as to enable Rudolf Steiner to give a practical demonstration.

In order to help the interested and astonished onlookers understand what he painted, which was executed with a wonderful color sense and the most delicate yet deliberate strokes, he clarified each step as the picture arose.

Here the attempt will be made to give a tentative account of what was said. The basis for this undertaking is, however, very imperfect. No official (stenographic) report was made of these lectures. Thus it is a matter only of personal notes made by various young people, which all in all, are difficult to decipher, as most did not themselves understand *what* they were taking down. So there is only a certain maze of thoughts to go by. I myself did not make any notes during the two lectures on painting. An alternative is to rely on memory. This was supported and strengthened by the fact that the young people came up into my studio, located on the grounds of the Waldorf school, after each lecture. The color problems were then discussed in a lively manner.

After the Youth Course had ended, a number of young friends stayed on in Stuttgart, and we attempted jointly to work out the indications of Rudolf Steiner in my studio. Certainly, the best way to shore up one's memory is to become thus actively involved in seeking to enter into the problems for oneself. And as a result, the indications and guidelines of Rudolf Steiner were put into practice and not lost.

But it is becoming more and more apparent that the many new co-workers joining the various institutions of the anthroposophical movement are no longer so easily able to find access to this color world, so rich in promise and curative potential. Thus the attempt has been made here to convey something of those lectures of 1922, partly from all sorts of notes, partly from personal experience, and from gradually remembering the original words of Rudolf Steiner. In the various rough outlines, words and sentences are found here and there which reproduce what Rudolf Steiner actually said. Often it is a matter of only partial sentences. These are distinguished by being in italics.

On October 13, Rudolf Steiner spoke, in the first lecture held during the Youth Course on painting, first of all about art in general. He said that *"Kunst"* ("art") comes from the word *"Können"* ("ability").

Human beings have learned to see colors in the sense world to be sure, but color is still dead to begin with, and has on that account to be ensouled. If the activity of the artist necessary for this dies away, art dies as well. Color may not be merely seen externally and painted, for example, yellow.

In front of Rudolf Steiner there stood a painting board on which a white sheet of paper was stretched, ready for him to paint on. He said, "*The starting point* for painting is the surface. What is a surface? In the surface the will cannot come to expression, for the will is three-dimensional. *The will works in the three-dimensional, feeling lives itself out in the two-dimensional. The surface is two-dimensional; I can only experience the surface in as much as I have a world of feeling in me. Thoughts I cannot paint at all, because thoughts have only one dimension.*"

Then Rudolf Steiner pointed out that the surface here was white. "*In white the colors fade away.*" With that the white was meant, when *next* to it a color is painted on the surface. For later he said: "*We penetrate by means of white as though through a door into all colors.* Practical experience shows that the pure white must indeed be completely overcome in painting. It has to become light. Even the most delicate yellow laid over the pure white causes it to become ensouled. And by means of color, if it is properly experienced, everything should become ensouled."

Then Rudolf Steiner began to paint. He said: "*I want to paint some muted blue. I have to be able to experience a dull blue surface, the color must be completely in me. I can possibly fetch something out of the dull blue. But if something is to emerge, the blue experience must pass over into something or other.*"

While speaking these words he had painted a subdued blue with the plant colors on the right and on the left sides of the painting surface in rich tones, corresponding to the particular blue. These became like a large gesture enclosing the middle of the page. The blue of the night-sky reposed within it, and yet it was already as though softly lightened by another color. The blue experience went over into something else. "*I want to paint something that comes towards me,*" he said. "*I have something on the surface that wants to work out of the surface.*" And thus he began to paint the empty middle of the page with the radiant forms of a shining yellow. These plant colors, the yellow in particular, had at that time a glowing quality, and thus an effect came about in Rudolf Steiner's hands capable of taking hold of and inwardly affecting one with intensity. However, the plant colors unfortunately soon lost their luminosity and faded quickly. Having painted this, he said: "*That is much too restless; the only thing I can do about it is to add a support below.*" He then painted, in cool rose-reddish tones, the earth's surface. Then he said: "*Out of the blue, lightened in the middle by means of something reddish-yellowish that exercises its influence all around, and that acquires a support from below – thus a sunrise is to be experienced out of the color.*

I must experience that not only while painting, but continually. In painting the point is that everything must be fetched out of the color. As far as possible one should not draw. For drawing in painting means lying and not living in the color."

Rudolf Steiner now turned to a second board stretched with white paper and began to paint something new on it. He then said: "*I want to experience something out of the blackish blue that bores itself into it like a hole, like a cosmic hole. That can be something reddish. I now play a little with the strong blue. Then I give it a support. In the support there can be something of another color. In this way I have a moon mood.*

As a result of one's own color experience one's heart opens up for the colors of nature. The physicist only looks at the corpse of the world. What floats, gleaming and shimmering over things, plays over them, there is future in that. Color is the child of the cosmos."

In the middle of the board stretched with white paper the moonrise had arisen in this manner. To the right of it he placed another exercise on the page above, which, however, had nothing to do with the moonrise. It was once again an attempt to help the young people to appreciate something of the nature of color. He did this in painting a head in profile, calling it: "*the first element of a face in profile: blue/yellow.*" Then he said: "*The yellow wants to fray out.* (Nose, eyes, mouth, chin.) *The blue withdraws.*" Like hair, the blue enclosed in a rounded, quiet shape the "frayed out" features formed by the animated yellow. Here the gestures of the single colors were brought out in an impressive manner: the yellow, which wants to ray out from within – and the blue, that withdraws itself, that closes itself off and becomes darker outside, but lighter within.

In a face in which the forehead is bowed, two colors are again next to each other, red and yellow. The red comes toward one in the forehead inclined forward. The yellow lies further back in the lower region of the face, which, thus withdraws in relation to the red. "*You must remind yourselves that a thoroughly creative element lies in the color world. You will yourselves become creators if you play with color, although you must retain the necessary modesty for this.*

If I want to paint something devilish, I shall have to begin with vermilion red – and then paint soft, delicate blue. The red, after all, always wants to come out and everything devilish also always wants to pounce on me.

If I want to paint an angel, who merely lets himself be looked at (the gentlest activity of all), then I can only paint him in the most delicate blue; it is the gentlest color of all."

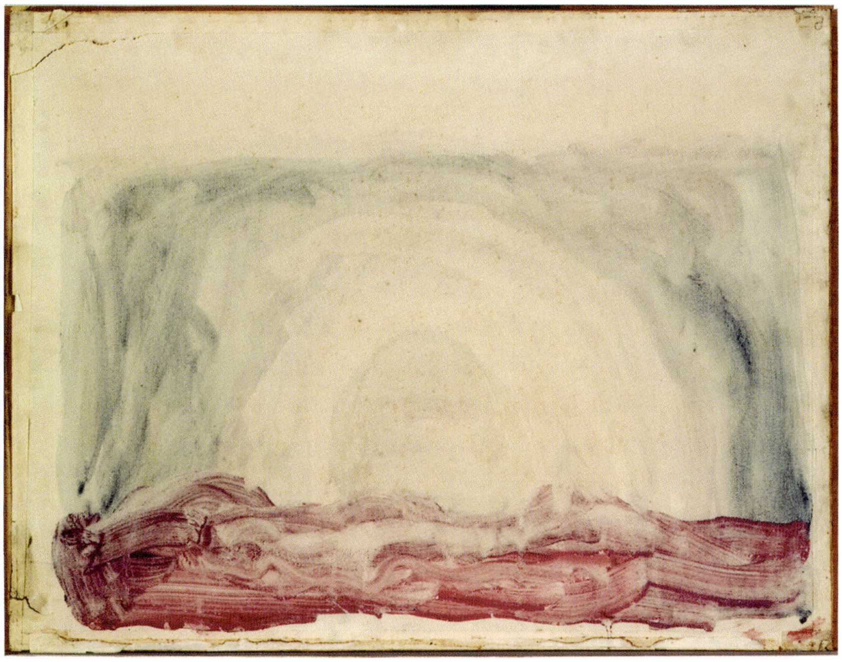

Sunrise Rudolf Steiner Archive (Dornach)

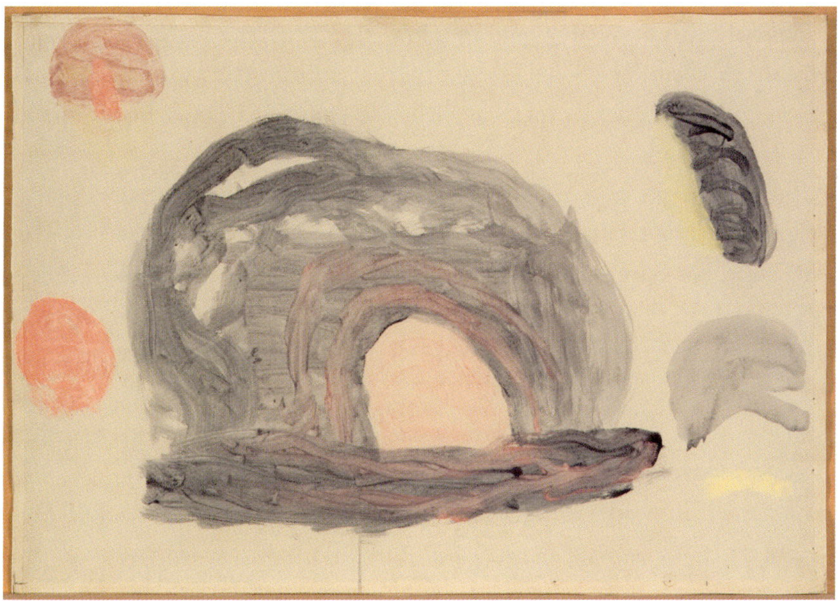

Moon Mood Rudolf Steiner Archive (Dornach)

Rudolf Steiner's original "Sunrise" and "Moon Mood" plant color sketches:
Maria Strakosch-Giesler's description of how Rudolf Steiner himself painted out of the color remains unique in being practically the only eye-witness account of this kind. Unfortunately, due in part to the inadequate light-fastness of the early plant colors used, the original studies reproduced here are in a very imperfect and unsatisfactory state of preservation. This is most obvious with the yellow, which in the *Sunrise* has not merely lost intensity and faded, but has essentially disappeared altogether.

Second Lecture of October 15, 1922

In this second lecture on painting, Rudolf Steiner did not demonstrate in front of his onlookers. With the two painted sheets, the sunrise and the moon mood, he had given an abundance of suggestions which now had to be worked out in constant further activity.

Rudolf Steiner wanted in this second lecture to appeal to and awaken the artistic sense in his listeners. First of all he said a few words about plant colors. He spoke of how necessary it is to find the right painting medium. In Stuttgart he had occupied himself in great detail with this problem in the laboratory where the plant colors were produced. The result turned out to be very satisfying. It was a milky-looking painting medium made from eight different resins and etheric oils.

In May 1921 Rudolf Steiner held his three lectures in Dornach on the nature of color. In the last of these lectures he indicated view-points for representing and giving shape to the three kingdoms of nature, stone, plant and animal, out of the color.

In the lecture of October 15, 1922, he briefly went into the mineral and animal kingdom and then mentioned the human form as well. He indicated how one would have to adopt a different attitude to each of these kingdoms. However, he occupied himself more closely with the nature of plants and showed how with the plant, colors particularly arise in the blossoms. One's attitude to lifeless objects has to be quite different than to plants.

With the plant we have to experience how it is earthly and yet sun-related, and look for what the sun brings about in it. First of all, the plant has the upward direction. It strives toward the fruiting-point. The upward direction originates from the previous year and presents everything the plant has that is most of all useful.

That which is color, and is at the same time of great beauty, spirals as leaf and blossom around the upward-striving stalk and comes from this year.

Indications now followed, contained in aphoristic statements of Rudolf Steiner; he said:

"One cannot arrive at concepts concerning the beauty of Nature. Every specimen of Nature is a revolt against aestheticism. Nature is beautiful when she entwines the useless with the useful.

The flower already bestows color on itself, and the painter has to be able to experience that.

All painting after the model is completely incompatible with artistic development, but artistic feeling must learn from the great artist herself, from Nature!

Today we can only begin to find the way to free creative activity with difficulty, but the world of color is in itself creative and we must immerse ourselves completely in it.

Then we must above all learn again to feel how a patch of blue takes us into the depths of space – how a patch of red, on the other hand, comes out, approaches us. In its two-dimensionality the surface is the life-element for our feeling-perception. It catches hold of what is the life-element of color. Blue comes as if from behind onto the surface. Red and yellow want to come onto the surface from in front.

Color has to be experienced as perspective. Linear perspective is dead, it is linked with intellectualism. In color-perspective it is necessary to experience how on the dark (cool) side the color recedes, on the light (warm) side it approaches us. The color must be, as it were, caught on the surface. If one wants in teaching to help someone to appreciate color-perspective, it can happen in the following way: *One has a round blue spot painted, surrounded by a yellow. Then one attempts to awaken a feeling for how the blue goes back and the yellow comes forward. The blue makes the impression of being a hole. After that a red spot is painted with a bluish-greenish border around it. The red then has the effect of being embossed.*"

Rudolf Steiner then indicated that one should work out of the material. He took sculpture as an example. He said: "*If you work in wood, then you must as though scrape everything out, scrape out the hollows; but if you are working in marble, then it is as if everything had to be added on, for example the nose.*"

Then he mentioned that the question of the frame is in itself inartistic. The gold frame is the last remnant of the gold backgrounds of the old masters. They saw, in looking spiritually, human beings and other figures proceeding out of the shining gold.

Rudolf Steiner now once again attempted to awaken in his hearers the sense and the proper receptivity for the artistic, particularly in contemplating visual art.

He took Dürer's well-known copperplate engraving *Melancholia* as an example. He indicated that Dürer had not wanted to depict a state of melancholy, but as the word melancholy – which means black – suggests, to have this blackness of color overcome by the light. The picture shows how light gives form to the space. It is a light-dark study, which has as its purpose to study the secrets of light in relation to mineral, plant, animal and human being. Then he said: "*Sentimental people ask, 'Did Dürer not feel something else, something deeper?', for the age does not feel the urge to experience what is truly artistic. Yet this does indeed have to be experienced in its purity, also in regard to painting. The form has to come out of the color!*"

Thus Dürer wanted to study the manifestations of light. Here it may be permissible to add what Rudolf Steiner personally said to me about this copperplate engraving of Dürer, in giving me the task of transposing Dürer's *Melancholia* into color.

He first had me investigate how many shades of light and dark Dürer had made use of in the polyhedron located in the middle on the left side. It is a matter of all the shades to be found in the picture being summarized in this solid. In thoroughly studying, for example, a *Reichsdruck* (a high quality print) that really shows all nuances, I discovered twelve of them, going from the brightest light to the deepest black.

When I told Rudolf Steiner this, he nodded in agreement. *"And now translate the whole picture into color, but pay attention to the fact that there are two light sources. One comes from outside onto the picture and illumines the objects and one bursts out from the picture itself."* With that he laid his expressive hands in a gentle gesture onto the picture so that the left hand lay lightly on the sphere at the feet of the angel-like figure. This sphere is lit from outside.

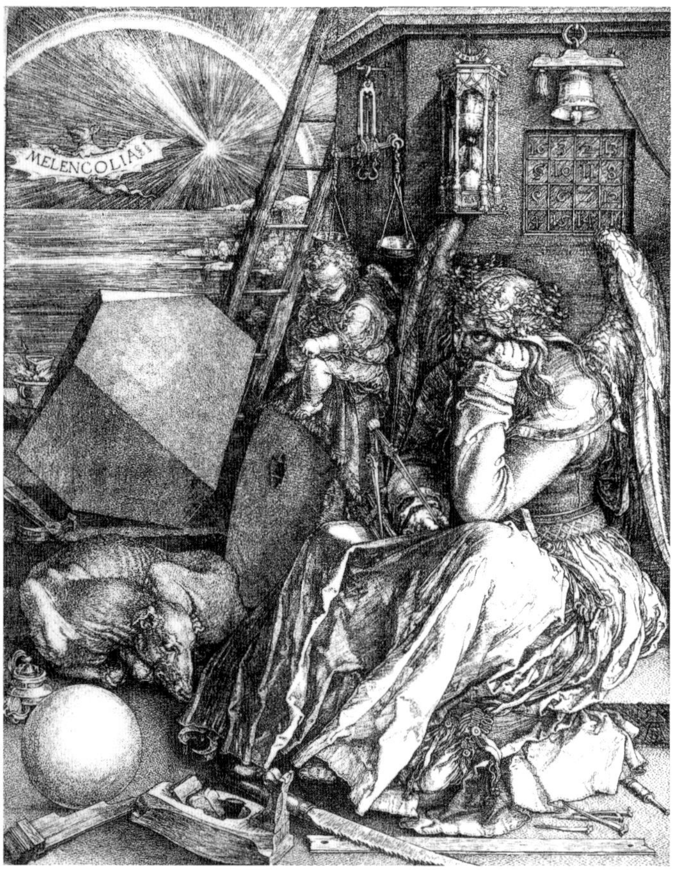

Melancholia, 1514. Albrecht Dürer (1471–1528). Engraving, 241 x 192 mm.

He laid his other hand on the light that breaks out powerfully from the clouds above over the sea and land. A rainbow arches over this light source and a dark bat flees from it. It bears a kind of banner in front of its wings with the inscription: 'MELENCOLIA-I'. Melancholia-flee! The sphere and its whole surroundings are illumined by the sun, which shines on them from without. This light-effect will organize itself in yellowish tones. On the other hand, the light flooding out over land and sea will appear in the color of peach-blossom. The colors that mainly come in question for the darkness in the case of the yellowish light are blue and violet. In the case of peach-blossom, all the colors of the rainbow.

Hereupon Rudolf Steiner again spoke about the nature of color itself in greater detail. We must experience color perspective artistically; spatial perspective does not really enter into space. We must also learn to live with the material. In regard to color perspective Goethe's color theory is a gold mine, especially the chapter on the "sensory-moral effect of colors." It does not penetrate the head, but the fingers, and one can after all only paint out of the hands and not out of the head.

Rudolf Steiner now gave further valuable indications as to how the nature of color presents itself with regard to the human being. By means of color one has really to experience the inner core of the human being. That is possible by means of experiencing the color of a person's countenance.

With the animal it is not possible to experience the inner being by means of color, even if the fur were to be removed. But in painting the human being, one will seek to penetrate the color of the countenance, and all around it one will then see the astral body in color.

In all of Nature there is nothing similar to the human countenance. It is that which is most of all human. And as the outer manifestation of the inner core, its color is something of the greatest value as regards the human being. The brain is not the most valuable part of the human being. The human head is true on the outside and hence cosmic and to be found nowhere else.

The legs are formed from outside out of the earth's force of gravity. From the earth the legs place themselves onto our organism.

A geometrician becomes one, because he clearly experiences the brain. And we become mathematicians by experiencing our limbs right into the bony system. The gift for mathematics does not come from the nervous system; in the brain there is only a mirroring.

The human nude reconstitutes itself in us, becoming color experience.

Nowadays living in color has been lost. Incarnadine is no longer truly experienced in painting. Raphael and his contemporaries were not yet able to disregard the external human form. He brought the color of the human being to expression in the manner in which he clothed the human being. Mary and Joseph are represented in blue and red: feminine and masculine. In Paris we have the Dionysus and John by Leonardo. With John, we can observe how all color coming from outside bounces off, while with Dionysus all color comes from within.

Painting must proceed from the hands. It must be possible to recognize the personality in each brushstroke. In the most amorphous patch of color one must be able to see the hand of the artist and must know whether the painter painted the red patch from left to right, or otherwise.

"But it is essential to paint out of the paint-dish, out of the mobile, flowing color, not from the palette with viscous (semifluid) paint." The advice quoted in conclusion was given by Rudolf Steiner in one of his three lectures on the nature of color; it is necessary for understanding the statements concerning the handling of brushstrokes.

Translated from *Die erlöste Sphinx* (The Sphinx Redeemed) by Maria Strakosch-Giesler. Novalis Verlag, Freiburg im Breisgau 1955.

Other written works of Maria Strakosch-Giesler: *Concerning Wassily Kandinsky's Early Work. (Vom Frühwerk Wassily Kandinskys,)* Manuscript, ca. 1945.

About Maria Strakosch-Giesler
1877–1970

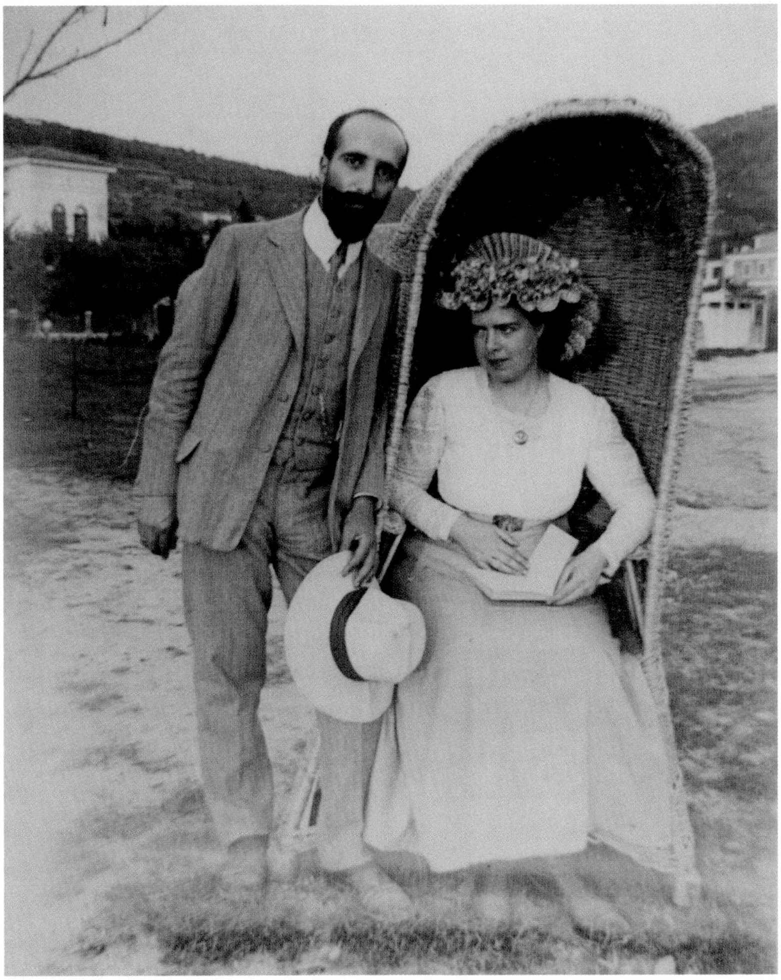

Maria Strakosch-Giesler and Alexander Strakosch

Maria Giesler was born in Siegen, in the state of North Rhine Westphalia on August 6, 1877, the daughter of a leather manufacturer. In various draft-outlines of her life (written later for exhibitions) she mentions that the cathedral in Cologne (75 km away [about 46 miles]) was for her as a child the epitome of what is beautiful. At 17 she left her parents' house to study at a private painting school in Berlin with a classically-based training. Her already strongly developed sense for color was not entirely satisfied by the portrait and nude studies as well as still lifes she made in this school. At about the age of 20 she won first prize in a competition for fairy tale illustrations. After a time she switched her studies to a well-known flower painter, making a variety of flower pictures, some of which she was able to sell. This put her in a position to finance her further studies herself.

Hearing of Wassily Kandinsky in 1902, Maria Giesler made a spontaneous decision to travel to Munich. Together with the group of artists known under the name "Phalanx," Kandinsky had founded a painting school there in 1901. One of his students at that time was Gabriele Münter. Upon seeing his pictures, Maria Giesler at once decided to study with him. With the dissolution of "Phalanx" eighteen months later, the school also came to an end and it was thus not possible for her to continue studying with Kandinsky. Kandinsky went on study-trips to a number of different European countries with Gabriele Münter, later settling in Murnau until 1914. However, the friendship begun with Kandinsky, as well as with other artists with whom Maria Giesler had become acquainted in Munich (e.g., Alexej Jawlensky, Marianne Werefkin, and Paul Klee) proved lasting, especially in the case of the "Blue Rider" painters. These all strived to get away from mere naturalism. Of this period, she later wrote:

> Destiny had granted my coming into closer connection with this circle. I was the only anthroposophist among them, and Baroness Werefkin liked to introduce me as "*Frau* Strakosch, an anthroposophist." Thus I gained a certain insight into the inner attitude this circle had toward anthroposophy, and ascertained a certain spontaneous interest. Werefkin once said, she envied my inner quiet and single-mindedness in the realm of color and painting; she herself, however, could not go this path. – Why, she did not say.
>
> That was also the case with some of the others in this circle. But it seemed to me that they were at the same time transformed and deeply affected by all the indications and impulses Rudolf Steiner brought to expression in his books as well as in his lectures. Yet they did not have the courage to devote themselves to this anthroposophical spirit-world, or did not do so for other reasons. There were other circles in Munich also that viewed this world in a similar way.

> The one who occupied himself most seriously and more in depth with the thoughts of anthroposophy was Wassily Kandinsky. When we [Maria and Alexander Strakosch] spent some time with him in Berlin in the spring of 1908, and first came into contact with Rudolf Steiner ourselves, he always accompanied us to the lectures of Rudolf Steiner in the *Architektenhaus*, which we regularly attended. For his part, Rudolf Steiner also showed particular interest in the work of Kandinsky. It was a matter then of, for example, exquisite colored woodcuts which Kandinsky had created, prompted by the spirit-imbued, pictorial language of Rudolf Steiner in his lectures. Once I was able to show such a woodcut to Rudolf Steiner. In a warm, friendly tone of voice, he responded by saying: "He is capable of something, he knows something...."

While studying in Munich (also with a painter by the name of Exter), Maria Giesler met Alexander Strakosch, then a mechanical engineering student from Austria at the Institute of Technology. Their friendship led to marriage in 1906 in Meran, where he had been posted by the Austrian Railway upon being hired as a construction engineer. In 1907 Alexander Strakosch was transferred for one year to Innsbruck and was required to stay for several weeks in Berlin in March of 1908. There the young couple met friends from their time in Munich, including Kandinsky, and attended their first lecture by Rudolf Steiner on March 26, 1908, at the *Architektenhaus*. When the speaker had finished, they looked at each other and said: "That's him." They became personal pupils of Rudolf Steiner.

Between 1908 and 1912, Alexander Strakosch was stationed by his employers in Trieste. In the summer of 1911, Rudolf Steiner came with Marie von Sivers, who needed a cure after a severe illness, to nearby Portorose on the Adriatic, leading to seven of Maria Strakosch-Giesler's paintings being chosen by Rudolf Steiner and shown at the Theosophical Conference in Munich that year.

A relocation to Vienna followed in 1912, where the Strakoschs' lived until 1920 and where Maria Strakosch-Giesler became a member of the artists' group *"Freie Bewegung"* ("Free Movement") and participated in a number of exhibitions. During 1914 she joined in the work of carving the capitals and architraves of the first Goetheanum.

On June 1, 1918, Rudolf Steiner held a lecture for about 60 invited guests in her Vienna studio, entitled "The Sensible-Supersensible – Spiritual Knowledge and Artistic Creation."

In 1920 Maria and Alexander Strakosch moved to Stuttgart, where he had been asked by Rudolf Steiner to become a teacher in the first Waldorf school. Requested to give painting classes, Maria Strakosch asked Rudolf Steiner in 1921 for lectures on color, whereupon he held the course of three lectures in Dornach from the 6th to the 8th of May (published as *Colour*. Rudolf Steiner Press 1992). In 1922 she founded a painting school in Stuttgart, which had on average thirty students from various countries. The school existed until 1937, by which time it had become impossible to continue under the increasingly threatening conditions prevailing in Germany. Alexander Strakosch was of Jewish descent and they had to leave Stuttgart practically without financial means and resettle in Dornach. A difficult time followed in which they were dependent on the help of anthroposophical friends for support.

After the end of World War II, Maria Strakosch was able to regain a footing in the art world, organize exhibitions and sell her paintings. She held exhibitions in as many as twenty different cities: Basel, Bellinzona, Bern, Dornach, Dortmund, Frankfurt, Heilbronn, Innsbruck, Karlsruhe, Krefeld, Milan, Mannheim, Munich, New York, Nizza, Rome, St. Gallen, Stuttgart, Ulm and Vienna.

An utterance of Rudolf Steiner makes it clear in what high regard he held Maria Strakosch: He told Alexander Strakosch at the time of the impending move from Vienna to Stuttgart in 1920: "And when *Frau* Strakosch is here, I shall be able to think of realizing my artistic intentions."

In addition to having her book *Die erlöste Sphinx* (The Sphinx Redeemed) published in 1955, Maria Strakosch also wrote for periodicals such as *Das Goetheanum* and *Die Kommenden*. She survived her husband by twelve years. Her eyesight weakened to the point where she was unable to work. She spent her last years totally blind and confined to bed, and died in Dornach on September 4, 1970, at 93 years of age.

– *Peter Stebbing*

HILDE BOOS-HAMBURGER

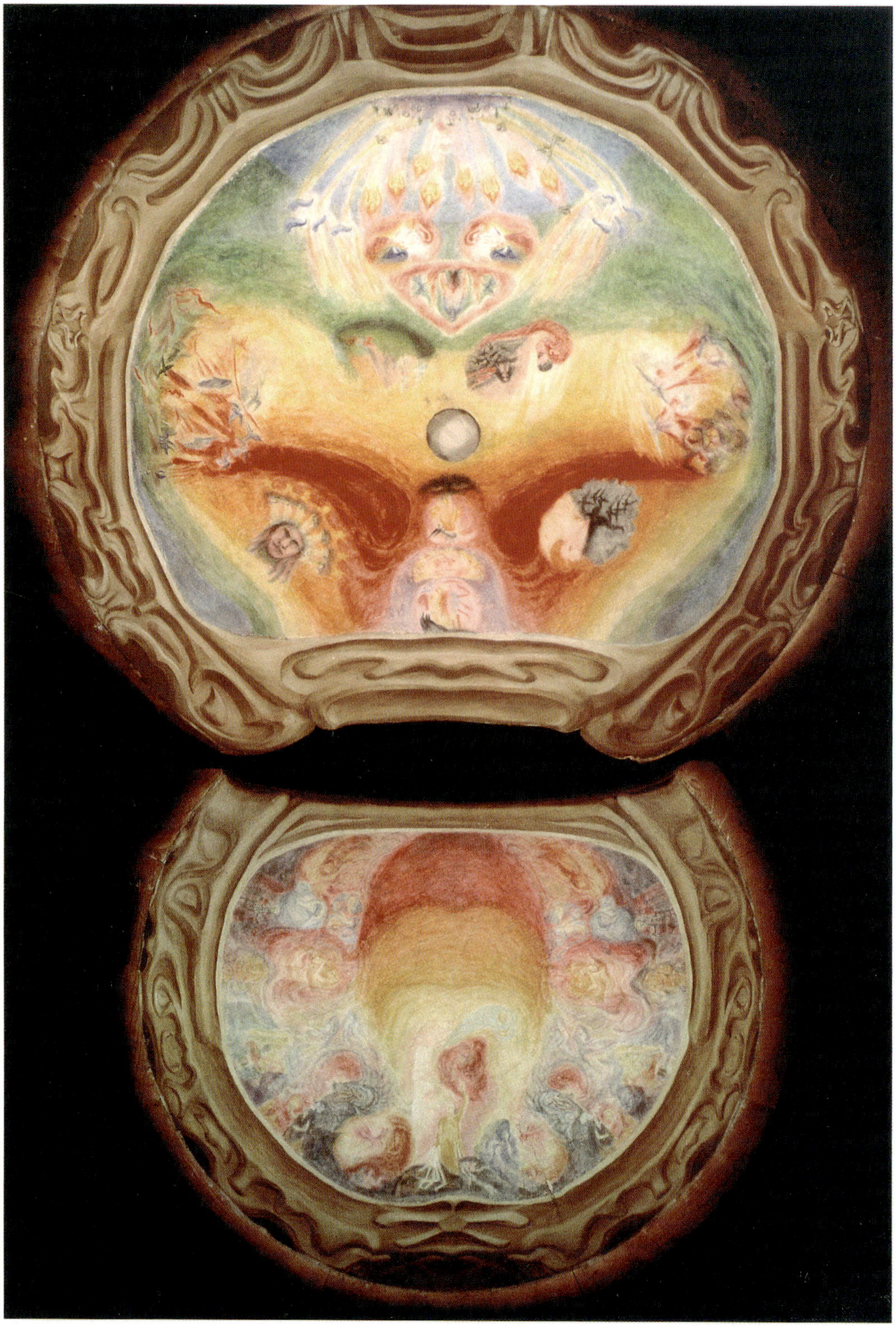

View looking up into a scale model of the large and small cupola, built by Carl Liedvogel and painted by Hilde Boos-Hamburger. Exhibited as part of the Goetheanum art collection in Dornach, Switzerland. Reproduced by kind permission of the copyright holder: M. Boos-Egli (Basel).

Preliminary Remarks

In reliving memories it is not easy to present them so that the self-centeredness that normally clings to them does not push itself to the fore. This applies even for someone who undertakes a daily retrospective view of the circumstances of life, for the sake of gaining objectivity.

If statements are nonetheless made in a few places here which appear important only for the author personally, the reasons are as follows: A great deal was talked about and wrestled with in the years of striving to establish Rudolf Steiner's painting impulse. Much also was said that was not objective. Younger friends no longer having had the great good fortune of being able to work with Rudolf Steiner, expressed at various times the opinion that what he had said to pupils personally was only of subjective value for them and lacked a more general validity. Those not having directly experienced his way of doing things were certainly not at once able to distinguish in what instances a pupil had received purely objective answers, or when the great teacher had felt himself obliged to take into account the wish-filled attitude of the questioner. These are the reasons why personal considerations were touched upon where it seemed justified in illuminating matters having to do with painting. Personal conversations and recollections as such are not included here. Whoever takes painting seriously will find no contradiction between what is communicated – often difficult to bear at first for those with an academic training – and what is expressed in Rudolf Steiner's lectures. The conversations related here seem to me to extend the practical path set forth in the book *The Creative Power of Colour,* which has as its purpose to offer help in putting Rudolf Steiner's indications into practice.

H. B.-H.

EXPERIENCES IN PAINTING THE CUPOLAS OF THE FIRST GOETHEANUM

Hilde Boos-Hamburger

Every artistically striving person making closer acquaintance with Rudolf Steiner and his anthroposophy is likely to have experienced in a quite individual manner the agreeable shock: here lie all the possibilities for the further development of art. In one way or another it may have gone with him as with the writer of these recollections when she first read through (not yet actually studied!) the book *Theosophy*[5], without understanding the essential, yet rivetted by the crystal-bright formation of this work, and having to say to herself: Even if I cannot survey it, it is nonetheless evident: Here lies a comprehensive work of art! This first impression did not deceive, for with every subsequent work taken up, every book, every lecture, not to mention the Mystery Dramas, there opened up new experiences and vistas previously undreamed of. – These will surely be found most felicitously expressed in the poem by *Christian Morgenstern* (1871–1914) dedicated to Rudolf Steiner:

To beauty does your work lead:
For beauty in the end
Streams in through every revelation
That surrounds us.
Out of human-sufferings
Upward to ever higher harmonies
You release the dizzying feeling,
Till, united
In accord with the
Inestimable proclaimer of GOD
And HIS never-to-be-grasped splendor
It vibrates in the love-light
Of blessedness. . . .
From beauty does your work come, to beauty does it lead.

---

[5] *Theosophy: An Introduction to the Spiritual Processes in Human Life and in the Cosmos* by Rudolf Steiner. Anthroposophic Press, N.Y. 1994.

In view of such lofty aims, the aims of the Expressionists of that time (1910) seemed narrowly circumscribed. In the first conversation I had with Rudolf Steiner, I therefore did not venture to mention the Expressionist movement, sensing his far-reaching knowledge. This dealt rather with general points of view. Repeatedly, he emphasized that the painter must devote himself again and again with intense interest and enthusiasm to the phenomena of light and air. And "work a great deal" (*"viel, viel arbeiten"*), he urged.

Those were the years when every August the Mystery Dramas were performed. In 1911, I was first able to participate in the work of preparing the scenery along with many artistically zealous individuals and other friends in the Munich *Schrannenhalle* (the old granary) under the direction of the three scenery painters, *Hermann Linde* (1863–1923), Haass and Volkert. The work began already in June and was continued over the next two months. Scenery, which sometimes included arches, had to be cut out and for the most part, as with complicated contours such as those involving foliage, sewed onto nets. Some pieces of scenery such as that for Scene 7 in *The Guardian of the Threshold* and the Cosmic Midnight in *The Souls' Awakening* were completely sewn from layers of organdy; various colored surfaces one over the other. Rudolf Steiner had made sketches for these, which I still recall quite well. Self-evidently, he had provided indications for all scenes, while still leaving artists maximum freedom. We also produced numerous smaller pieces of scenery for the stage, and in the last two years I was permitted to paint some side panels and the like for Hermann Linde.

As our "reward" we could go to scenery-rehearsals in the *Gärtnerplatz* Theater and in this way be present for the rehearsal of a number of scenes under Rudolf Steiner's direction. In the goodness of his heart, Hermann Linde asked Rudolf Steiner's permission for our participation at all dress-rehearsals as well, and right away brought along a number of entry-tickets signed by him. In this way, it was possible to take in these plays still more intensively and retain many details better in memory than when seeing them only once, since the wealth of impressions was overwhelming. One was dealing after all with comprehensive works of art. There were innovations as regards color and painting as well. The Cosmic Midnight scene had the most intense after-effect, particularly the colors of Luna's garments, orange and violet, the strongest color impression of all. It seemed incredible. How on earth did Dr. Steiner come to such a provocative, marvelous color-chord? The answer only came in studying Goethe's color theory several years later! *Imme von Eckardtstein* (1871–1930), who made the costumes according to the *Doktor*'s indications, had an unusually fine sensitivity for coordinating colors with each other; thus she showed us some fabrics she had "treated" so as to get the most varied nuances. These fabrics were often only obtainable in tones that were too garish. She hung them for weeks in the open air in the shade, where they mostly faded only a little, taking on a fine silvery tone, and afterwards showed themselves to be splendidly attuned to each other.

In these years, keen negotiations were carried on with the purpose of erecting the *Johannesbau*[6] on the land acquired on the Ungererstrasse. When this project had to be given up on account of the building prohibition, and it became possible to choose the *Bluthügel* ("Blood Hill"[7]) in Dornach instead, many artistically striving individuals went there in the spring of 1914. *Sophie Stinde* (1853–1915), whose name and noble being is quite unknown to the majority of members today, was not only one of the most outstanding pioneers of the anthroposophical movement, but also the first and most energetic of those initiating the erection of our building. A few months earlier, in reply to the question as to whether I would also be permitted to join in the work there, she said: "Yes, we can use you. – I know you!" Her answer seemed to me brief, straightforward and clear – like her whole being, that consisted of truth and clarity. When she departed from us only a year and a half later, Rudolf Steiner dedicated the most moving words to her.[8]

Directly after the laying of the foundation stone on September 20, 1913, the preliminary excavation of the ground was begun. At that time there were only a very few members in Dornach. From March onwards, more and more came, since it became possible to begin with the sculptural work. On June 28, 1914, the ominous day of the assassination in Sarajevo, I found around 150 friends there, occupied with the most varied tasks. It was a Sunday morning. That afternoon the *Herr Doktor* held the third of the lectures given at the building site in the Carpentry Building. On ascending the hill, one came upon the eagerly awaited sight: already the cupolas were to be seen in their noble dimensions, though they did not as yet shine out into their surroundings, being still not yet covered with the greenish blue-gray shimmering slate from Norway. The whole building in its proportions had an effect, such that one directly sensed: there stands the fulfillment of all striving and all longing for the distantly-surmised and hoped-for renewal of the visual arts... Rudolf Steiner spoke to us of it in those lectures held in the Carpentry Building concerning the underlying impulses of

[6] Later renamed the Goetheanum.

[7] In a tumultuous battle, Swiss confederate forces gained the victory here over 3000 Swabians on July 22, 1499. The "Peace of Basel" was signed the same year, recognizing Swiss independence.

[8] See memorial addresses, pp. 150–179, in Rudolf Steiner: *Unsere Toten* (Our Dead) (GA 261), Rudolf Steiner Verlag, Dornach, Switzerland 1984.

the new building: how the element of time, of movement, would have to be incorporated into the visual arts, if they are to be re-enlivened.

Wishing to have me as an assistant and co-worker, Hermann Linde sent for me. The next morning I discussed with him in his studio (the former office in the Carpentry Building) the first tasks to be done. As he was showing *Frl.* von Eckardtstein and me the first two sketches Rudolf Steiner had made for the painting of the large cupola, it so happened that Rudolf Steiner himself entered the room. *Herr* Linde interrupted himself and pulled out the early edition of the newspaper he had brought with him from the city, announcing in large headlines the murder in Sarajevo. There was as yet no radio! Never shall I forget Rudolf Steiner's expression at that moment. Tremendous horror and grief lay in his wide-opened eyes as he uttered the words: "Now the catastrophe has overtaken us!"

As a matter of course, the work went on as before. Hermann Linde had already done a number of experiments with grounding, and these were continued with united energies. Stress was laid by Dr. Steiner on finishing the building by September on account of the anticipated outbreak of war. As regards the practical work of painting the large cupola, it was conceived that the five painters who had been chosen by Dr. Steiner would each form a staff of co-workers. Thus *Herr* Linde assigned to me the task of making various studies, e.g., arm-studies, but also attempts at shaping the Elohim beings in the west. The two first motifs, the lowest of the triad in the west and east of the cupola, the *Herr Doktor* had sketched with both pencil contours and pastel, while all later ones are worked only in color and the details of form retained in separate black-and-white studies. The desired color nuances were often not available to him. Thus he added verbal indications. In the case of the Elohim, he said they would have to be painted entirely in warm yellow, with a golden shining effect. Nowadays we can hardly imagine the difficulties that arose with such tasks. *Herr* Linde and his colleagues were very capable, talented painters – pictures by the former hung in various museums – but they had come completely out of the naturalistic school, had worked more with light-dark values and less in terms of color. Thus their activity in Dornach signified a total readjustment. Right into the details, everything had to be worked out from scratch.

One day a long-standing acquaintance, *Johanna Wagenmann,* close friends with the spouse of the leading architect *Schmidt-Curtius,* drew me mysteriously into *Haus Brodbeck* (the old part of what is today the *Rudolf Steiner-Halde*). When she had me slip into a small room and under the enclosed interior model worked entirely by Rudolf Steiner, it was the height of all happiness. An unspeakable impression presented itself; for he had only quite recently painted the curves of color into the model of the large cupola – with a tremendous intensity. It was

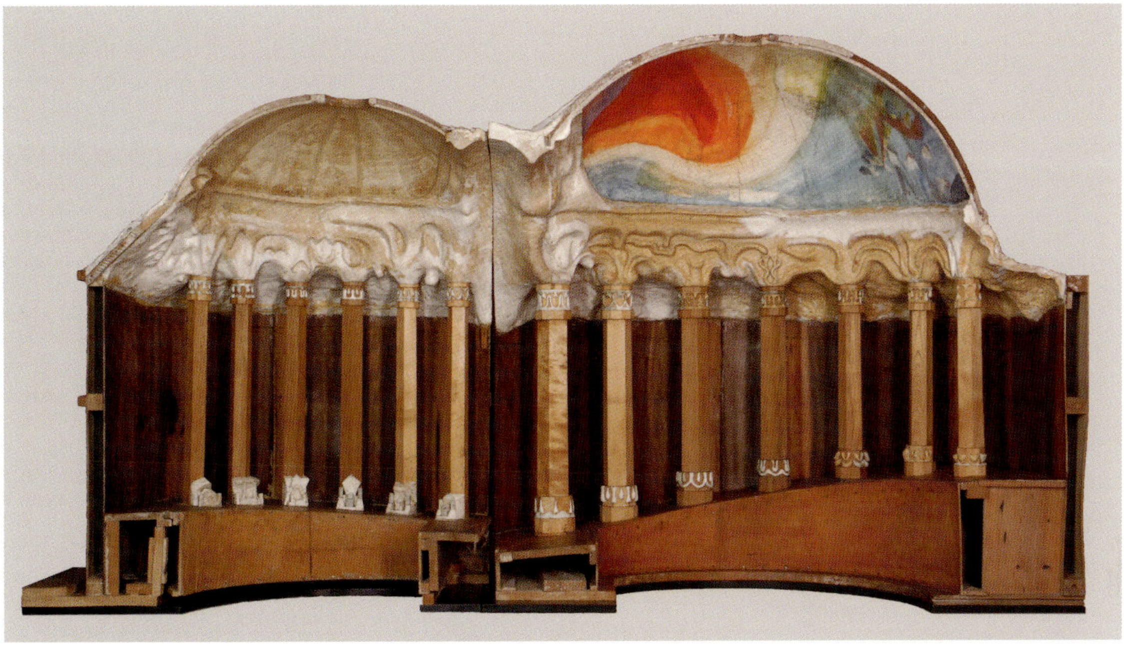

The interior model of the first Goetheanum by Rudolf Steiner. Scale 1:20. 1913. Goetheanum Art Collection (Dornach). Rudolf Steiner Nachlassverwaltung (Dornach). Restored 2005. Photo Haiggi Baumgartner.

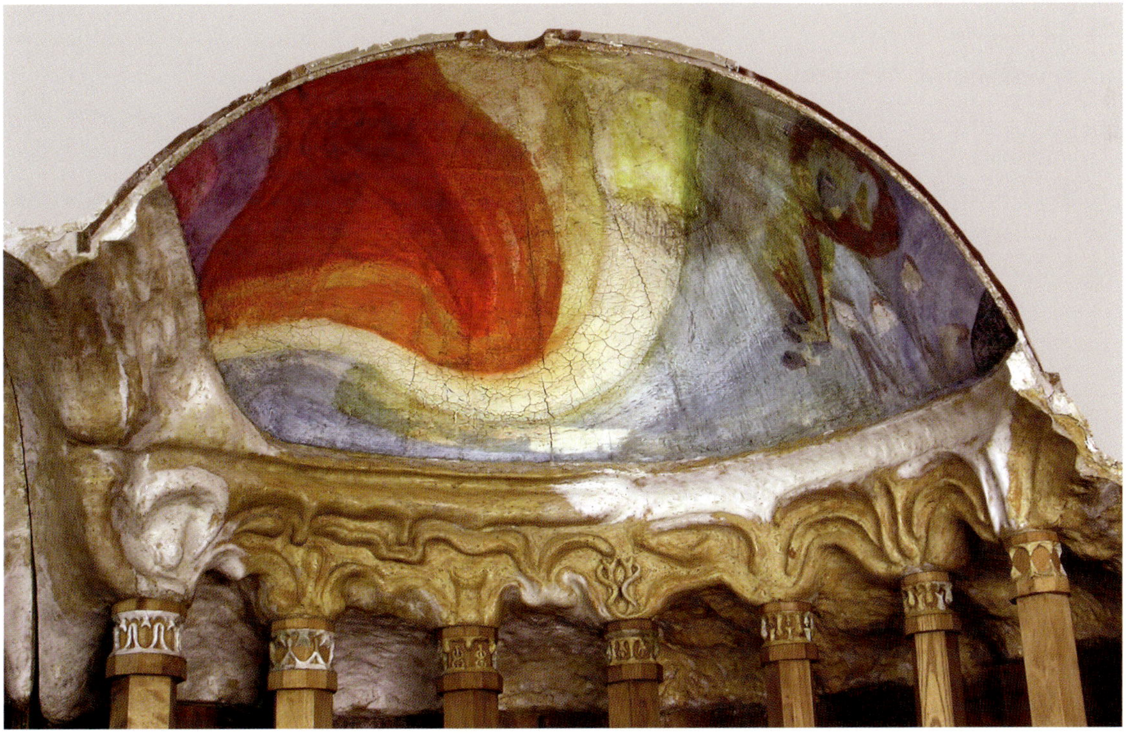

The interior model of the first Goetheanum. (Detail of the large cupola).

not the color alone which worked so powerfully, but the whole, quite new, singular formation of this sea of color with its flowing curves. One sensed something blossoming, growing and as though turning in on itself and out again: mysterious processes of becoming!

Soon many things changed: war had been declared! Many of our male friends were called up. *Herr* and *Frau Doktor* were at the Wagner festival performances in Bayreuth, but managed to get over the border just in time. *Frau Doktor* described this graphically. Hermann Linde had also gone north to fetch his wife and child, and remained absent for many weeks. In this way, a lot of tasks had to be postponed.

After a month or two, it was possible to form a picture for oneself of what was happening on the hill where our building was going up. Where so many artists were together, in order to serve a common goal out of enthusiasm, it could not be otherwise than that human weaknesses broke through now and again in the course of the work. Whether it was, for example, that more talented individuals found it difficult to look on while those perhaps less talented than themselves were able to accomplish certain tasks; or other things having to do with the various shades of temperament. At that time, however, it was moving to see how Rudolf Steiner always clearly indicated a particular necessary attitude, as the moment required, without ever moralizing. With rare exceptions, the indication was always heeded. In this way, each person's striving could keep pace with the work as a whole. He emphasized several times: For world events it was quite indifferent who carried out a particular task, if it is a matter of whether this task is done at all! The previous year, he had spoken of how impulses consciously held back, e.g., a seven-year renunciation of a favorite occupation, transform themselves into certain capacities. And in the last cycle of lectures held before the outbreak of the World War in Norrköping, he explained how, after death, Lucifer most easily spins a web around the human soul by means of its own ideals, and is then able to make its fruits his own, if the soul does not willingly during life give these ideals over to the spirit of humanity.

The situation of the Goetheanum, of the human race at that time, weighed heavily on the soul; the feeling reinforced itself, that only in attempting to give meaning to such teachings in one's own case, would one be doing one's part as an individual. Dr. Steiner had offered me the opportunity to involve myself in several other painting tasks. From similar motives to those given above, I renounced these and opted instead to take care of the grounding of the cupolas and the preparation of the painters' study-panels.

At that time a number of us also prepared the many thousands of oak shingles with which the exterior wall of the small cupola-space – actually of the storeroom (or magazine) surrounding it – was to be covered. Each one was dipped in a hot bath of wax dissolved in turpentine, which was then vigorously brushed in. However, this recipe proved to be insufficiently weatherproof. Later, this wall was covered with another waterproofing agent. In such simple tasks, important friends took part. Among others, *Walo von May* (1879–1928), the ingenious illustrator, keenly involved himself the whole time in this shingle-brushing, for the most part silently, only now and again making a kindly-ironic remark.

After various tries, I learned only somewhat late from *Frau Dr. Thekla Schmiedel* (1886 – 1963), that together with her husband she had developed a painting ground, which was at first rejected by some painters, as it did not seem white enough to them, being mixed with ordinary chalk instead of with so-called champagne-chalk. All experiments showed, however, that the ground made with the latter was far less resilient than the former and did not withstand washing very well. In addition, the grounding of *Dr. Oskar Schmiedel* (1887 – 1959) had wax mixed into it, lending the colors a wonderful luminosity. I decided in favor of this one after *Herr Doktor* declared the color tests on it to be satisfactory. Thus in the course of the next two years, apart from the 650 square meter surface of the two cupolas, approximately another 800 square meters of study-panels were produced for the various painters. For this purpose, two square meter plywood panels were used, made from Gabonese mahogany. The painting ground consisted of two different layers: the first was a mixture of chalk, casein and saponified wax. It had the magnificent advantage that a second coat, by definition the thickest, could be applied in any desired degree of graininess. The second layer consisted of a mixture of dissolved cellulose, wax and medium. This was to prevent the watercolor from penetrating too deeply and grant it corresponding luminosity.

The following episode is reported because it could point the way in some cases. In the early summer of 1915 we had finished grounding the large cupola up to a point. The painting ground consisted – as already mentioned – of two main layers. The first, of chalk, wax and casein-glue had to be painted three times onto cork panels, which were screwed onto plywood panels. These cork panels, used for acoustic reasons, had previously been washed down twice with a strong solution of aluminum acetate so as to bond the tannic acid. This would otherwise have struck through the white ground and caused stains. Between each of these three chalk coatings it was necessary to wait two weeks so that the casein-glue set completely. As a precaution, however, we let each layer dry still longer – for how much depended on our cupolas being well grounded and durable! As stated above, it was possible to give this painting ground any degree of graininess with the final coat. The wishes of the artists in this regard were diligently followed up and, in good time, we had made samples for them to try out. Even the most demanding requirements appeared to have been satisfied. However, one afternoon as I climbed down the scaffolding-steps 30 meters into the depths below, spattered from head to toe, eyes, nose and ears bespeckled with the precious white ground with which 450 square meters had been painted that day, I was met by one of the artists, asking for the key for the cupola lighting, saying he wanted to smooth the painting ground on his surface area with sandpaper right away. Horrified, I explained that we had made every effort to do all that was desired and that such an intention could definitely only be carried out in eight days time, after complete drying of the paint surface. To my astonishment, I got the answer: "The *Herr Doktor* has permitted it"! Assuming a misunderstanding, I climbed down to the bottom, and on meeting *Herr Doktor* in front of the Carpentry Building, I attempted to clear the matter up. "And why should N.N.[9] not do that on his part of the cupola?" he asked. "We have been working for months to prepare this ground properly so as to accord with all requirements, and the responsibility for it lies with me," I retorted. "But if you have delivered on and completed your work, you bear no further responsibility; only the painter himself does," Dr. Steiner replied. That did not make sense to me. "I can't understand that," I cried out, "aren't human beings there for the Goetheanum? Is it excusable that the work is knowingly impaired in this way?" But with a tone of extraordinary earnestness the answer came back: "No, the Goetheanum is there for human beings!" However, only the next few months shed light on this answer. The individual in question was in a somewhat unstable state of mind, and on that account it was important to put the person first in everything. Such a word of Rudolf Steiner has its effects throughout one's life and becomes decisive in certain situations.

Rudolf Steiner had as an ideal to use only organic plant material where possible for the interior space. Thus he also wanted specially produced plant colors rather than the usual mineral colors. These new plant pigments were developed and produced by *Frau* and *Herr* Schmiedel in their own laboratory. The old masters had already placed value on grinding the colors for as long as possible, since by this means the brilliance of the colors can be considerably enhanced. Thus a number of diligent hands applied themselves to grinding a portion of the pigments on matt plate-glass for up to 100 hours. These were mainly elderly friends who lacked the strength for carving and who now enthusiastically devoted themselves to this necessary work.

---

[9] In more than one instance, where no name is to be given, Hilde Boos-Hamburger indicates this with the letters "N.N." They do not necessarily stand for any actual initials.

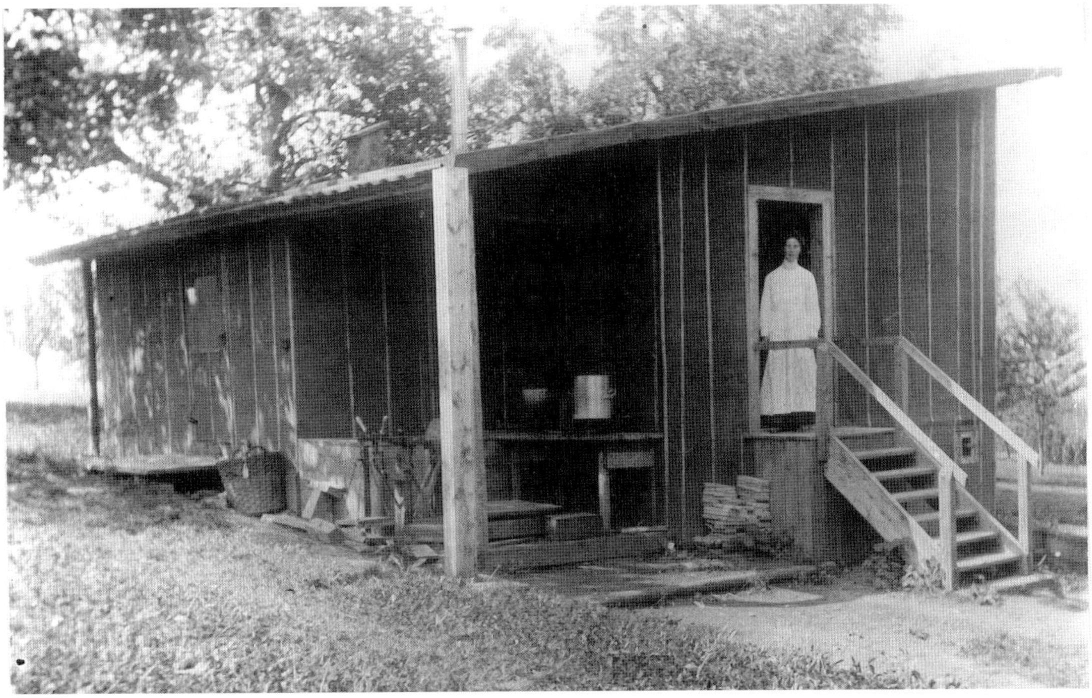

The plant color laboratory at the Goetheanum, 1914. Verlag am Goetheanum (Dornach).

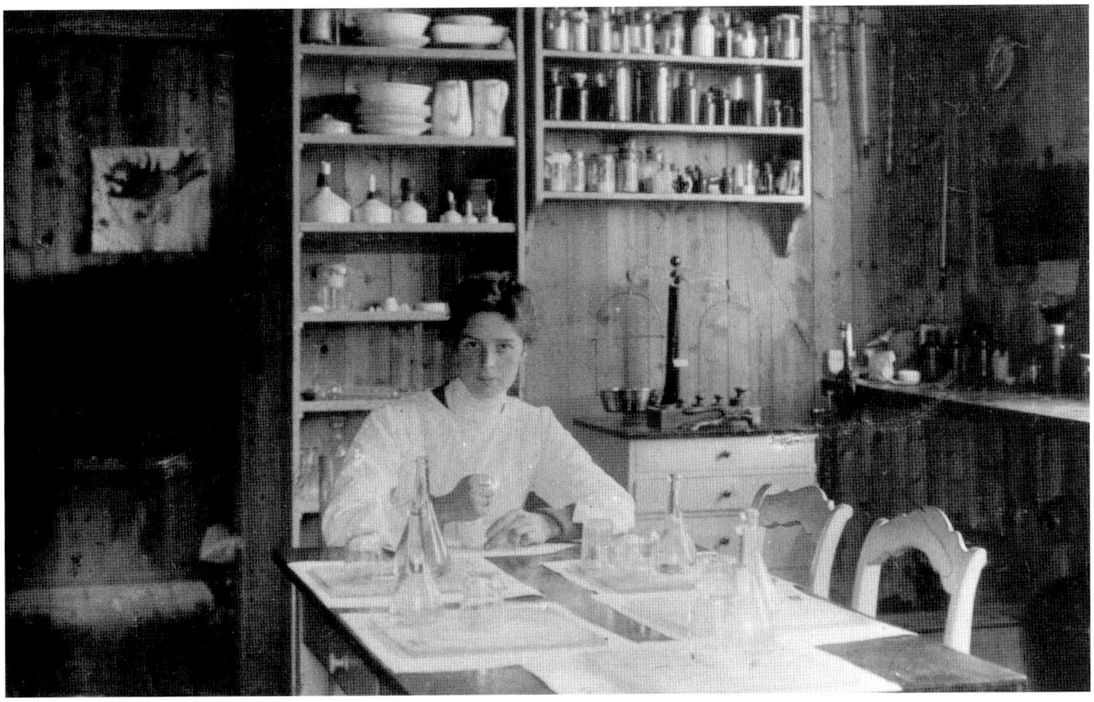

Thekla Schmiedel preparing plant colors in the laboratory. (When the first batch of plant colors stood ready for use, Rudolf Steiner was presented with a sheet of paper, on which he spontaneously painted the mythical beast dimly seen here in the background to the left.)
Verlag am Goetheanum (Dornach).

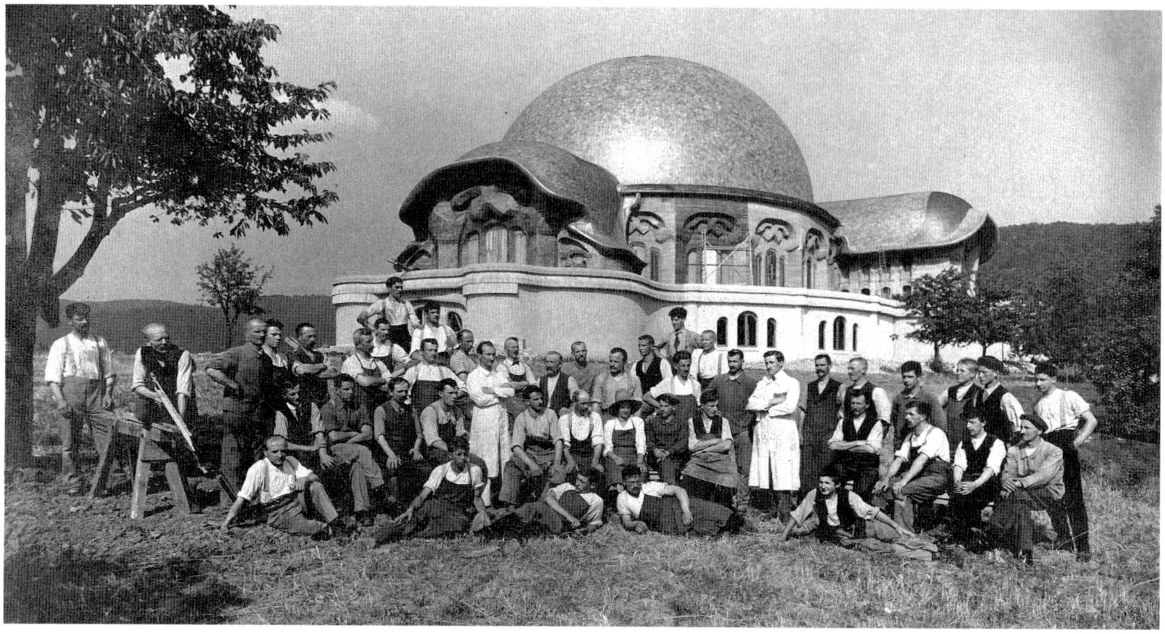

The team of carpenters in front of the first Goetheanum. (To the left, holding a saw, is the lead carpenter, Heinrich Liedvogel, who worked with rousing energy on the construction of both the first and the second Goetheanum.) Dokumentation am Goetheanum-Bildarchiv.

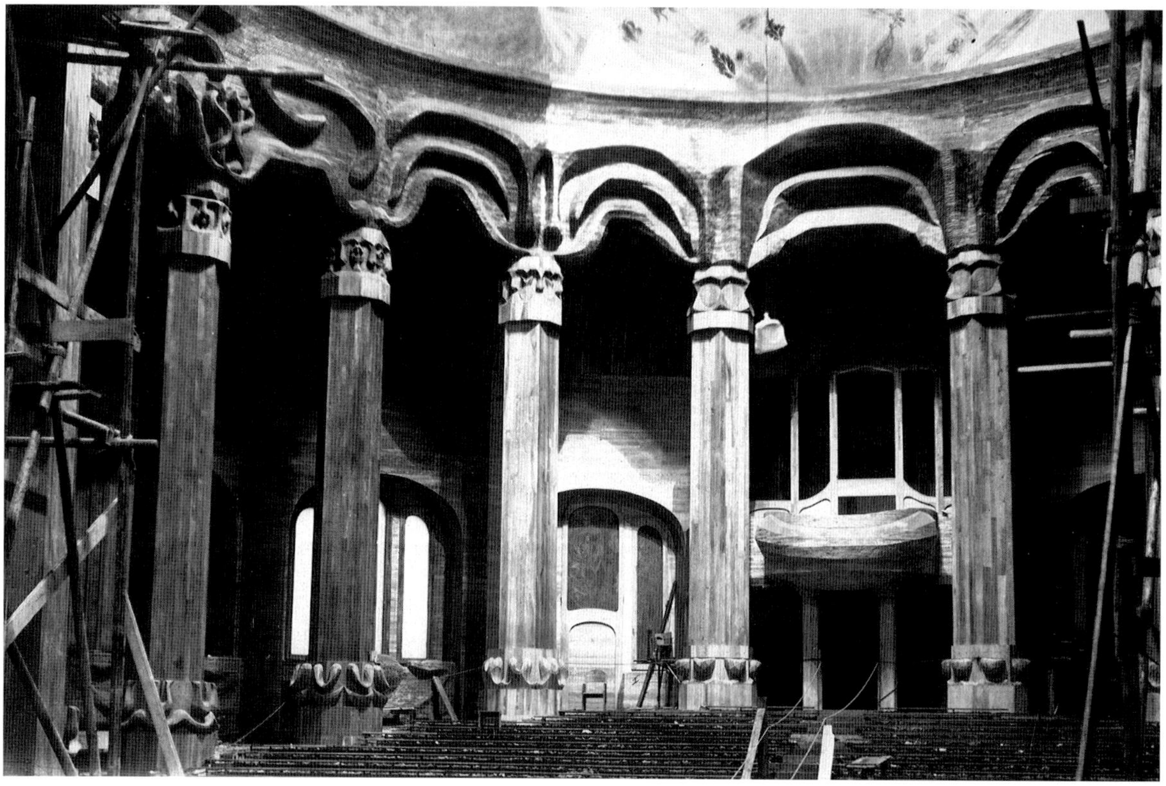

The auditorium and part of the large cupola (toward the southwest). Rudolf Steiner Archive (Dornach).

The plasticine which Rudolf Steiner required for the 9.5 meter high model [about 31 feet] of the great wooden group of the *Representative of Humanity*, which was to stand in a central position in the Goetheanum, was produced by *Frau Dr.* Schmiedel in the laboratory. It was a matter of approximately 2000 kg. [4400 lbs]. After the mass of plasticine had been duly mixed, it was kneaded by *Herr* and *Frau* Schuurman and then delivered to Miss *Edith Maryon* (1872–1924) in the studio. Together with our exceedingly dexterous carpenter *Sonderegger* – here I am reaching ahead somewhat – she had built up the scaffolding for the large model, based on the small, approximately two meter high model and the calculations of the architects. The individual framework for each of the six large figures of the group was made according to her specifications. These consisted of iron rods and wire mesh, the latter being already adapted to the main forms. Miss Maryon was rather well known in England in the years leading up to the first World War. I had heard her name mentioned there years ago. She worked with an unparalleled devotion and selflessness for Rudolf Steiner, placing her considerable abilities entirely at his disposal. I myself helped at that time in the preparatory work of spreading the plasticine onto the rods and wire mesh, roughly shaping the forms so that it was possible to relieve Dr. Steiner, who was continually occupied in all manner of places, of the most onerous part of the work. Thus I experienced something of her manner of doing things. In his memorial address for Edith Maryon, Rudolf Steiner emphasized how necessary such selfless help was for his work, and held her up as exemplary in this regard. At the very beginning he had said, in the lecture of June 17, 1914, printed in *Ways to a New Style in Architecture:* "True healing from evil to good will in the future lie for human souls in true art sending a spiritual atmosphere into human souls and human hearts, so that these human souls and hearts, when sympathetically surrounded by what has come into being in architectural sculpture and other forms, if they are predisposed to lying, cease to lie, if predisposed to disturb the peace, cease to disturb the peace of their fellow human beings. They will speak a language which human beings today have as yet no presentiment of!"

Not only could these words be felt as profound truth, but increasingly also as an earnest admonition as, oppressive and threatening, the dull thunder of cannons began to roll across from nearby Alsace.

The work itself was a source of much satisfaction. While the fourteen painters – since Christmas 1914 those assigned to work on the small cupola had also begun making their studies – struggled intensively with the new painting problems, they needed an immense number of study panels, as already indicated above. I had to provide these according to need, so there was often the opportunity of visiting their work places and taking part in many conversations and discussions. Ever new riddles came up: it even emerged that Dr. Steiner had said something to one artist which seemed to contradict what he had said to another. Much confusion arose on this account among the painters. We first had to learn to understand how subtly he entered into the various questions, answering them out of the whole mood and context from which they proceeded. It then occurred to one: you must first learn how to ask questions – how to formulate objective questions, free of wishes, that willingly accept either confirmation or denial in answer.

In the autumn of 1915 when difficulties had arisen in connection with several personalities that needed settling to clear the air, a number of evening sessions were scheduled for this purpose. Rudolf Steiner often let people talk for hours and began speaking himself only when a great deal had already come to light. Among other things, he tried to make comprehensible to us how problematic it is for the esoteric teacher, that he is under the strictest obligation not to encroach in the slightest degree on the free will of the pupil. He said: "If for example someone comes to me and says, 'I know I was the Mother of God in my last life'" [a crass case, which had actually occurred – *the author*], "then as an esoteric teacher I do not even have the right to say: that is not true. Why? Because, if someone comes to me with a statement of that kind, the desire for confirmation is in fact already contained in it. And this I have to take account of. Thus I can at most reply: If you think so – but this answer is then taken as confirmation!"– (quoted from memory).

As a result of the outbreak of war much had changed, affecting the work. Of necessity it had to proceed much more slowly. Hermann Linde had returned in the autumn with his wife, who was also a painter. It then came about of itself that the artists now had the time and the leisure to bring their studies for the large cupola to a conclusion on their own. Linde took on the three motifs lying one over the other in the west and later also the ones in the east which lead over to the small cupola. *Richard Pollack-Karlin* (1867–1943) and his wife painted "Lemuria" and "Atlantis" as well as the Greek cultural period. Baroness Paini-Gazotti – known at that time as *Lotus Péralté* (1862–1953) – painted the "Indian" period; *Fräulein Ottilie Schneider* (1875–1957) from Prague the "Persian" and "Egyptian" period. With all these colleagues, who differed in age, I was good friends in later years as well. Hermann Linde was well-known as an artist in Germany. Among other places, he exhibited regularly in the Berlin Secession. He was an Impressionist in the best sense of the word and a subtle chiaroscurist. Especially charming are the many studies in which he was able to capture in the most exceptional way a sense of life and movement. It was admirable how he struggled for the changeover to immersing oneself in the life of color. His final picture series of the *Green Snake and the Beautiful Lily*[10], created on commission for the wife of privy councillor Röchling and often exhibited in the Goetheanum, bears witness to this.

Richard Pollack-Karlin was from Prague and had been associated in his youth with the circle around *Gustav Meyrink,* though he went rather his own way. He sought mystical deepening. When a number of friends, including Meyrink, had connected themselves with "*Meister Johannes*" ("Master John"), a significant, though outwardly unassuming man in Frankfurt, who was also known to Rudolf Steiner, Pollack visited him once, but continued following his own path, as he told me.

Knowledge of higher things shone from his eyes, which sparkled with great kindness. A deep seriousness and feeling of responsibility permeated his whole manner of striving. After a number of years he had come far enough that the stigmata could be seen to emerge, and a great weakness tied him to his bed. At this time he and *Hilde Kontanyi,* later his wife, heard of Rudolf Steiner and requested a visit from him. Dr. Steiner said to Pollack: "This is not a path for you" and gave him instructions leading onto the modern, Rosicrucian path. This was told me in later years by Pollack himself. I had often visited him and his wife in their studio in Vienna prior to 1914 and made friends with them. Both faced life with great interest and were connected with a wide circle of people. Hilde Pollack was a plump, unusually lively woman who in like manner turned out *Buchteln* (yeast pastries), *Strudel* and *Zwetschgenknödel* (plum dumplings) and enjoyed inviting her friends to an excellent "*Kaffeetscherl*" (coffee party), just as she also worked out with loving care her – albeit *Jugendstil* (art nouveau) stylized – "*Viecherl*" (animals) for the task assigned her in the cupola painting, while Pollack had been allocated the "*Engerl*" (angels) by Dr. Steiner. They worked jointly on the Greek, Lemurian and Atlantean motifs. Hilde Pollack had seized the initiative in painting small program-posters for the eurythmy performances which, from 1915 on, took place regularly on Sunday afternoons. This pleased *Herr* and *Frau Doktor* so much, that they regarded the painted program-poster as an integral part of the event and retained this custom.

Admittedly these posters looked very different from those of today. They had rather something of Viennese *Jugendstil* about them. They were more like decorative drawings tinted with color. When the paintings in the large cupola were completed, *Frau* Pollack began to live out her phantasy in fine silk-embroideries. Several friends had made their view known, that her style would lend itself most favorably to a kind of embroidery or needlework-painting. Although her attitude was to reject this at first, she did in fact attempt

---

[10] Goethe's fairy tale.

it, and came to astonishing results. She then later produced a great deal in Prague – where the couple had moved after the separation of the Austro-Hungarian monarchy – and acquired a name for herself. So much so, that when these loyal friends were both brought, under the Nazi regime, to Theresienstadt and were to go after a time to Auschwitz, the German National Socialists offered to spare her life, if she would embroider for them. In her upright, brave manner, she declined and preferred to go with her husband to her death. At the age of 76 he held hundreds of anthroposophical lectures for his companions in suffering in the camp. In view of such greatness and tragedy, one first comprehends the old biblical saying: "Be true even unto death, and I shall give you the crown of life." May they now, adorned with this crown, help perhaps thousands of their blood-companions find paths into the future in earthly life.

Shortly before Christmas 1914, Dr. Steiner had allocated all the sketches for the decoration of the two cupolas. I could now yield to a long cherished wish to show him some work without seeming to drop a hint. I hoped for a fruitful conversation.

Upon stating my wish, he first of all replied: "Yes, but I have unfortunately already given out all the sketches for the cupolas." I explained to him that I knew that and had intentionally waited so long with my request, in order that he would not think I wanted to force myself on him. He went into the studio of Lotus Péralté and looked at a number of my watercolor sheets there. Stopping at one in particular he suddenly exclaimed: "I shall still give you something to paint even so!" It was a somewhat naive-bold attempt, inspired by his description of the Old Moon evolution in *An Outline of Esoteric Science.* To my astonished question, whether there was anything at all left to paint, he answered: "Yes, in the *Skyoptikon!*[11]" And just what was to be done there, I ventured to ask. "It will be esoteric things," was the reply. This story should be told, since almost no one knew about it, not even *Herr* Linde or *Herr Aisenpreis,* both of whom I asked about it. Only *Fräulein* Stinde had learned of it from the *Doktor,* but without further particulars.

Unfortunately, I forgot to ask *Frau* Dr. Steiner what she knew.

In these days, Rudolf Steiner also gave a sketch for the stage curtain.[12] It has the wanderings

---

[11] Though it seems to suggest an observatory, *Skyoptikon* was then still a current term for what had been an early form of slide projector, as first used by Herman Grimm for his lectures on art history. This was a room designed to admit direct sunlight from an aperture in the ceiling.

[12] This sketch measuring 30 x 44 cm [12 x 17 in] is available in a full-size color reproduction published by the Rudolf Steiner Verlag, Dornach.

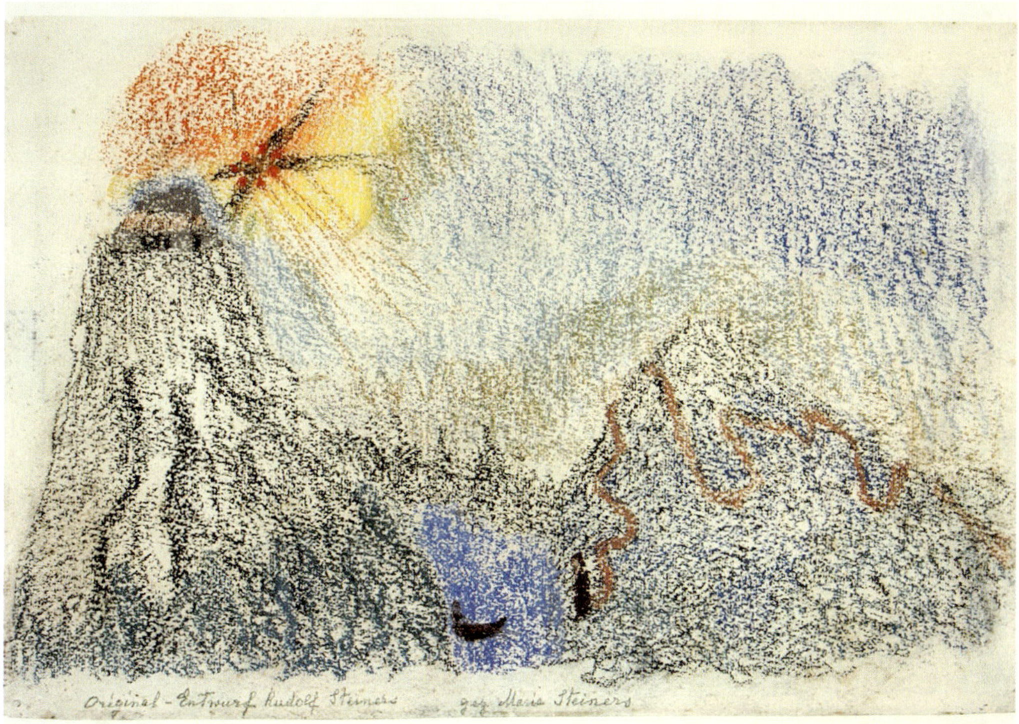

Sketch for the stage curtain in the first Goetheanum by Rudolf Steiner. Oil crayon. 1914. Rudolf Steiner Archive (Dornach).

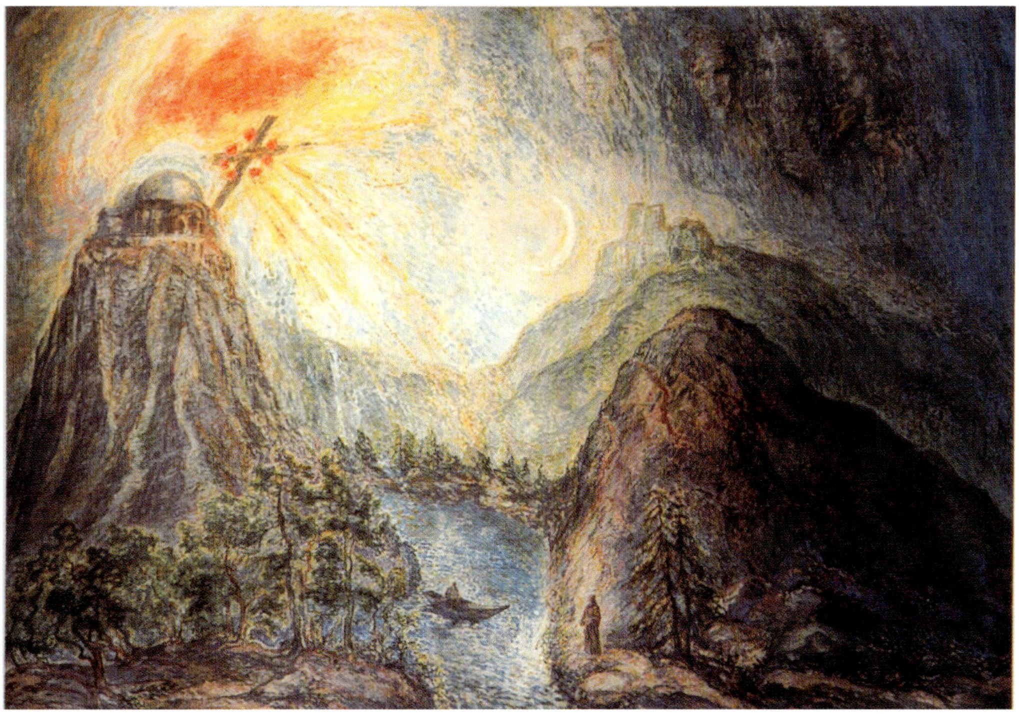

The stage curtain in the second Goetheanum painted by William Scott Pyle. 1937.

of Brother Mark from the *"Geheimnissen"* (Mysteries) by Goethe as its motif. He said that Goethe had in some respects not fully grasped the underlying imagination. For example, the rose-cross which comes into question here is not chiseled in stone, but floats from the spiritual world over the monastery. This is actually the first Goetheanum, which has to stand on a crag of primary rock, while the mountain over which Brother Mark strides would have to show a limestone formation. It appeared to me decidedly odd that the painter [*Camilla Wandrey*]who carried out studies based on the sketch, wavered, because, as she lamented, she did not know the difference between primary rocks and limestone. Hence she wrote to Dr. Schmiedel in Innsbruck, who had been obliged to do his military service there in the hinterlands, requesting photographs of primary rock crags. I wanted to assist her, and when the opportunity presented itself, I asked the *Doktor* whether he had rock formations of a particular region in mind. Animatedly, he replied: "Well, you know the *Rosalien* chapel near Wiener-Neustadt. It stands on the foothills of the *Wechselgebirge* and that is primary rock!" It was for him simply a matter of the characteristic kind. The mountain range he mentioned subsides gently, undulating down towards the Hungarian lowlands; it shows bare rock in only a few places. On the other hand, the crag in the sketch juts up steeply. Nothing came of this painted curtain so far as the first Goetheanum is concerned. One problem lay in the difficulty of producing a suitable painting ground for a curtain which is to be gathered up, and maybe Rudolf Steiner also did not find it artistically satisfactory to gather up a painted curtain. Many years later our now-deceased American friend *William Scott Pyle* (1888–1938) painted the motif as a curtain for the new building – one can say, as his legacy.

Time flew by. The two cupolas were grounded, and the painters worked for the most part on painting them. We had performed several *Faust* scenes in eurythmy under the unforgettable direction of *Herr* and *Frau Doktor*. On Assumption Day on August 15, 1915, Faust's ascent to heaven was presented on the stage of the Carpentry Building. A mood of consecration prevailed which recalled a similar one at the Munich performances of the Mystery Plays. *Jan Stuten* (1890–1948) had created the first version of his music for the Prologue. The previous Easter the Easter Night scene, and at Whitsun the Ariel scene, were performed. – All with the simplest means, for it was crucial to save. Yet these performances often had the strongest effect, arising quite especially from the specifications, the outstanding knowledge and ability, the true artistry of Rudolf Steiner. Those more qualified have already given an account of this.

It seems to me that too little is told of the wonderful humor of the great teacher. When describing the hats appropriate for Faust and Wagner to our old friend *Ellram*, who was

60-ish, but devoted herself with skill and enthusiasm to costuming, he took hold – for lack of other means at that moment – of the blue silk turban she always wore wherever one saw her. Startled, the poor woman shrieked, "Oh, *Herr Doktor,* my wig, my wig!" And, with a slightly mischievous, yet beaming smile, he said: "Excuse me, please!" It was his subtle way of treating people with humor. Years ago, our spirited friend had been in actual fact, as she often recounted, director of the boarding school of the officers' daughters in St. Petersburg. One of her duties was to teach the girls the formal curtsy. She once declared to me grandly: "Never have I felt better than when these 500 girls, in practicing, sank to their knees in front of me!"

When we were rehearsing the scene in which Mephisto, in order to get away from Faust, calls upon the spirits who are to delude him with magical pictures, Dr. Steiner explained that these were the group-spirits of "flies, fleas, bugs and lice" which were being summoned hither by their lord and master. Noticing the startled faces around him, he said these beings were, however, very beautiful to look at. Thus this song was now rehearsed. During one of the pauses, a Russian friend asked: "*Herr Doktor,* what does it mean if one has great antipathy to spiders?" Beaming, Dr. Steiner looked at her and answered genially: "That means that one has great affinity with these creatures!" – eliciting shock.

He then fetched another eurythmist and showed her how to do the movement she was to carry out as a leaping rat sent for by Mephisto, in order to gnaw at the pentagram on the threshold. She likewise showed no enthusiasm at first for the role intended for her!

When the Easter march was rehearsed, it turned out that most of us were not good dancers, in many cases not even being able to dance a simple waltz properly! *Herr Doktor* almost despaired that no rhythm and fire could be infused into it! It should not be forgotten that he had grown up in Austria. *Mieta Waller* (1883–1954), who in her lively way at that time often liked to play the *enfant terrible,* suddenly cried out: "Oh *Herr Doktor,* couldn't you demonstrate a *Schuhplattler* (Austrian folk dance) for us?" "Oh yes, certainly," was the immediate answer, and already he prepared to climb onto the stage. "Oh," *Frau Doktor* quickly exclaimed, "it is already much too late, we absolutely must go home." In her concern, she wanted, where possible, to avoid his overtaxing himself by such strenuous exercise.

A while before that, at Christmas 1915, the *Shepherds Play* and *Three Kings Play* had been performed for the first time in Dornach. Dr. Steiner held various lectures on this subject. The plays took place at that time only within the limited circle of the members. It was wartime. Once he described how these plays gradually came about, how at first only a small crib was set up; but then every inhabitant of the village went up to it and wanted to rock the child in it. It often came off rather crudely. Joseph was performed in a somewhat oafish manner – not yet as a worthy "alderman." At this he stepped onto the stage himself and mimed this figure. All at once he stumbled and fell flat on his face. Taken aback and concerned, everyone jumped up – however, he was already up and said cheerfully: "Yes, but that belongs to it!" It had seemed so genuine that no one had the idea that it could have been intentional.

Herr Doktor devoted particular care to the scenes of Faust's death and the battle for his soul. The burial scene had an unusually eerie effect. Jan Stuten, who took on all manner of difficult things and applied himself diligently to solving them – at that time he always played Faust as well – had skilfully sawn out the skeletons of the "Lemures" from wooden boards painted white, and these "bones" were then sewn onto black costumes. With the gestures indicated by Rudolf Steiner, the audience got the impression of real tottering skeletons on the stage. The Scrawny and Fat Devils had their realistic costumes. The latter, with short, straight horns, had a stomach protruding out almost a meter, made of a wire frame with which it was not easy to get around the scenery. Once, *Herr Doktor* was almost blown over by it! Having had enough of playing angels, I asked *Frau Doktor* to let me play a devil. "You are an angel, I think?," she replied. "Angels are a bit boring in the long run," I said. "May I not play a Fat Devil?" This she laughingly took note of.

Dr. Steiner gave us an additional lesson in how these beings move. He explained that walking – in a way that comes clearly to expression in "threefold walking" – has a purely Christian element about it: establishing balance again and again in the act of walking. These sub-human demons are incapable of this. The Fat Devils, for example, can only move along, with their short, stumpy legs and broad, flat feet, in a half-shuffling, half-hopping manner, which Professor Petz, the violinist from Neuenburg, *Fräulein* Elisabeth Vreede (1879–1943) and three others among us then faithfully practiced. The Scrawny Devils did likewise – among them *Jeanne-Marie Bruinier* (1875–1951), who painted in the small cupola, and Richard Pollack-Karlin. They were to jump so as to hardly touch the ground. When Rudolf Steiner himself played the whole burial scene as Mephisto for the actor of Mephisto, *Max Schuurman* (1889–1955), most of us felt a cold shiver run down our spines. It was played with such realism, and to double effect, since it adhered to the boundaries of the artistic.

In her book *Eurythmy* (Verlag Waldhaus, Malsch), *Tatiana Kisseleff* (1881-1970) has reported a number of things concerning the rehearsals for the Romantic and Classical *Walpurgisnacht.*

Before the building in Dornach was begun, Rudolf Steiner had already held lectures on artistic questions and artist-individualities. Fundamental in this respect are "Goethe as the Father of a New Aesthetics" and, in 1909, "The Being of the Arts." In the lecture cycles there are many further indications. In 1911 on the occasion of the cycle given in the *Prinzensälen* in Munich, he had selected and hung a number of pictures by *Frau Maria Strakosch-Giesler* and said certain things about them. The reader is referred to the report of *Frau* Strakosch in her book *Die erlöste Sphinx* ("The Sphinx Redeemed"). (See p. 6–7 of this volume.)

The actual basic lectures on painting with their far-reaching perspectives for the future were, however, held in 1914 and 1915. Again and again, he gave new indications. But as yet it could not easily be surmised how these new impulses would take effect. Of course, artists were still strongly tied to their old ways of expressing themselves and it was necessary to wait till the new seeds could really begin to take root. Apart from Rudolf Steiner's sketches for the painting of the cupolas of the first Goetheanum, there was as yet nothing really new to be seen. Some things threatened to cause confusion! Other painters who visited Dornach brought along their own attempts. One case was interesting. Already a year or two earlier, following a lecture in Germany, Rudolf Steiner had once shown a few such attempts. He showed them again later on the occasion of the General Meeting in Berlin in 1914 and said, these were mirrorings in the objective world-ether. Very few people could make anything of this. That winter there was a circle of people who particularly interested themselves in these paintings. Among them, the paintings produced by two women were especially admired. One could hear of experiences in "lofty, spiritual realms." Admiringly, the "initiation" of the person in question was spoken of. It continued like that for a while. Then, however, Rudolf Steiner began holding his clarifying, unambiguous lectures on "head and abdominal clairvoyance." He also emphasized at that time that precisely those who were most affected usually did not apply the distinction to themselves. From spring into the summer, he spoke about these questions again and again as was his wont, illuminating them from new sides. Among other things, the nature of Imagination was described, how it can be attained by means of a spiritual-scientific training, in contrast to the visions that easily arise as a result of the organic activity of the human body.

One of the personalities referred to had left Dornach for a time. When she reappeared, *Frau* Stinde let me know, adding that it would only be possible to grant this painter support for her stay if she were to obligate herself to do the necessary practical work, and not only to turn out her own paintings, as in the winter. She would need to actually assist in the work of grounding as planned. I then asked Sophie Stinde whether she could say how matters stood with those paintings of which such a lot had been made in some quarters the past winter. I believed I had understood something of the recent lectures mentioned above, but even so, I did not trust myself to pass judgment immediately.

Fräulein Stinde then told me that Dr. Steiner had, at the special request of *Frau* Dr. Steiner, *Countess Kalckreuth* (1856–1929), and herself, explained most of those painted sheets, since this painter had handed over her portfolio each time to Dr. Steiner. He told these ladies, it was a pity this artist had not been more modest and had again and again wanted to show her work in the Carpentry Building. If her paintings had not in this way become so generally known, one would now have the most beautiful anatomical atlas for the doctors of the movement. And with that, he began to describe each of the paintings exactly, showing how they brought to expression miscellaneous processes of digestion, of the sexual organs, etc.

In the lectures which Dr. Steiner held a short time later in the Carpentry Building, in connection with the premiere of "Faust's Ascension" on August 15, 1915, he referred once again to this question from a wider point of view. On account of its interest, it is perhaps permissible to add a longer quotation from one of these lectures here[13]:

> If you now disregard everything else – one can't after all enumerate everything – you can then more or less imagine this physical part of the human being arising from the etheric organization in such a way – including, of course, everything else that I have presented in *Esoteric Science* and elsewhere, – that female and male forms arise. Whatever else plays a part, we now disregard, but female and male forms arise. If Lucifer and Ahriman had not participated, then female and male forms would not have arisen, but rather that which I once described in Munich: an intermediate. Thus we can really say; it is to be ascribed to Lucifer and Ahriman that the human form on earth became differentiated in a male and a female form. And in fact, if we already imagine the condition in which the human being approaches the earth, which gradually consolidates by means of the mineral kingdom, if we imagine in addition, that the earth planet forms itself, physically densifies, that in the circumference of the earth there is the ether permeating the earth, we can then picture to ourselves that human beings form themselves out of the ether of the whole earth and thereby in their character also approach the physical of the earth, that at the same time the etheric-

[13] Rudolf Steiner: *Spiritual-Scientific Annotations to Goethe's Faust,* Vol. I, "Faust, the Striving Human Being" (GA 272) (not yet published in an English translation).

mineral-physical in them meets with the mineral-physical of the earth. But Lucifer and Ahriman are there, are really at work there. They have a lot of means by which to exercise their influence on the evolution of humanity. And these diverse means they make use of for this or that process that they call forth.

Lucifer has above all the tendency to develop the spirit of what is light; he would actually always like to not let human beings become properly physical, would like to not let them quite descend to earth. Lucifer remained behind at the stage of the Moon evolution and wants to gain human beings for himself, not letting them enter into Earth evolution. He strives for this in such a way that he takes possession of the forces of warmth-ether and of light-ether. These forces he utilizes in his own way in the processes that now take place with the human being becoming physical. Lucifer mainly has power over warmth-ether and light-ether; he chiefly governs these. He prepared himself well for this already during the Moon evolution; he organizes them in his manner. By this means he can influence the development of the human being in a quite different direction. In letting the human being become physical out of the ether, he can by virtue of making use of warmth- and light-ether and asserting his power in these, give rise to the human form in a different way than would have been the case without this happening. As he now holds sway and weaves in the warmth-light-ether, it is not the intermediate human being that would otherwise come about, but the female form of the human being that arises. The female form of the human being would never have arisen without Lucifer. It is in fact the expression of what emerges from the ether when Lucifer takes possession of the warmth-light-ether.

Ahriman has power particularly over the tone- and life-ether. Ahriman is at the same time the spirit of heaviness. Ahriman has the desire to counteract Lucifer. By this means equilibrium is in a certain way substantially brought about, in that the ahrimanic power is placed by the wisely acting, progressive gods over against the luciferic power that wants to lift the human being above the earthly. Ahriman actually wants to draw human beings down into the physical. He wants to make them more physical than they would otherwise become as intermediate human beings. Ahriman is prepared for that by having power especially over the tone- and life-ethers. In tone- and life-ether Ahriman acts and weaves. And in this way the human physical form, in going out from the ether into the physical, becomes physical in a different way than it would have become through the progressive gods: it becomes the male form. Without the influence of Ahriman, the male form would not be thinkable at all, would not be possible at all. So that one can say: the female form is raised through Lucifer out of the warmth- and light-ether, in that Lucifer infuses this form etherically with a certain upward striving. The male form is formed by Ahriman so that a certain striving toward the earth is implanted in it.

This, which is now at the same time thus willed out of macrocosmic world evolution, we can really observe in the human being by spiritual scientific means. If we take for the moment the female form, schematically drawn, then we have to say, there is etherically woven into it by Lucifer in his fashion, warmth and light. Thus the physical female form is so woven, that in the light- and warmth-ether not only the regular progressive gods have developed their forces, but luciferic forces are woven into this female ether body. Let us now assume, in this female ether body, that which the earth in particular has provided, the "I"-consciousness, the unifying consciousness, is dimmed down, a kind of subdued consciousness enters in, that some people already call "clairvoyance," — a kind of dreamlike, trancelike seeing. Then, in such a case, there emerges what Lucifer has woven in the warmth- and light-ether as a kind of aura; so that, if visionaries are in their visionary state, they are surrounded by an aura that has luciferic forces in it, namely those of the warmth- and light-ether. It is now a matter of this aura surrounding the female body not being seen as such when, in mediumistic fashion, visionary states enter in. For, self-evidently, if the female body is in the midst of this aura (a drawing was made), then the female organization sees into this aura and projects on all sides what it sees in this aura. It sees what is in its own aura. The objective observer sees something that can be designated as follows: the human being rays out Imaginations and has an aura that is in fact made up of Imaginations. That is an objective process which does not affect the one who observes it. That means: if this imaginative aura is viewed from outside, viewed by another, then quite simply, an aura is objectively seen as anything else is seen; whereas, if this aura is looked through from within by the visionary herself, then she sees only what Lucifer spreads out within her. There is a big difference whether one sees something oneself, or whether it is seen by others — a tremendous difference.

With this is connected the fact that when visionary clairvoyance occurs in a woman, great danger exists if this visionary clairvoyance appears in the form of Imaginations; there caution is especially necessary on the part of the woman. And it is always required that development be taken severely in hand, that it be a healthy development. — Not stopping short at everything one sees, for that can actually simply be one's luciferic aura seen from within, which was necessary in order to mold the female body. And some things that visionaries describe are interesting for quite other reasons than those the female visionaries consider interesting. When they describe or regard what they see as though it were an interesting objective world, they are quite wrong, they are quite in error. When the corresponding aura is seen from outside, however, then it is that which made the female form possible out of the ether in the first place in earthly evolution. So we can say that the woman has to exercise particular care when visionary, imaginative clairvoyance begins or shows itself; for there a danger can very easily lurk, the danger of falling into error.

The male organism is different. If we consider the male organism, then Ahriman has power to enter into his aura but now woven into the tone- and life-ether. And as with the woman it is mainly the warmth-ether, so with the man it is mainly the life-ether. With the woman it is mainly warmth-ether within which Lucifer works and with the man, the life-ether within which Ahriman works. If the man now gets out of his consciousness, if the cohesion that expresses him as an "I"-consciousness is dampened-down, if a kind of passive condition occurs with the man, then one can once again see how the aura around him asserts itself, the aura within which Ahriman has his power.

But it is now an aura that chiefly contains life- and tone-ether within it. There is vibrating tone in it, so that one actually does not see this aura of the man directly. It is not an imaginative aura, but is rather something consisting of vibrating, spiritual tone that surrounds the man. All of this has to do with the form — not with the soul, of course, that has to do with the man in that he is physical. So that one who observes this form from outside can see: the human being rays out — one can now say — Intuitions. These are the same Intuitions of which his form is comprised, by means of which he is there as man in the world. There it resounds with living-vibrating tone around one. On that account another danger is present in the case of the man, if consciousness is dampened-down to passivity, the danger of now hearing one's own aura, inwardly hearing it. The man must take particular care that he does not let himself go, when he spiritually hears this aura of his, for there he hears Ahriman holding sway in him. For he has to be there.

THE STRUGGLE FOR THE UNDERLYING PRINCIPLES OF A NEW SPIRITUALIZED PAINTING IMPULSE

Hilde Boos-Hamburger

After quite a few attempts in painting that had arisen on Sundays and during the midday break, I ventured once again to request an opportunity to show these to Dr. Steiner. About two years had passed since the first time. From this point on, I was able over a number of years to learn from him, among other things, how he proceeded as a real pedagogue with all these paltry attempts. Everywhere he looked for the positive features, taking note of the intention with each exercise. He stressed how important it was to "study Goethe's chapter on the 'Visual-Moral Effects of Colors'. – It is a gold mine for the painter." At a few of my efforts he smiled in a friendly fashion. Even so, he objected to an angel's wing on a larger work as being not right. In response to my complaint, that I couldn't after all know how such a thing is formed in reality, he tapped me on the shoulder blade and said, smiling, "You have one there yourself, you only have to feel it!"

Only months later did my friend Pollack tell me that Rudolf Steiner had afterward expressed himself to him as quite hopeful regarding those attempts, which naturally encouraged me to continue striving.

Prompted by my various studies, I also asked him one day, whether it could be helpful to one's quest in the field of painting, to occupy oneself with significant painters from the past, entering intensively into their works. "Of course," he replied animatedly, "but one must keep to the right time-period! The soul should have gone through the portal of death not too long ago and not too recently. Rembrandt, for example, has already been dead for too long..." "But," he said after a moment's reflection, "occupy yourself with Alfred Rethel (1816–1859), that would be a good thing."

As the opportunity presented itself, I now did this, procuring books about him – though not much was to be had. Many years later, I also saw his frescos in the town hall in Aachen. I did not feel I had made real contact with him, however, which had quite certainly to do with my own inability. On the other hand, in later years an intensive preoccupation with Philipp Otto Runge (1777–1810) seems to me to have been in a certain way more fruitful. It may have been easier inasmuch as this painter stands somewhat closer to us today, especially in his writings, which bring out his intentions more clearly than he had been able to express them on canvas in his youth. This does seem to me a fertile pointer for painters.

This was the beginning of the time of the "Threefold" movement, about which *Emil Leinhas* (1878-1967) and *Dr. Roman Boos* (1889-1952) have reported authoritatively. The latter and I had at that time accompanied Rudolf Steiner to Bern where in March 1919 the first "pacifist" meeting of the League of Nations took place (before the Treaty of Versaille). Rudolf Steiner and a few friends had hoped the possibility would arise there, even in this turbulence, for him to speak and be heard. But that circle of people felt no need of this, although many among them had known him from earlier days. Almost more than is usually the case, everyone seemed only to want to speak and be heard themselves. Many there regarded themselves as cultural leaders. But no one asked whether Rudolf Steiner had some advice to give amid the great chaos of the time. Thus we spent several days in that meeting hall, and the results of observing the state of awareness of those conference participants may well have been quite oppressive for the outstandingly wise man who sat so quietly among them. From that hall we were then able to accompany Dr. Steiner each time to the hospitable house of *Johann Daniel Hirter,* a member of the National Council, where he spent the night.

One day while en route he asked: Have you seen a specific picture, hanging on such and such a gallery wall in the art exhibition forming part of the Georges Buchet[14] Collection? – He described everything exactly and in detail. "It is painted completely out of the spiritual – but it is the only one of all his works!" This painting did not present distinctly recognizable physical forms, but rather decidedly abstract ones. It had many in fact almost cubistic, as well as some expressionistic elements in it, one could more or less say. "The modern movements are nothing new to me," I answered, "but, viewed externally, this picture appears to me extraordinarily abstract." "Yes," Dr. Steiner replied, "that is so: the last that one still has of the physical world, when one ascends to the spiritual world are abstract thoughts, and the first that comes to meet one there, are abstract Imaginations." I attempted to pursue the conversation further: "But I can't find anything special in the picture in terms of color. Though beautifully composed in terms of light and dark, it has only decidedly murky gray and brown tones and two white and two pale blue patches." "Exactly, he has overcome color," said Dr. Steiner. "Excuse me, *Herr Doktor,*" I cried, flabbergasted, "that I can't understand: color is after all the basic element of painting, why

---

[14] The staff of the Museum of Fine Arts in Bern have indicated to the translator that this name is unknown to them. They suggest that Hilde Boos-Hamburger may possibly have mistaken the first name, and actually have had in mind the Swiss artist *Gustave Buchet* (1888–1963).

then should one overcome it?" "I did not mean it as praise," he replied, "the artist has already departed from color and gone too far over into what is musical."

That was a tremendous revelation to me. Rudolf Steiner had presented to us the harmonious interaction of the arts, with painting in their midst as a two-dimensional art between those that are three-dimensional and one-dimensional: architecture/sculpture/*painting*/music/and poetry. These are followed by eurythmy as a synthesis of them all. It then became an important question, *how* to find for each art, in this case especially for painting, the ideal, middle way. That would necessarily require in each case a recognition of their pure means of expression. If, for reasons of historical development, the pendulum had swung too far in the direction of the spatial in recent centuries, there remained the opposite danger in the first two decades of the twentieth century, of going too far over into what is musical. However, Rudolf Steiner had tirelessly shown the way to pure, inherently lawful, inner color experience, which, without great discipline, is not so easy to follow in reality.

Heaving a sigh, he continued: "You see, one is glad even if one only ever once sees something really painted completely out of the spiritual!" For a painter, that cut to the quick, and so I was only able to say: "Oh, *Herr Doktor,* there are so many of us painters in the movement, putting ourselves to so much trouble for so many years, and still we don't manage to come up with the right thing! The fact is, you have already given us so much, and I hardly know what I should still ask for: Could you please give an indication as to how one attains to real spiritual content?" (Today, I have to admit, however, that this question did not exactly give evidence of profound understanding – on the other hand, there was as yet no possibility of working all these things out, as could be done later on in the course of the years afterwards). But the ever-helpful teacher went into it immediately, even so: "If in the evening or in the morning you have done your meditation – it does not matter when – be attentive to how your ether body emerges up there from the crown of your head. Then do not, however, let the Imaginations which arise condense to visions. If after that you paint in the course of the day, something will certainly appear!" Thanking him, I nonetheless remarked that this indication could only remain a goal after all, for the time being, toward which one would have to strive. Yet I allowed myself the further question as to what he thought on the other hand, on the purely technical-practical side, about exercises of the kind I attempted out of the moral experience of color: Placing, for example, a color on the paper and then adapting a next one to it, as far as possible always out of the sensory-moral experience, and so on, till the greatest possible harmonization is reached. "That is a very good path," Rudolf Steiner exclaimed, "do it just like that!" "I've already attempted this quite often," I replied, "but it was always off-putting to me, that in doing so I had the feeling of not being able in this way to penetrate everything sufficiently with my consciousness." "Yes, if one proceeds in this way, then this consciousness comes only at the end. But try it in this way all the same," he added.[15]

For me there was now nothing more to lose, since I had had my fill of many of the older ways of working, right up to my association with the first Expressionists. However, there had been no satisfaction or fulfillment to be found. Accordingly, a period of frightful daubing began. Intentionally, to start with, I left aside everything I had of so-called ability, in order as far as possible to live unconditionally in color, and in doing so to observe my own soul-processes exactly, as becomes possible with meditative activity. I constantly reflected on what I had heard from Dr. Steiner.

The indication, not to let Imaginations condense to visions, seemed especially important. It became apparent, of course, that this difference had not been clearly worked out in people's minds, which became noticeable in general with painters of the movement. As one of the main differences, it had often been emphasized that real Imaginations could not be retained in memory. If one wanted to re-experience them, one would have to transpose oneself once again into the same soul-state. This distinction is presented very clearly for painters as well at the beginning of the second lecture of the cycle, *Initiations-Erkenntnis,* held in Penmaenmawr, August 20, 1923.[16] A few passages are quoted here:

> Let us once more call up before our souls whither modern Initiation leads, after the first steps to Imaginative knowledge have been successfully taken. We then come to the point where the previous abstract, purely ideal world of thought is permeated with inner life. The thoughts coming to us are no longer lifeless, passively acquired; they are an inward world of living force which we feel in the same way as we feel the pulsing of our blood or the streaming in and out of the air we breathe. It is therefore

---

[15] Goethe's "sensory-moral" ("*sinnlich-sittlich*") experience of color may also be characterized as a "feeling perception" of color. This subtle and more inward response to color, as opposed to retinal or optical color impressions as such, becomes indispensable for an artistic training based on color. Such a training to develop the feeling perception of color is set forth in more detail in *The Individuality of Colour* by Elisabeth Koch and Gerard Wagner (Rudolf Steiner Press, London 1980). A reprinting of this important handbook is planned for 2008.

[16] Rudolf Steiner: *Initiations-Erkenntnis* (GA 227), published in English as *The Evolution of Consciousness* (Rudolf Steiner Press, London 1979).

> a question of the ideal element in thinking being replaced by an inward experience of reality. Then indeed the pictures that previously constituted our thoughts are no longer mere abstract, shadowy projections of the outside world, but are inwardly filled with living existence. They are real Imaginations experienced in two dimensions, as indicated yesterday, but it is not as though a human being were standing in front of a painting in the physical world; whoever experiences them like that, experiences visions, not Imaginations. Rather it is as though, having lost the third dimension, one's being were itself moving about within the picture. Hence it is not like seeing something in the physical world; anything that still shows itself as in the physical world will be a vision. Genuine Imagination comes to us only when, for, example, we no longer only see colors as we do in the physical world, but when we experience them. How are colors experienced? When you see colors in the physical world, you have different experiences. You perceive red as something that attacks you, that wants to spring at you. A bull will react violently against this aggressive red; he experiences it far more vividly than does a human, in whom the whole experience is toned down. When you perceive green, you have within you something like a sense of evenness, no pain, nor anything particularly arousing; whereas blue induces a mood of devotion and humility. If we allow these various experiences of color to penetrate right into us, we can realize how it is that when anything in the spiritual world comes at us in the aggressive way red does in physical life, it is something corresponding to the color red. When we encounter something that calls up a mood of humility, this has the same effect as the experience of blue or blue-violet in the physical world. We can simplify this by saying: we have experienced red or blue in the spiritual world. Otherwise, for the sake of precision, we should always have to say: we have experienced something there as when red or blue are seen and experienced in the physical world. To avoid this cumbersome way of expressing oneself, one says simply that one has seen auric colors which can be distinguished as red, blue, green, and so on.

With this it seems necessary to remind oneself of the remarks which Rudolf Steiner made in the lecture of January 1, 1915, when he spoke about the moral experience of the world of color and tone[17]:

[17] Rudolf Steiner: "The Moral Experience of the World of Colour and Tone," contained in the volume *Art as Seen in the Light of Mystery Wisdom* (GA 275) (Rudolf Steiner Press, London 1996).

> And as has been said, we can see a time coming, in which the preparation the painter will undergo as an artist, will signify such a moral experiencing of color, where the experience that prepares the artist for artistic creation will be much more inward, much more intimate than it ever was in the past... We can see a time before us – if we immerse ourselves fully in the perceptions and feelings which can proceed for us out of the spiritual-scientific world conception – a time when the path to the artistic will be in many respects different than in times gone by, when it will be much more full of life. That which is the medium of artistic creativity will be experienced much more intimately by the human soul than in times past; color and tone will be much more intimately lived through, lived through morally and spiritually; and in the creations of artists we shall confront at the same time traces of the experiences of artist-souls in the cosmos.

In the months following those conversations with Dr. Steiner, at all events, unexpected and for the most part rather sorry results had arisen from my efforts. Yet when he saw them on a visit to Zurich, about half a year later, he exclaimed at one attempt: "That is just what I want, there natural forms appear!" Mindful of the experience we had had in the first years of the War and which was described above, I asked, half pleased, half astounded: "When I made this study, I was uneasy, being afraid that perhaps, unconsciously, organic processes had found their way onto the paper; is there nothing of that kind in this work? – How can one protect oneself against that?" "No, no," Dr. Steiner replied briskly, "if one *really* paints out of the color, there is no danger of such a thing happening. But if one draws with the brush, works in a linear fashion" – and with that he made a sweeping movement with his arm and hand – "or even becomes symbolic, then one gets irretrievably into the visionary." At that, I showed him a small study which – as it seemed to me after this explanation – contained just such a critical tendency. Thereupon he said, were I to continue in this direction, I could quite well develop an "abdominal clairvoyance" (organic clairvoyance). With that a reference was clearly given as to how any possible strayings of that sort could be avoided, right into the practical application. It confirmed once more how he saw the healthy future development of the arts in again and again proceeding only from the fundamental elements, the artistic means of the art in question.

Rudolf Steiner's remark that the painter could tend to cultivate an unhealthy visionary experience by making use of the brush in a linear fashion, instead of in making flat surface-areas, applies, of course, particularly to working in a free manner with the color. In confronting nature, a human being with healthy tendencies will not proceed in a one-sidedly linear fashion. It is here as it is everywhere else: nature and life are the great educators and rectifiers and do not so easily allow us to lose the ground from under our feet. The above indication is suited to preserving the painter from hazardous one-sided tendencies in trying new things. It can also be of practical help to teachers. If one has experienced in oneself first-hand the temptation deriving from a one-sided experience of line – if one tries for example to follow all the linear rhythms of a picture, to consider them in their subtlest effects – one soon discovers a state of blissful self-enjoyment that rises, however, to a point where revulsion sets in, in becoming aware that with such rhythms one is trapped as though in a labyrinth. It is also possible to feel as though caught in a spiderweb and inwardly become paralyzed. If line leads a life of its own in this way (here it is a question of the characteristic extreme, not of transitional states), it leads to rigidity – in the end even to arabesques, from which all life has been squeezed out. For that reason, line has been able to find its purest expression in Islamic art, since in the Muslim religion, as is well known, the representation of the living is forbidden. As these connections seemed obvious to me, I asked Dr. Steiner, whether one can say that everywhere in painting where line leads a life of its own, the luciferic temptation was in play. He answered at once in the affirmative. I then recalled a lecture in which he had described how in the Muslim advance on Spain, a last attempt was to be seen on the part of Lucifer to divert the culture of the West into other channels.

This finding sheds light on the tremendous significance that learning to live in the surface, in two dimensions, has for the would-be painter. For only by this means can the essential weaving life of color be grasped, continuously bound up as it is with the surface-element. In order to recognize this more fully, the painter has also to have an experience of line taking on a life of its own and become aware of that peculiar enjoyment-of-self mentioned above with its refined egoism. If one knows the dangers, one learns to avoid them. For that reason, in painting it is not a matter of dabbling about in dreamy or shallow feelings, but of striding a path in clear consciousness which leads into realms where archetypal forces of artistic creation are to be found. Thus I had right away to put the question to Rudolf Steiner: "But what is the ahrimanic error in painting? I've not been able to make this clear to myself." With a faint smile, he replied: "It is copying! – Photography shows it in the most pronounced way – but copying of any kind belongs here; copying of any kind!" That was clearly stated, and so the obvious conclusions had to be drawn.

How often had he not spoken about the fact that working strictly from the model, copying nature, could produce only an "after art." It has been "attempted in these Mystery

Plays actually to present something artistically in the way something presents itself to our soul, when it tries to let itself be taken up by cosmic forces, when it empathizes with the spirits of the cosmos. That was in reality the beginning of all art. Then, however, the materialistic age necessarily came, and this ancient art in which the spiritual as something inward revealing itself by means of matter, had to convert itself into secondary 'after art.' This is essentially the art of the materialistic age, an art which cannot in fact create, but only imitate. And it is the sign of all secondary art, all after-art, that it can only imitate, that it needs models to work from, and that it does not produce the form primarily out of the material."[18]

Receiving such an answer, one feels an obligation to consider everything Rudolf Steiner ever said about such questions, and to think it over as carefully as possible. For it implies finding the middle path in one's own consciousness, so as to work with the proper awareness. "Copying of any kind," he had said. – Not only copying from Nature was meant: if one has a dream or even something like a vision and then paints it from memory, one also copies in actual fact, since the memory picture is placed as a mental image before the mind's eye and then copied. It amounts to the same thing. This accounts for the fact that one sometimes sees very "beautiful motifs" in anthroposophical circles, produced in such a manner, however, that one prefers by far the well-painted "Butcher's Shop" by *Lovis Corinth* (1858–1925), for example, to put it plainly.

Rudolf Steiner emphasized again and again in lectures and in conversations that a renewal in painting can only come about if painters really learn to immerse themselves in the essential nature of color. Then out of the forces of colors themselves the forms take shape, in that one "listens in" on the color. (Needless to say, this cannot happen as the result of any sort of accidental daubing, but only from truly coming to terms with the inner lawfulness of color itself). To comprehend this in its full significance, I endeavored to acquire a clear idea of the creative process in painting, by means of alert observation, and by taking into account all that Dr. Steiner had said on the subject. Obviously, with each creative individual this process takes on different nuances.

One comes to realize: As content of the world, color can be made the content of meditation, as set forth in the lecture cycle *The Spiritual Beings in the Heavenly Bodies and in the Kingdoms of Nature,* as well as in *How to Know Higher Worlds.* An essential feature of spiritual-

---

[18] Rudolf Steiner: "The Moral Experience of the World of Colour and Tone," contained in the volume *Art as Seen in the Light of Mystery Wisdom* (GA 275). (Rudolf Steiner Press, London).

scientific training is that meditative contents of such a kind are chosen, and that the one who meditates is able continually to survey everything taking place in the soul. In doing so one has to exclude intellectual activity and mental images on the one hand, and memories on the other, so as to prevail in one's meditation. Solely in such activity can one in fact attain to an actual experience of the present. In such a state one knows oneself to be more awake than in normal daily life, in which one is actually given over to a continual state of dreaming. This is characterized from various sides in spiritual-scientific literature, and every meditator is acquainted with this experience. In this active state of soul, Imaginations can be experienced with the greatest degree of wakefulness. As already mentioned, these should not be permitted to condense into visions. Such lines of thought represent a kind of ideal. In order to receive confirmation that it can be so expressed, I put the question, whether in such devotion to color while painting (as described above) there is justification for saying one is in a meditative mood? The answer followed promptly: "Yes of course, that is altogether the case with any true creative activity."

To help us appreciate the full import of what has been put forward here, a further quotation is added from a Dornach lecture of October 9, 1920:[19]

> But if one passes over to painting, it is then a matter of thoroughly rejecting any sort of thinking in lines and of going over to pure feeling which creates out of the color.
>
> And as strange as it appears to anyone who speaks in a misplaced abstract sense of the spiritualization of art, it has to be said: for one who thinks in terms of painting, it is a matter above all else of the fact that at a particular spot on a particular surface there is a nuance of color, and that if one goes from this color or color-nuance over to another spot on the surface, there are other color-nuances there. It is a matter of creating out of the color. The artist will then be supported in this creating, however, by means of what I should like to call the experience with blue, the experience with yellow, the experience with red. What he has when he experiences the yellow, the red, as though it attacks one; what he experiences with blue, as though he would have to run after it with his soul, as though he would have to extend himself beyond himself *— that is what transforms itself in him to artistic creation, and that gives him the possibility of reshaping the color-feelings into that which is to become the work of art.*

[19] Rudolf Steiner: *Der Baugedanke von Dornach* (GA 287) (italics by the author).

> If, for example, one confronts the task of painting some surface or other, it then becomes a matter of making gradations between so-called light, warm colors, and between dark, cold colors. With color experience one is able to create out of this color experience as the musician creates out of the experience of tone; then it is a matter of form arising out of color itself. In this way, one does not draw and then smear the color into the spaces between the lines arising from drawing, rather does it become a matter of proceeding from color experience in the first place, and the experience of line, of form, first arises for one from the color experience. For this reason I said already in the first of my Mystery Dramas in a certain place, or had a character say, putting into his mouth that "the form" would have to be "the work of color."
>
> Basically, all drawing — *one has to be aware of this — all drawing and all thinking in terms of drawing in regard to painting is actually false.* For, if I see for example a blue sky and beneath it the green of the sea, the surface of the sea, then I simply have, above the blue of the sky, below the green of the sea, and the line, the horizon, arises simply out of seeing the colors. I lie, actually, if I do something that really is not there, if I draw a line into it.
>
> That is what really has to be faced in a thorough manner. Otherwise one does *not enter that world which can be experienced in all artistic mediums of expression,* which can be experienced in the colors and their nuances, *just as in concepts and ideas,* if these concepts and ideas are not abstracted from ordinary human consciousness.

Nowhere else, as far as I know, is it so clearly expressed that the imaginative world, experienced in pure thinking, can be experienced in the same way by means of all artistic mediums of expression. If this were fully comprehended and taken up in methods of teaching and self-education, then no compromises or purely subjective opinions in regard to the new painting impulse of Dr. Steiner could be carried out into the world. Furthermore, it needs to be taken into account that all artistic creation and appreciation takes place within the rhythmic system of human beings and that in this system we normally *dream.* Anthroposophy, however, and the art inspired by it is meant to bring us to an awakening precisely there. What is the best way to practice this? How do we set to work, once we are in that active, meditative mood? We shall always first *act* out of this mood, create, paint a surface of color or two onto the paper or canvas, then however, we step back — detaching ourselves and make ourselves conscious of what we have done in taking a look at it. And in looking at it — which in this case is identical with artistic appreciation, and that once again takes place in the region of the rhythmic system — in this looking we form our judgment. Then we immerse ourselves once more in active doing, and yet again, we look at what we have created – at what it expresses and presents to us. It becomes a rhythm that we then practice. If it has become a habit through practice, then it usually happens fairly rapidly; on the other hand, it can also slow down to a considerable extent, depending on the individual and on the particular artistic process. But *only* in this way do we raise to consciousness the dreaming into which we have immersed ourselves while artistically creating: if we look at what we have done and again and again acquire perspective, and do not blindly or compulsively muddle on and finally lose ourselves altogether in dreaming. For in such a state of dreaming another entity than the "I"-conscious human being (that knows itself in the state of inner balance) can often guide one's hand.

In quite a humble way at first we thus learn to practice a part of that vast, imaginative consciousness: we act, and then view what has transpired. For further clarification a quotation from Rudolf Steiner may be brought here:[20]

> The moment we look into the past we have to regard what is past as being a necessity. And if we look at ourselves and produce the past again as deeds of the present, so long as we do this consciously, we are still free in what we bring into the present of what was prepared in the past out of necessity. Thus that person is freest of all who knows in full consciousness: With that which I do, I do nothing else than what is spiritually necessary. These things cannot be understood by means of pedantic logic but only by fully grasping reality in a living way.
>
> There is still another approach that can help us understand this completely. We can ask ourselves the following. If we look at animals, we know they have a dimmed consciousness. I have often described that. Human beings have a level of consciousness in which freedom can come to expression. But what kind of consciousness do angels have, the beings immediately above human beings? What is the consciousness of the angels like? It is actually very difficult to have an immediate perception of the consciousness of the Angeloi. When we as human beings want to do something, we consider what form our action is going to take. And if it does not work out on the physical plane as we imagined it should, we have failed. If someone sews two pieces of cloth together, and when he has finished it they come apart, the endeavor has not been a success. This can happen with a sewing machine. If things do not turn out as we had

[20] Rudolf Steiner: *Necessity and Freedom* (GA 166) (Anthroposophic Press, Hudson, New York 1988) (*italics, the author*).

envisioned they would on the physical plane, we say the deed has miscarried. That is to say, people aim their will at something they picture happening on the physical plane. This is how our human willing proceeds. It is not so with the Angeloi.

With the Angeloi everything lies in the intention. An Angeloi's intention can be carried out in many different ways and the effect can still be exactly the same. This is quite true, though it is of course contrary to ordinary logic. Only in the *artistic sphere,* if this is taken in a *human* sense, can *one feel oneself approaching nearer this consciousness.* For you will always find that if the artist is able to take things in a human way – he may not always be in a position to do so, but if he can – he may possibly appreciate what turns out contrary to his expectations, even to the point of failure, and regard it as of greater value than what he did exactly as it was supposed to have been done. We then come a little closer to what is so difficult to grasp: that with the consciousness of the Angeloi, their will, everything depends on the intentions, and that these intentions may be realized in the most varied ways on the physical plane, even in polar opposite ways. That is to say, when angels decide to do something, they choose something quite definite, but not in such a way that they say, "On the physical plane it must appear thus and so." That is not in the least implied. They will only know that when it is there.

We have seen, and I have drawn your attention to the fact, that this is the case even with the Elohim. The Elohim created the light and saw that it was good. This means that what comes first for human beings, the mental image of what is on the physical plane, does not come first at all in the consciousness of the spiritual beings standing above human beings. With them the intention comes first, and how it is to be carried out is quite another matter. Now in this respect humans are of course midway between animals and angels. Therefore, they tend on the one hand to descend to the unconsciousness of animals. Whenever a criminal deed occurs, it is essentially due to the animality in human beings. On the other hand, however, we also have a tendency to ascend to the consciousness of the Angeloi. We have within us the possibility of developing a higher consciousness, a consciousness beyond the ordinary one, in which intentions take on a different aspect than is normally the case.

Thus we can say that, if as human beings we get involved in some of life's important problems, we cannot then make plans in the ordinary way. Suppose that as a teacher – a proper teacher this time – you have a particular child to educate. Now an average person has his educational principles. He knows when to give punishment and when not to; perhaps that he should never give any punishment at all. He knows how to do that. But

> if you look at the matter from the point of view of a higher consciousness, you will not always judge in this way, but will leave everything in life's hands. You will wait for the results of observation. Your one intention will be to bring out all the latent talents. But these potential talents *can be drawn out in various ways.* This is the important thing.

Modern human beings may hold back from accepting the prospect such a quotation calls forth in them. Yet on the other hand, we come to see, in all gratitude and humility, how human beings may affect the course of the world. The craving for momentary success will fade more and more, while they draw creative power from the wealth of existence, unconcerned whether they are despised or misunderstood. If painters in their journeyings have come to such definite experiences, they will increasingly recognize the following:[21]

> You have this or that impulse out of the spirit; you devote yourself to it, making yourself into an instrument for carrying it out! A first failure occurs – it doesn't matter! A second failure occurs – it doesn't matter! And if a hundred failures occur – it doesn't matter! For no failure is ever decisive for the truth of a spiritual impulse, the efficacy of which is inwardly seen and taken hold of. For only then does one have trust, the right trust in a spiritual impulse which one has come to at a particular point in time, when one says to oneself: A hundred times I have failed, but that can at most prove to me that the conditions for realizing this impulse are not given me in this incarnation! That this impulse is right nonetheless, I perceive by means of its own character. And if only after the hundredth incarnation were the forces for realizing this impulse to accrue to me – nothing can convince me of the effectiveness or ineffectiveness of a spiritual impulse other than its own nature! – If you imagine this developed in the minds of human beings as the great faith in some spiritual goal or other, if you imagine that human beings can adhere unwaveringly to something that they have once recognized as spiritually victorious, adhere to something so firmly, that they do not let go of it, no matter how much the external world opposes it, – if you imagine that, then you have an idea of what the power of Michael actually is, of what the Michael-being wants of human beings; for then only do you have a conception of what the great faith in the spirit is.

---

[21] Rudolf Steiner: "Die Anthroposophie und das menschliche Gemüt," contained in the volume *Das Miterleben des Jahreslaufes in vier kosmischen Imaginationen* (GA 229).

Noteworthy was still another conversation: The well-known Swiss painter of genius, *Augusto Giacometti* (1877–1947) once came to see us in Zurich. He had himself made many interesting experiments; I showed him my first color tryouts, made with no other intention than to proceed only from color as described above. He disputed, however, that forms of any consequence could arise out of the activity of color! Admittedly, those attempts were not as yet convincing enough; that has certainly to be conceded in Giacometti's favor. First signs could, however, be noted even so. Yet, as stated, he disputed the possibility of such a goal and said: The highest goal is abstract art (it was 1919), ultimately only geometric forms were to arise! – Plainly to be seen was the marked reserve he had in coming from the abstract into the concrete. For he was, in spite of his tendency to abstraction, which in itself already lies in the direction of the spiritual, caught in materialistic ideas, in the belief that the path from the abstract to the concrete went only from above downwards, from abstract art to concrete copying of the details of nature; and that it does not also lead from below upwards, namely from the abstract to the concrete grasp of spirit-reality beyond.

On a brief visit of Rudolf Steiner's to Zurich following this conversation, we told him about it. He explained it in approximately the following words: it depends on what the painter has filled himself with spiritually. If he lives only in the material, then only material things will slip into the color by means of the brush. If, however, he were to strive in the spirit, then the living content of the spiritual world with which he has united himself – effective in the soul of the artist – will take hold of the material colors and in this way form themselves.

Thus a spontaneous utterance of Rudolf Steiner became more and more comprehensible to me: We were walking through the streets of St. Gallen in the autumn of 1919. He was conversing with several gentlemen about social questions. Suddenly, however, he abruptly turned to me and said flatly and definitely – without anything having previously been said about artistic matters that day or on preceding days: *"The motif, which until now has been the starting point in painting, must become the result in the painting of the future!"*

These words rang out like a decisive call, and can seem a distant goal which he set for many centuries to come. And yet, if we hold onto everything he communicated in lectures and conversations, if we above all practice all this, then by means of this practicing, experiences will be gained which make this future ideal appear self-evident. Furthermore, this ideal is brought to expression in various lectures of Rudolf Steiner. And yet in attempting to represent this ideal with enthusiasm (which often perhaps did not let itself be sufficiently restrained), one frequently met with the strongest resistance precisely in our

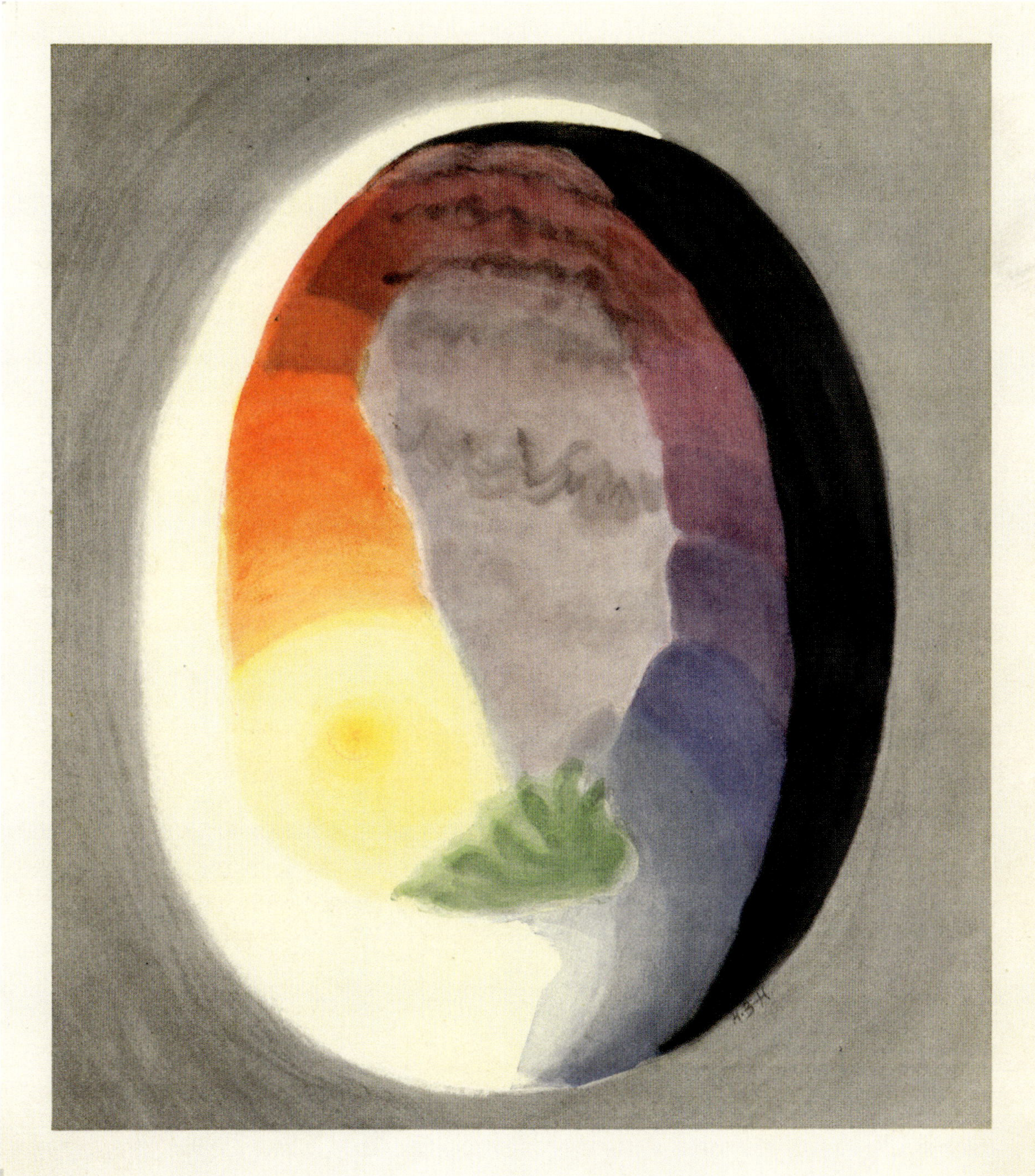

Color circle by Hilde Boos Hamburger. Watercolor.
(Based on indications of Rudolf Steiner in his lecture on color, May 7, 1921)

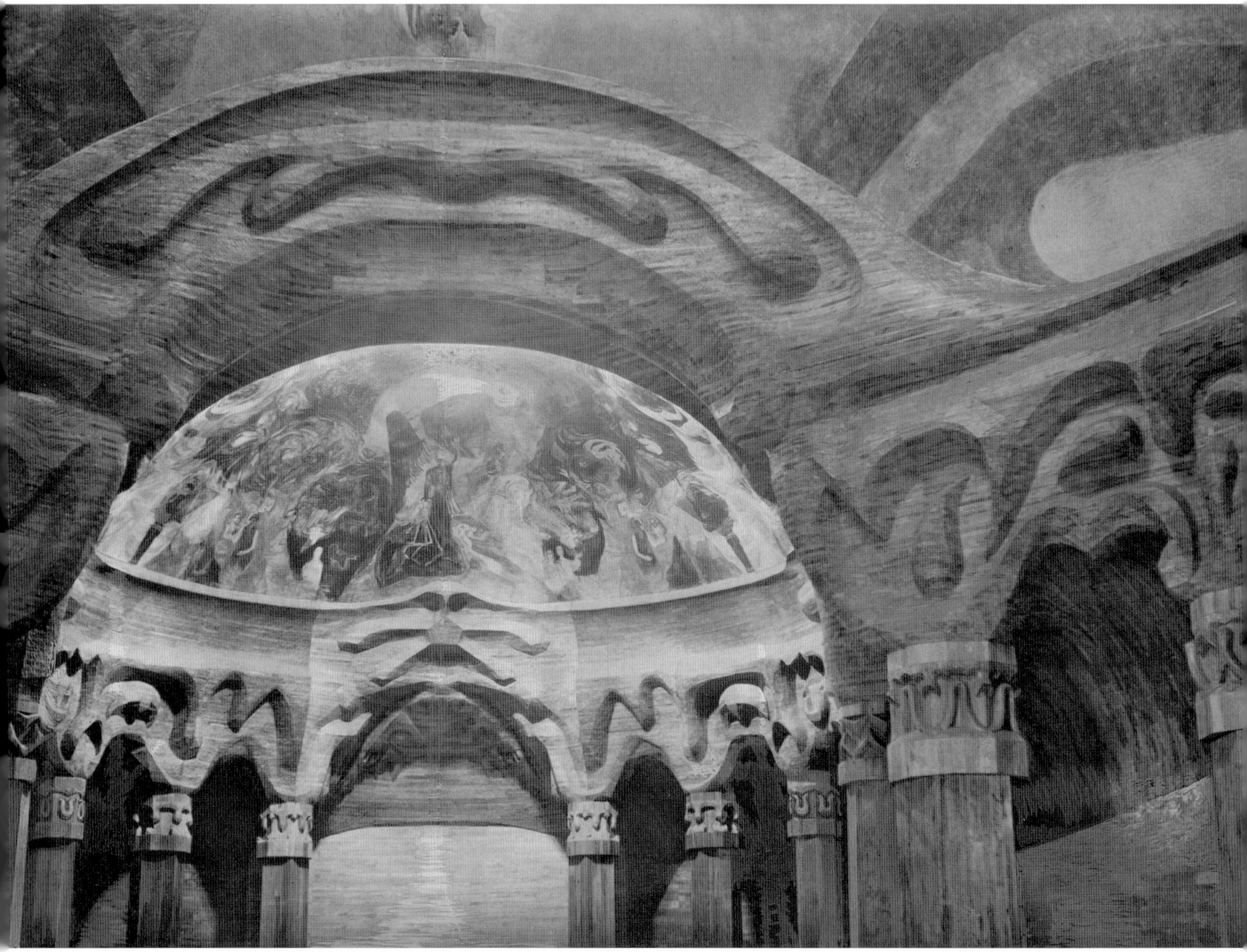

View into the small cupola of the first Goetheanum.
Photo: Rudolf Steiner Archive (Dornach)

ranks. Certain it is, that leaping into the void is not comfortable for everyone and strikes some people as uncanny. Once, when I had told him how much this goal had become an ideal for me, mentioning such a vehement rejection in a conversation with two colleagues, he at once assured me very strongly: "But it is so, it really is so!"

In order to acquire complete clarity, I asked: "Tell me, how is one to go about it, if one wants to set oneself a motif and yet to solve it in such a way that it is painted as far as possible out of the color without compromises? Can one do that?" "You see," Rudolf Steiner answered, "the artist who has to earn his daily bread nowadays is still bound to the motif in most cases, if for example he is to carry out a commission. Then it will be a matter of his transposing such a commission, such a motif entirely into a color experience, and then painting out of the color experience. If he has correctly transposed it, then the motif will arise in the right way."

That would seem harder than anything else! Yet it only appears so; for at this point it will become apparent, whether one has deceived oneself, or has gone about it quite honestly, and has struggled for definite experience and sound judgment in one's work. Mere dreaming has no place here – but neither does anything rationally thought-out!

If one wants to follow through on all these indications of Rudolf Steiner, one must come to realize that it is a matter of a "dying and becoming" in Goethe's sense, a heightening of one's awareness by means of self-education, so as to make oneself gradually into a "self-aware instrument" of those forces and powers that hold sway and live in the world of color. It is as in all fields in which one wants to carry out spiritual-scientific impulses: in artistic as in scientific fields.

Whenever I was able to visit Rudolf Steiner, I brought along a few examples of my work. Right at the beginning when, for a time, I also painted with tempera and pastels, he said: "Why don't you use pure watercolors instead!" He continually pointed to the purest, most luminous places on each sheet of paper, approving of them. In his characteristic positive manner he emphasized the best in each piece of work. One had to tell oneself, if one didn't want to be deluded, that the well-meaning praise was relative and meant as encouragement, and could never be taken as absolute! With such praise some people have often all too easily forgotten to take it as being relative, not bearing in mind what immense perspectives and lofty aims must have stood before Rudolf Steiner. What presumption, to think one's own product came anywhere near! Great harm has been done by some in not acquiring sufficient power of judgment and not making the acquaintance of one of the enemies of spiritual development, namely of "The Right-Honorable Baron Deficient in Powers of Discernment"! (*"Herr Leberecht Baron Mangel an Unterscheidungsvermögen"*) (Rudolf Steiner).[22]

I proceeded from such designated places once again, endeavoring to enhance and develop them further. Of a certain place, he said: "That is excellent, only the color ought to shine still more and glisten." – An argument had once taken place between me and a very diligent colleague of mine. She maintained that one should only work with pure colors, and not with broken tones. I protested against this and observed that one would never ever be able to paint a picture without broken colors. Otherwise such a picture would look like a "carton of sugar," nice and pink, green, blue and yellow! Shortly afterwards I was able to visit Dr. Steiner, and before I had even said anything, he pointed to the place in a painting where, over a red floating figure, a greenish mist had been drawn, and said: "That is a very good place!" I told him about the conversation with my colleague, whereupon he replied: "Of course one cannot paint a picture without broken tones, for only in one color surface shining through another can a certain spiritual element come to expression."

Here it is appropriate to allude to the lecture of September 24, 1921,[23] in which it is stated:

> We look out into nature and see the colors, all the colors of the spectrum, from the red at one end to the violet at the other, with all the shades in between. If we were now to mix these colors in a certain way, tingeing them with each other, then they would take on life. Then they become the human, so-called flesh color, incarnadine, the color that emanates from the human being. When we look out into nature, we are looking in a certain sense at the outspread colors of the rainbow, the sign and symbol of the Father God. If we look at human beings, however, it is the incarnadine that speaks out of the inner human being, for in the human being all the colors interpenetrate, thus taking on life, becoming living in their interpenetration. Gone is that which takes on life, if we only look at a corpse. There, that which is human is thrown back again into the rainbow, into the creation of the Father God. For the source of what makes the rainbow into incarnadine, making it into a living unity, human beings must look into their inner being!

---

[22] Rudolf Steiner named the other two "enemies," *Dr. Illusion* and *Fräulein Naivität.*

[23] Rudolf Steiner: *Cosmosophy,* Vol. 1, pp. 30–31 (Anthroposophic Press, Spring Valley New York 1985).

The statement of Rudolf Steiner that one brings a spiritual element to expression by means of the color, in letting one color shine through another, clearly reveals the reason why he wanted the old glazing (or "veiling") technique taken up again in a new way. In wide circles this is now practiced and propagated in a quite one-sided manner, as if it were the sole, supposedly blessed dogma. But it should not be forgotten that no real artists can *ever* express themselves by means of, or tie themselves to, a single technical means, if they are not to fall into mannerism. Certainly one should master every technical means, so as to have them at one's disposal as needed – self-evidently. If a spiritual element of color can be brought to expression with translucent veiling, then soul qualities on the other hand will show themselves more by means of a damp merging and weaving together of colors, which naturally has to be technically mastered in the same way. One only needs to study Rudolf Steiner's large watercolors and one will see that he never held to any dogma. In every field nothing could have been farther from him, as with anthroposophy itself.

Once we were traveling by train through the middle of the country; in the foreground the yellowish-brown, withered winter grass of the meadows, clumps of leafless trees in front of the blue mountains, a gray sky above. He looked out of the window and said: "You see, you can paint such a landscape-mood on the basis of these colors. But you could just as well make something totally different out of them that has nothing more to do with this landscape at all. It is a matter of starting from the color and remaining with it – not leaving it – then it will yield the form." – He never tired of emphasizing this. If one only takes the trouble to think things through and to experiment, then one knows the reality of such a procedure. One gradually learns to deny oneself personal moods and sympathies or antipathies in regard to these questions.

The following little episode throws a sidelight on the kindhearted, great teacher and knower of human beings:

After several years absence, our old friend and colleague, *Baron Arild Rosenkrantz* (1870–1964) had returned with his wife to Dornach. With bated breath, I showed him, the great academician, the shameless daubings I had dared to make. At first he was somewhat taken aback, but then he said: "Those are actually, rather interesting, stimulating studies. You should now work them out, form them and carry them further. Out of this one, for example, you could make a hand holding a large sphere, and so on."

It seemed to me that this would all too easily lead to a kind of symbolism, which was after all to be avoided. On the other hand, I asked myself whether it was not time, in my case, to combine what had been acquired in earlier years with the new attempts? Shortly after that a visit with Dr. Steiner became possible, and I brought him the same work-sheets that Baron

Rosenkrantz had seen, and told him about our conversation. When it came to the matter of the hand, I permitted myself the question: "Would this not actually be symbolism after all, which is not wanted?" "Well, yes," Dr. Steiner answered, "Rosenkrantz often is a symbolist!" Still, it has to be said that Dr. Steiner valued highly the great ability of this artist, so much admired in some circles in England. – Everyone could sense his noble, inward humanity. Then I also mentioned the remarks he had made about a more careful attention to technique. At that, it was wonderful to see how the earnest countenance brightened with a well-meaning smile. Pointing to a few places, he said almost mischievously: "Well now, that does look rather as though you had thrown the paint pot over it, doesn't it!" At that I was quite relieved, as the moment seemed to have arrived for a cautious combining of old and new experiences.

One of the last questions I was able to submit to him was this: "How must painters project themselves into Nature, unite themselves with her, so as really to be able to bring her to expression in painting in her essential character?" At the same time I told him of attempts I had made on the basis of the book *Knowledge of the Higher Worlds and Its Attainment* [*How to Know Higher Worlds*], and the results of these. He seemed pleased, as indeed he showed himself in his kind-hearted way, even with the most primitive attempts, and answered: "That is good, very good, if you do it like that. Just continue further with it." – What indescribable amazement and good fortune it was, when about ten to fourteen days later, after a brief journey, he began in three lectures to speak about this very question and to answer it thoroughly from still another side. It was an example of how much he continually united himself with the search of the questioner. At the beginning he even included in his statements formulations with which I had tried to make clear to him my attempts in this field. To receive answers from the lecture podium in a more comprehensive way than one could ever have expected was always the most exhilarating, because one could be sure that it was divested of all personal character and had its validity also for every other person. These three lectures are the first three in the book *Mysteriengestaltungen*, of the 23rd, 24th and 25th of November 1923 (GA 232).[24]

As he maintained that those working at the Goetheanum should always keep him informed, if they undertook work leading in some way into the outside world, it was incumbent on me to notify him of a commission for pictures in a book of fairy tales. He wished the studies for it to be shown to him. Thus in spite of his being then particularly overburdened with work, I had to go and see him at an appointed time in his studio.

---

[24] *Mystery Knowledge and Mystery Centres*, Rudolf Steiner Press 1997.

There were about fourteen pages of pictures. *"Frau Holle"* he looked through without questioning anything. But looking at the title page for *"Joringel und Jorinde,"* he said: "This cat is painted without fantasy!" – I was speechless, since I considered this the best page. It conveyed the eerie mood: the evil witch, who either prowled as a cat around her castle, or appeared as an owl, waylaying harmless wanderers. The black cat with arched back and evil, gleaming eyes, sharpening its claws on a barren tree, in the background, the bleak castle in the greenish moonlight... Thus I only managed an uncomprehending, "Without?" He looked up: "Without *color-fantasy!*" [As opposed to "motif-fantasy." — Ed.]

I understood only that I would have to begin over again and look once more for a solution. He said the same of the transformed little nightingale. But understanding did come in getting started on a new attempt. It became clear: the cat did indeed show fantasy in its form, but not in its color, since the animal was dealt with as a silhouette kept uniformly black. The general effect was of course much enhanced by a treatment in color.

On parting, Rudolf Steiner said to me: "In the new building we shall have many walls; a lot of painting will need to be done inside. If you see that your situation allows it, and you can combine it with your family duties, then let me know!"

It was the last actual conversation in May 1924, but it always lingered on like a warning cry. In the autumn of that year he had wanted after the course in speech formation, to give a course in singing, and in November a painting course. Certainly in the painting course – as in the two eurythmy courses of the last year – he would have integrated everything already given in lectures and color examples and drawn up a comprehensive training course.

Thus with our weak forces, we had, stumbling, to first gather together the stones little by little, in order to build ourselves a footbridge into the color world; each according to our individual abilities.

Since certain questions have frequently come up for discussion in artistic and pedagogical meetings, a few unique elucidating remarks are added from a question-and-answer session of Dr. Rudolf Steiner's.[25] They complement and illuminate what stands above:

---

[25] From a question-and-answer session during the "Summer Art Course," Dornach, August 26, 1921, (*italics by the author*). This course had opened at the Goetheanum on August 21, arranged on the initiative of the Danish painter *Baron Arild Rosenkrantz* (1870–1964), who lived at that time in London. Attending were predominantly English and American artists and others interested in the arts. They were given lectures in their own language, and the lectures of Rudolf Steiner, held in German, were translated each time immediately afterwards.

Whoever attempts to embody moral thought content in color, creates inartistically. *It is possible to embody in color only the spiritual element that can be experienced as spiritual in the color world itself.* To the same extent one has the moral intention beforehand and afterwards wants to give artistic form to what is morally conceived, to the same extent one falls into symbolizing, and allegorizing is always inartistic.

In order to illustrate what I actually mean, I should like to say the following: For the purpose of a *Faust* performance here, I once felt obliged to recreate the forms of the *Kabiri,* the gods of the Samothracian mysteries. They had to be shown while the text by Goethe was spoken. I believe that it was possible for me really to recreate these Kabiri out of spiritual seeing. Then the wish arose with one of our members – I do not say this from immodesty, but because a fact is to be communicated – to have these Kabiri as well, which had pleased them, and they were to be photographed. Well, to me photographing a plastically formed work is so dreadful, that every photograph of a sculpture is something I actually would like to run away from. This is because whatever really is created artistically, is created out of the spiritually experienced feeling for the material, and because it is impossible to directly experience in the form of a surface, what has been imagined in spatial forms. Hence I preferred at that time, since I wanted to accommodate this wish, to remake in black-and-white what I had produced as the three Kabiri, and this could then be photographed.

A person who thinks one can convert moral intentions into painting, imagines one can treat any content more or less in the manner of a novel, and then pour it into any material one chooses! *That is not true! It is artistically untrue. In a particular material something artistic can be formed in only one way.*

Question: "Would art under the influence of anthroposophical teachings not have a tendency to become monotonous, which is not interesting? Isn't there a danger that art would bear an anthroposophical stamp, as of a particular school of painting?"

Dr. Steiner: "If one understands what can actually proceed as art out of the anthroposophical spiritual direction, then one will not raise the question in that form, and one will not be tempted to believe that anthroposophy could ever aspire to influence art by means of anthroposophical teachings. To somehow think otherwise than that the artistic element arises from experiencing the spirit surging in the material, from living together with the material, cannot in fact be assumed at all from an anthroposophical point of view.

In a somewhat primitive manner, many anthroposophists conceive matters in such a way that they take what is given them, for example in the teaching of the rose-cross, and then paint this in some way or other onto a board. One then meets with these pictures in every branch. There, inner feeling, inner intention is captured externally. In regard to such 'artistic attempts' I generally help myself by not looking at them at all in the branches in question. For these are certainly primitive attempts that do not go far, to transfer what can be represented in the spirit – which has now become word, has become teaching – into artistic form. That is nonsense. One cannot incorporate doctrine into a work of art.

But that which is real anthroposophy leads, whether one approaches it in the form of teaching, or whether one approaches it in the form of art, to inner experience and to something more pristine than anthroposophical teaching is and anthroposophical art is – thus something that lies further back in the human being.

Thus on the one hand one creates artistic forms having nothing at all to do with anthroposophical teachings; and if one then adjusts oneself to the word, to thoughts, then one links ideas out of the same foundations. Both are branches stemming from the same root. But one cannot take one branch and stick it into the other!"

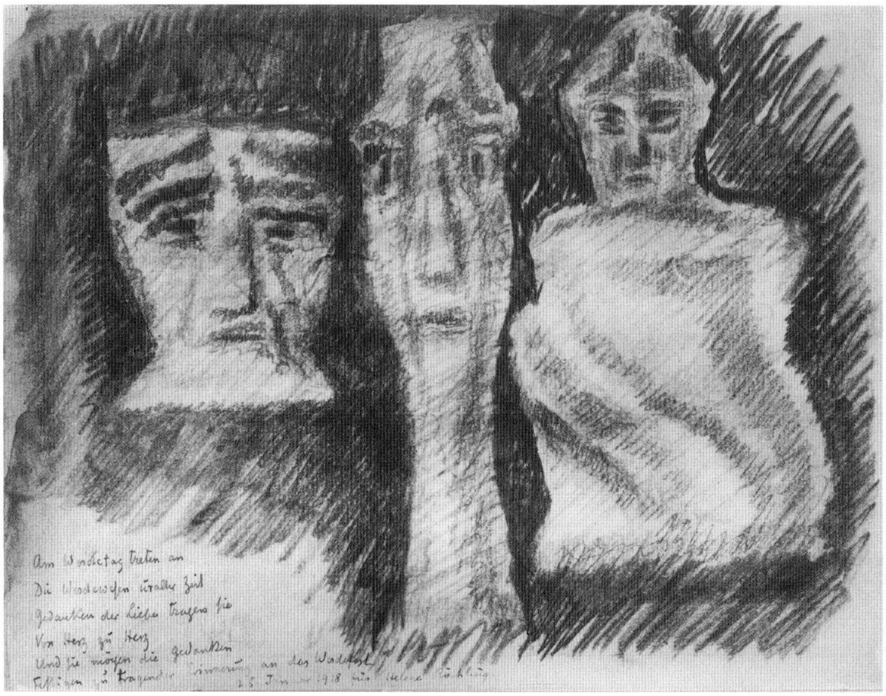

The Kabiri,[26] drawing by Rudolf Steiner (ca. 8½ x 10½ in.)

Rudolf Steiner had created his three sculptures of the Kabiri in 1917. Helene Röchling (1866–1945) who had supported the building of the Goetheanum with considerable sums, requested Rudolf Steiner to send her a photograph of the Kabiri. As he considered photographs of sculptures to be inartistic, he instead sent her a drawing of the Kabiri on her birthday, January 28, 1918. He had carried this out in the shaded drawing technique described in more detail by Assya Turgenieff. – See her "Recollections of the Beginning of Studies in Light and Dark," included in this volume. See also Rudolf Steiner's lecture of January 17, 1919, entitled "The Samothracian Mysteries of the Kabiri. The Mystery of Human Becoming" in *Geisteswissenschaftliche Erläuterungen zu Goethes Faust* (GA 273).

The inscription by Rudolf Steiner can be translated somewhat as follows:

On the day of becoming appear
The beings of becoming of ancient times
Thoughts of love they bear
From heart to heart
And they would strengthen thoughts
To self-sustaining memory of the festival of becoming.

–January 28, 1918, for Helene Röchling

(As indicated in the lecture of January 17, 1919, the term "becoming" refers here to "the spiritual correlate of human birth.")

---

[26] Sea-gods of ancient Greece: Axieros, Axiokersos and Axiokersa. Dokumentation am Goetheanum-Bildarchiv.

SOME EXPERIENCES IN TEACHING OLDER CHILDREN

First painting-pedagogical experiences in the Continuing Education School at the Goetheanum on the basis of Rudolf Steiner's indications

Hilde Boos-Hamburger

In the autumn of 1920 a number of parents wanting a further education course started for their adolescent children joined forces. They asked Dr. Steiner to inaugurate such a course. For the time being, only three teachers in all came in question: one for language, history and eurythmy; one for the natural-scientific and mathematical subjects; and one for painting, applied art and art history. *Fräulein Marie Groddeck* (1891 – 1958), who has now (1953) been the soul of this school for more than thirty years, took on the first category of instruction, *Dr. Ernst Blümel* (1884–1952) of Vienna the second. Dr. Steiner had already asked me a number of times, whether I did not want to take on the last one. This nevertheless came so unexpectedly, as I had never yet entertained such a thought, that I felt completely at a loss and could not decide to say yes, suggesting in reply someone else instead each time, of whom I knew, they would have jumped at the chance if asked. Upon a renewed inquiry I tried the same hedge. There was almost something like impatience to be sensed in the categorical rejection of the *Herr Doktor*. When I objected that I certainly couldn't do it, as I had never done anything like that, he immediately said: "You can do it perfectly well." I had never worked with small children, I didn't understand them at all, I moaned. He reassured me that these were school-leavers.[27] Now there was the obligation to at least try it and not evade it. After all, from many years experience I knew Dr. Steiner's judgement well enough. He offered such work from insight into one's disposition.

In this way, I asked how one should begin working with children of 12-18? – "For the time being have them play with the color. Wait and see what comes of it. Endeavor to see that the children develop a relationship to color. What is created in this way should then be utilized for applied art. If, for example, one of the children has achieved a painting that appears to

[27] I.e., pupils of upper school age. The legal framework of that time did not permit the founding of independent elementary schools in Switzerland, only of educational institutions at the upper school level.

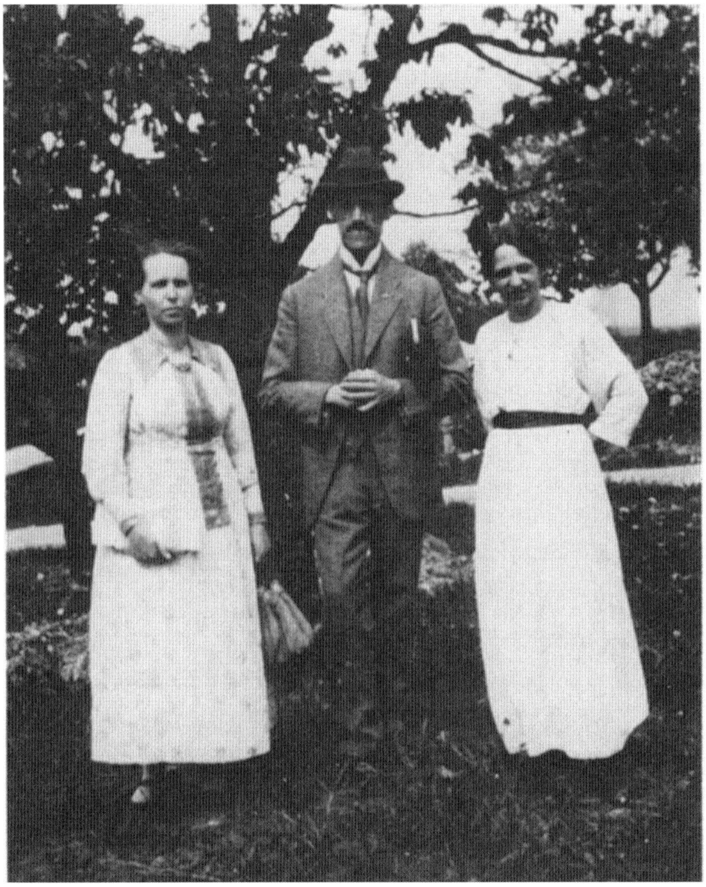

Hilde Boos-Hamburger, Ernst Blümel, and Marie Groddeck
Source: Dokumentation am Goetheanum-Bildarchiv.

you suitable for adapting, have it stylized a bit and then produce an article, a bag, a pillow, for example, and embellish it with the design. But shirts, dresses and shoes should also be sewn."

We began after a small opening festival on February 1, 1921, and boldly set to work on our tasks. Out of the general daubing a number of usable paintings emerged after about two months. At that point we turned to various housemothers for left-over pieces of material, and bought embroidery-silk and thread. After some thorough preliminary work, every pupil produced an article. Thus in a relatively short time we were able, since we worked every day for an hour, to submit the first results to *Herr Doktor.*

I shall never forget the kindhearted, joyful lighting up of his face, when he looked at these attempts, so diverse and so awkward. For one thing, the usual arts-and-crafts methods were not to be used. This showed itself at once in his advice and critique. No abstract decorations were to be, as it were, stuck onto an article. Rather should this arise from the actual, practical application of the article. For instance, he said: "With this book cover, one doesn't know *where* one has to open it! Here, the upper right corner should above all appear bright and light in weight in relation to the spine of the book, so as to show that it is to be opened *here*. With the spine of the book one should be able to feel that here the pages are held together – it is good if this is indicated by means of darker, heavier colors. The same is to be observed with bags: where they are opened, the color should become lighter, the forms should open themselves. Even if you have a flap, it has to be apparent where it is to be opened."

"These pillows here look very nice," he said, pointing to them. "However, one would not be able to rest one's head on them; it would prick one from all sides if one lay on it." – And Rudolf Steiner showed how a pillow design should be worked out, so that there is a quiet surface in the middle and the border is formed so as to protectively surround the head as it were.

With great enthusiasm, we of course then made the effort to follow these indications and had the joy of seeing that he was far more satisfied with the new attempts. In the course of the further work, he often said: "That really is very good. In a few days I shall be going to Stuttgart. I must tell the teachers in the Waldorf School, so that they can also try it out."

A girl wanted to embroider a dress at the neck, on the sleeves, belt and lower hem. That was a difficult task, which we were not able to solve out of our experiments with color in the way we had already done it for other things. The child also had special wishes. So I gave her a pencil and we worked out a little motif. Just at that moment Dr. Steiner came and at once intervened in a lively manner: "Yes, up here at the neck," he said, more or less, "the motif must be treated in the lightest fashion, so it can be seen that here there is no weight as yet, and that here the head slips through. At the sleeves it can get heavier and broader; at the waist it can properly metamorphose in color and form, so as to become heavier. And right at the hem below it should be wide and darkest of all, so that one really feels how the skirt hangs. If one now wanted to embroider shoes as well, they would have to be made so that (he began to draw) they are lighter where they are slipped on, becoming increasingly darker and finally here at the heel and sole, it has to become quite heavy and dark." He made a wonderful drawing in light and dark, which unfortunately got lost after my departure from the school.

These were his very first hints for applied art. *Louise van Blommestein,* who then carried on the lessons at the *Friedwartschule* for many years in this field, received a number of other indications from Rudolf Steiner. She faithfully recorded these in her little book, as did Hedwig Hauck in her large, beautiful compilation *Handwork and Applied Art*.[28]

In painting too the pupils had made progress. A quite withdrawn girl for instance, who always looked gloomy, though she was very pretty, had for two or three months produced only smeared-on cloud formations, stubbornly insisting on her way of doing things. Suddenly, this "consistency" appeared foolish to her and she began to paint in cleaner, purer tones. Others had come much further. New pupils came to the school, among them a girl of 14 years who refused very decidedly to make brush strokes as we did. Up until then she had copied flowers and landscapes from picture postcards and admired her own work. Why should I force her to paint things against her own inclination that she would only despise? It was necessary to appeal to her insight and show how things could be approached with more understanding. So I took her out into the spring landscape and indicated to her how she would need to look carefully at the color harmony of the soft blue of the sky and mountains, the shining yellow and bright green of the flowering meadows, the white clouds, and let all this have an effect on her. It was then a matter of giving form to this impression. When the end-result of her effort turned out to be fairly miserable, she became rather sheepish about it. The teacher then painted the landscape in the same color-tones and it appeared that the young girl then really learned something, showing genuine appreciation. At that moment – unexpectedly, as always – Dr. Steiner came into the room. He interested himself in the simple attempt, and challenged me then and there, to carry out in practical terms the indications concerning the nature of color given by him over the past few days in lectures in the Carpentry Building. He pointed out of the window, at the garden-path lined with flowers in bloom: an opportunity to study those things – plant-life and something mineral, the gravel pathway – on the basis of these indications. Unfortunately, this remained for a long time merely at the stage of good intentions.

From further away, a mother brought her adolescent daughter, whose original paintings showed great talent. It gave one reason to be astonished and glad. All the same I felt bound to tell Rudolf Steiner about it the same evening, after the lecture he held, since I did not want to assume the responsibility of letting the girl paint for the next two days in the same way as the rest of the pupils. From the whole manner and style of her work, it appeared to me that a mediumistic tendency was in evidence. The very next morning, he came over to the schoolroom, looked at the work with great interest and confirmed my assumption. This

[28] Louise van Blommestein, *Künstlerische Handarbeiten nach Richtlinien und Entwürfen von Rudolf Steiner*, Dornach 1934. Hedwig Hauck, *Handarbeit und Kunstgewerbe*, Stuttgart 1960.

was his advice: "Have the child for the time being paint the surface of the paper with only one color, while at the same time leaving a space in the form of a geometric figure. This should afterwards be filled out with another color. When she has become practiced in this to a certain extent, she can attempt it with several such figures that mutually interpenetrate, for example, a square, a triangle, a hexagon or octagon, and so on, and each of these forms would have to be painted with another color, so that the various colors shine one through the other. That will help her a lot, if she does it thoroughly enough."

And that's how it was. The girl worked with great joy at the new assignment, for she soon sensed how the stringent concentration required in coming to terms with it, consolidated her inwardly. Her all too dreamy nature became tauter. This exercise can be considerably extended, and is an important help for the teacher in such cases. In connection with the study of "negative" surfaces and "white exercises," it is particularly to be recommended. Such exercises are explained in more detail by the author in the book *The Creative Power of Colour.*

One day Rudolf Steiner came into the painting class again. He looked at the children's work, and pointing to an older girl's paper, he made a few remarks which I was not able to understand at all. When I apologized for this, he repeated everything once again. But it still remained quite incomprehensible to me, and even a third and a fourth repetition with his characteristic boundless patience proved fruitless. So much so that I could not as much as make out the words. Despairing and ashamed, I begged him to be so good as to clarify what he was saying by demonstrating it; after all, paper, color and brush were to hand. He at once took hold of the latter, dipped it into a pot of middle yellow, tested the color first on a paper palette, which he always made use of in this way (he recommended taking the same kind of paper as the paper one is painting on). Then he adjusted the color till it became a strong, almost golden yellow. This he laid on in a broad surface, giving the form a spiral tendency. To this he said: "If this yellow is now there like this, then a reddish tone *must* come in here." Again he mixed an exact tone, testing it on the palette, going somewhat toward a brownish red, and inserted it into the yellow shape. Then he continued: "If this is *so*, then a blue such as *this* must come there." And – I still see it in front of me – he dipped the brush into a dark ultramarine, and with a second brush took a drop of orange, mixed it into the blue – yet only so much, that the blue was still quite pure, but had lost the toxic quality that normally adheres to the factory-made colors, and had even acquired a certain warmth. He laid this tone of color underneath, as though supporting the yellow, which thereby (in terms of color- perspective, cold and warm tones) suddenly began to light up! "Then," he said, "some dull green has to come out there still against the yellow," which he mixed to a somewhat bluish green. "And now the whole thing must still

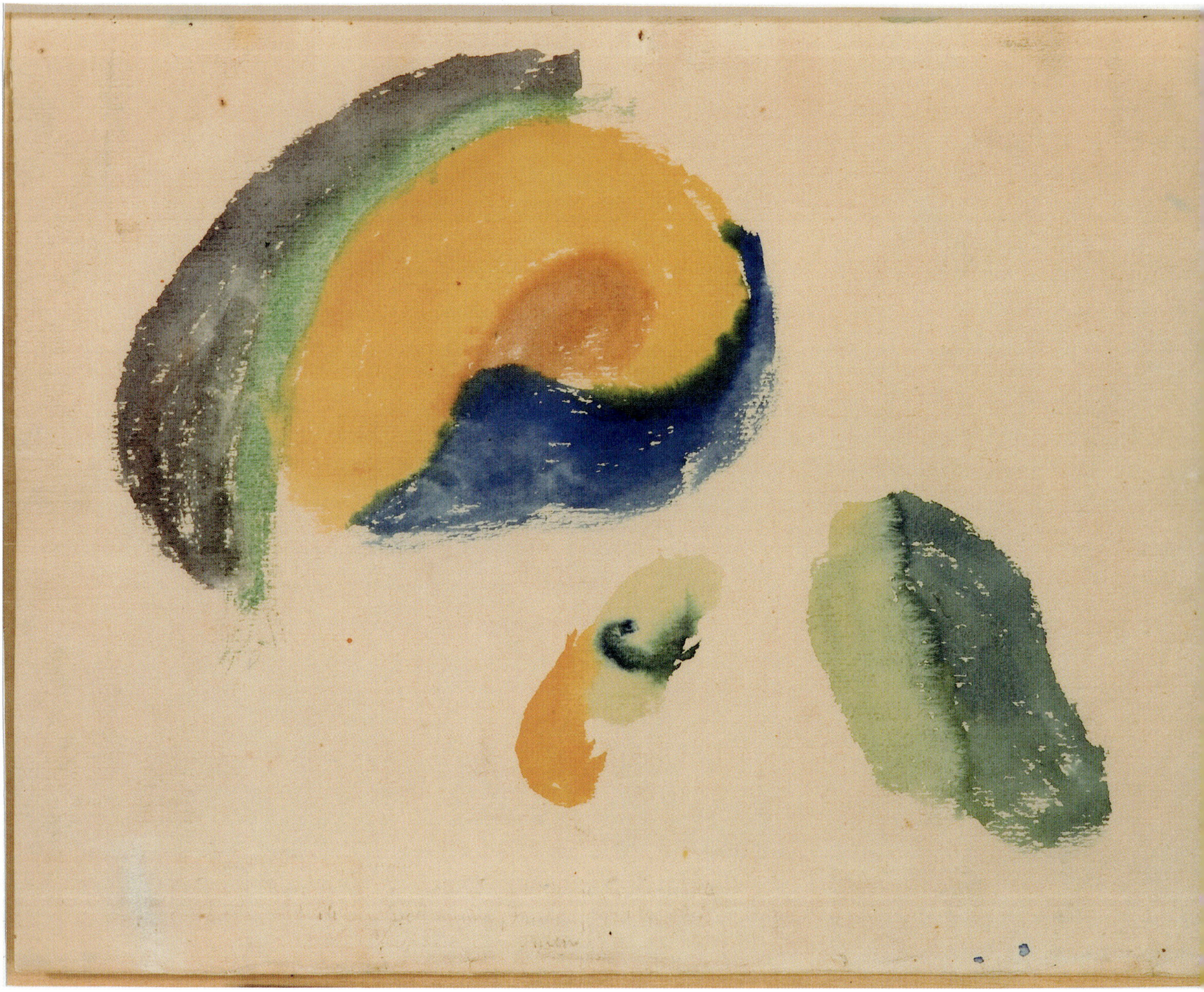

Sun Motif / Profile Head

Two watercolor studies painted by Rudolf Steiner on the same sheet of paper during a painting class in the Continuing Education School at the Goetheanum, also known as the Friedwartschule, in May 1921. (See pages 87–89).

be completed with violet!" This he adjusted to a middle, bluish-violet, somewhat broken. He then laid the brush down. (See *Sun Motif/Profile Head,* p. 88).[29]

At that moment, I did not know exactly what to make of it. On the other hand, in looking on, from the intense feeling of participation the thought arose: Rudolf Steiner knows the life of color in its lawfulness right into its subtlest manifestations! – As no one else does. Over the years, the question of finding the way to an experience of this became ever more urgent, and I tried hard to do so for a long time. Yet the question did not let itself be formulated. In my helplessness then, I asked Dr. Steiner, whether he would paint a head for me out of the color? He took the brush and painted the surface of a face (without features) in yellowish, dull green, adding in bluish green the surface of hair, and said, smiling: "That is a head!"

Disappointed, I replied: "Excuse me, but that is nothing new for a painter, *Herr Doktor,* – I meant a head with facial features!" He took the brush and began placing a few differentiated spots of color onto the same sheet of paper, but after a short time, laid the brush down and took his leave. (See *Sun Motif/Profile Head,* p. 88).

About two years later he painted a profile-head with blue surroundings for Louise van Blommestein, which can still be seen in the archives of the *Rudolf Steiner-Nachlassverwaltung* (the Literary Estate of Rudolf Steiner).[30] This was once again an example of how Rudolf Steiner occupied himself with the practical working out of a question, until solving it out of its full depths and also of how he went each time into the questions and strivings of pupils.

Many years after that, I began one day again to work through the chapter of Goethe's *Colour Theory* on the "Effect of Colour with Reference to Moral Associations," to which Rudolf Steiner had so often pointed as a gold mine for the painter. In doing so, I made use of colored crayons for all the color-combinations. This was repeated while taking into account the aspects which Rudolf Steiner had shown: of inner color movement and the qualitative distinction between image and lustre colors. It seemed to me at last that here the key was to be found for actually training the color-sense so far as the specific inherent laws of color were concerned. The first fruits of these studies were subsequently set down in the book *The Creative Power of Colour.*

---

[29] The essential thing here would seem to be the slight "breaking" or subduing of the color with its complement. By this means the three "lustre" colors, yellow, red, and blue take on "image" character, in the sense of Rudolf Steiner's lectures on color (GA 291). It becomes possible to paint them as flat, even surfaces.

[30] This pastel sketch, measuring 40 x 37 cm, is available in a full-size reproduction published by the Rudolf Steiner-Verlag, Dornach.

Preparing the lessons in art history was stimulating and valuable. Since the knowledge the pupils had was very slight at the outset, also in general history, it was necessary to start from the beginning. Thorough preparation was necessary, since experience was of course lacking in making such a subject attractive for this age-group. I began with the old Stone Age and attempted to give a picture in each case of the ancient cultures, enriching it besides with the help of one or another literary document and a lot of visual material. We unfortunately only got as far as the archaic Greek period; for then, after nine months, I had to relinquish, out of family considerations, the teaching activity which I had meanwhile grown so fond of.

At the *Herr Doktor*'s expressed wish, I had, however, to report to him now and again on account of certain matters, since preparations were to be made for the work in the future. With that, the opportunity was given to still put some of the questions to him which have been communicated here, as well as to submit practical attempts. Never did one go from him other than richly endowed with gifts, if he saw that one wanted to try to really unite oneself in the work with the problems of color. These occurrences had all been noted down either before or soon after Rudolf Steiner's death, so that they would not slip from memory. As just a few of us older pupils are still living, and have only put down in writing some of what was experienced, these recollections and conversations are being communicated in response to many inquiries. Those who strive to paint will find enlightening viewpoints regarding individual questions, which can facilitate their search.

Only in looking back does one see in what way it would have depended on one's own presence of mind and initiative to seize the possibilities offered by the presence among us of the great teacher of humanity in greater measure.

The comprehensive work lies before us; it is up to us human beings to summon the will for a sufficient deepening, so that it comes to life in each one of us.

Translated from *Aus Gesprächen mit Rudolf Steiner über Malerei und einige Erinnerungen an die Zeit des ersten Goetheanum* (From conversations with Rudolf Steiner about painting and some recollections of the time of the first Goetheanum), Verlag R. G. Zbinden & Co., Basel 1954. Reprinted 1961, 1985.

About
Hilde Boos-Hamburger
1887 – 1969

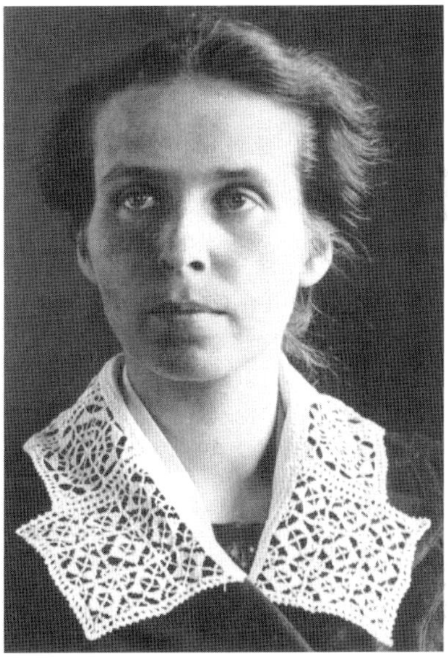

The central event in the life of Hilde Boos-Hamburger was the painting of the cupolas of the first Goetheanum building.

Hilde Hamburger was born in 1887 in Lower Austria near Pottschach into a well-to-do, cosmopolitan family. She was the youngest of five siblings who were taught by private tutors. Her interest in painting was supported early on by her cousin, Sir William Gordon Collingwood, who was her first painting teacher. In 1909 she studied at the art school in Karlsruhe under *Alexander Kanoldt,* who drew her attention to Rudolf Steiner. She heard Steiner's lecture of March 9, 1910, read the book *Theosophy* and became a member of the (German) Theosophical Society, which was later refounded to become the Anthroposophical Society.

In Munich she worked from 1910 to 1913 in painting scenery and making costumes for the Mystery Drama performances.

At Rudolf Steiner's suggestion, she moved to Dornach in 1914, to assist in the work of painting the cupolas of the first Goetheanum. She made preliminary studies for the Elohim figures and carried out the gesso grounding for the plant colors produced according to Steiner's indications. She participated in performances of eurythmy and in the Christmas Plays.

In 1917 she married Roman Boos in Zurich; they had two children. In 1920 the family returned to Dornach. For a time she was active as an art teacher in the Continuing Education School (*Fortbildungsschule*) at the Goetheanum, and painted according to indications of Rudolf Steiner.

Hilde Boos-Hamburger remained active in this field after the death of Rudolf Steiner, tending his artistic estate, holding slide lectures, and giving painting courses in Switzerland and, until 1940 as well as from 1945 on, also abroad.

Hilde Boos-Hamburger was not an easy person to get along with. She took clear and deliberate positions and often provoked arguments. Her greatest concern was to penetrate the subject area of the creative power of color in terms of knowledge, to formulate what she had recognized and to pass it on.

In the 1940s and 50s she reconstructed the paintings of the small cupola on six large panels. And with the help of *Carl Liedvogel*[31] she made a model of the entire cupola paintings on the scale of approximately 1:10, which affords a good spatial impression of the painted cupolas.[32] Her reconstructions were shown in 1978 in the large exhibition "The Goetheanum Fifty Years On – Rudolf Steiner's Architectural Impulse" and can be seen today in the Art Collection at the Goetheanum. In 1985 there was a special exhibition of her work.

– Roy Wilkinson / Jan Pohl

Translated from *Anthroposophie im 20. Jahrhundert. Ein Kulturimpuls in biografischen Porträts,* edited by Bodo von Plato. Verlag am Goetheanum, Dornach, Switzerland 2003.

[31] Carl Liedvogel (1879–1947), was the brother of Heinrich Liedvogel, mentioned on page 44. He was the master carpenter whose Heidelberg-based company was responsible for the construction of the columns of the first Goetheanum. From the beginning of the newly founded Anthroposophical Society, he was the branch leader in Heidelberg, with whom Rudolf Steiner and Marie Steiner often stayed when public lectures were held in Heidelberg. Described as a man of almost "unbelievable will," Carl Liedvogel adhered to a pure vegetarian diet, ingesting a minimum of food. Questioned, after the closing of the Branch during an interrogation by the Gestapo as to what he thought of Rudolf Steiner, he shouted out: "He was the greatest spirit we could have called our own!" Told later that this answer was extremely incautious, Carl Liedvogel replied that he was fully prepared to die for this answer at any moment. (Reported by Adelheid Petersen in *Nachrichtenblatt,* 1947).

[32] See illustration on p. 32.

HENNI GECK

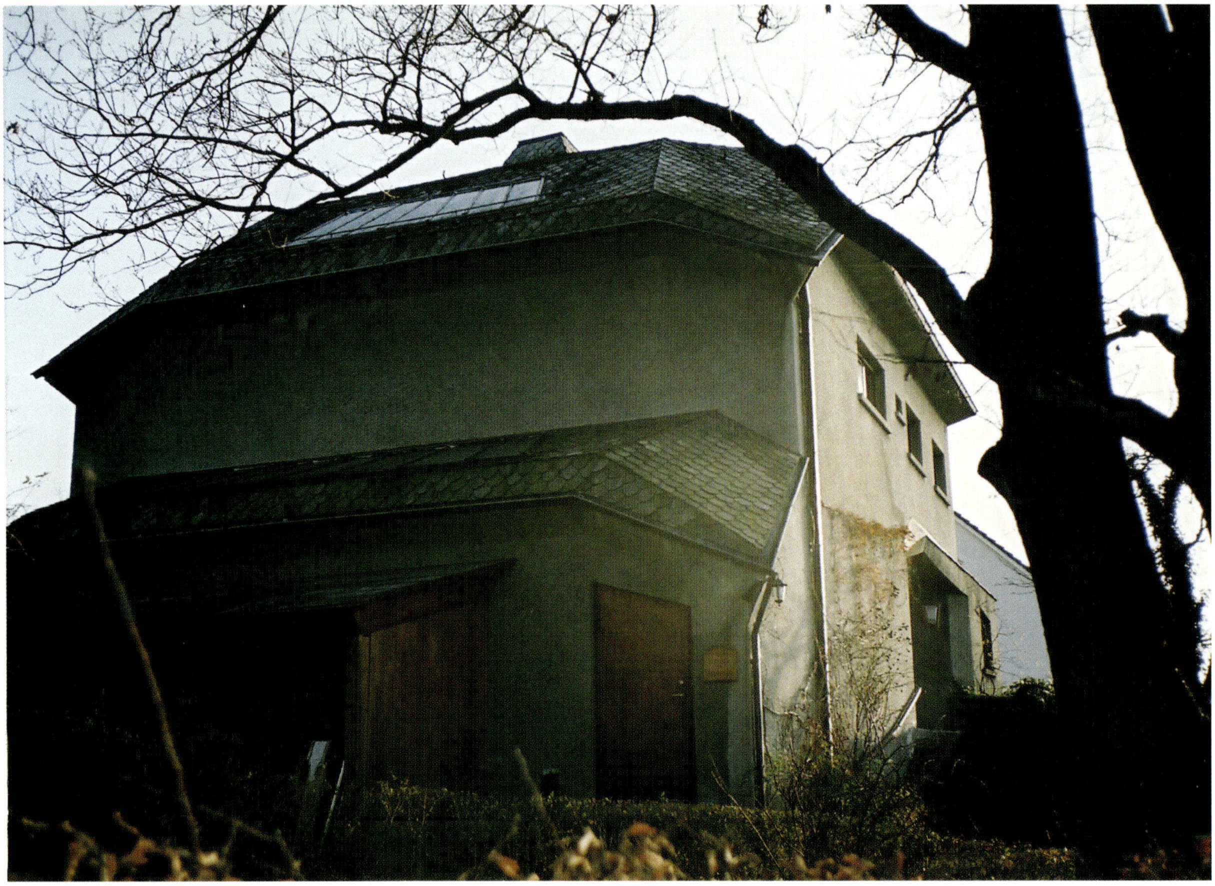

"Atelierhaus Farbentor." Henni Geck's house and studio. (Dornach).
Photo: Peter Stebbing.

THE SKETCHES GIVEN BY RUDOLF STEINER 1922–1924 FOR PAINTING COURSES AT THE GOETHEANUM[33]

(Nine Nature Moods, Thirteen Motif-Sketches, One Color-Beginning)

Henni Geck

Rudolf Steiner made these 23 color sketches for a new kind of painting training at my urgent request, when I had been asked to give a painting course by a few individuals alongside my carving work (nine years on the Goetheanum building and the central wooden Group Statue). This course had come about in consequence of my painting the program posters (for eurythmy and other performances), at Rudolf Steiner's instigation. Classes took place at that time mainly on Sundays. Only when I had carried out a sketch in watercolor did Rudolf Steiner make the next one. Since I mounted increasingly larger sheets of paper, which he filled out completely each time, the sketches became larger and larger. Experience showed me that an especially pure, translucent effect could be achieved by laying several sheets of layout paper (*Detailpapier*) one upon the other, and I therefore used such sheets.

The sketches were made by Rudolf Steiner only for the living process of mediating the teaching content. They are "picture seeds," not given in order to be "copied"or reproduced. On the basis of the paintings I executed, Rudolf Steiner went on to give indications in the course of time going far beyond the sketches, and varying and altering them altogether.

Just as the foundations of the art of eurythmy were first called to life and developed through direct collaboration between Rudolf Steiner and eurythmists, and can be carried further today, so I work further today in continuance of my collaboration with Rudolf Steiner in painting.

Since the sketches are "picture seeds" that have to be developed further in terms of painting in Rudolf Steiner's sense, they have a different task from his watercolors, which are self-contained works of art and hence can be "copied."

All 23 training sketches belong together and form an organism. I have painted and taught them from the beginning in exact sequence. When Rudolf Steiner came on the evening of

---

[33] From two letters addressed to the *Rudolf Steiner-Nachlassverwaltung* (Rudolf Steiner Archive) of December 1, 1949 and January 22, 1950.

August 8, 1924, before leaving for Torquay, in order (for the last time) to see the students' work, I was already able to show him not only studies in connection with the "Nature Mood" sketches, but also some done on the basis of the sketches following them.[34]

---

[34] Full-size reproductions of the "Nature Mood" sketches are contained in the portfolio *Rudolf Steiner: Neun Schulungsskizzen für Maler/"Naturstimmungen."* Rudolf Steiner-Verlag, Dornach, Switzerland 1962, 1999.
For reproductions of the later training sketches the reader is referred to *Rudolf Steiner: Ein malerischer Schulungsweg/Pastellskizzen und Aquarelle*. Rudolf Steiner Verlag, Dornach 1986.

The "Nature Mood" Sketches of Rudolf Steiner

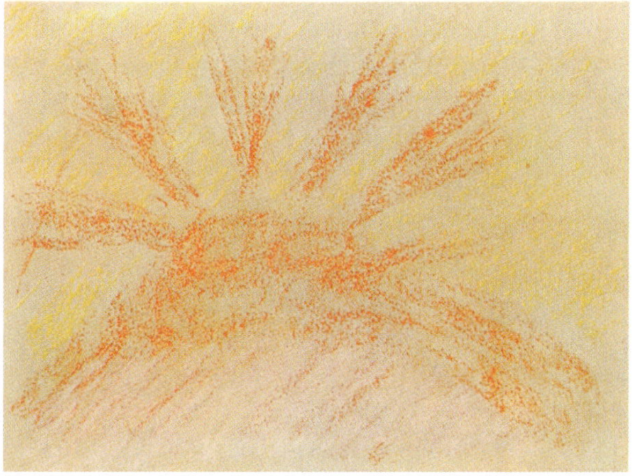

1

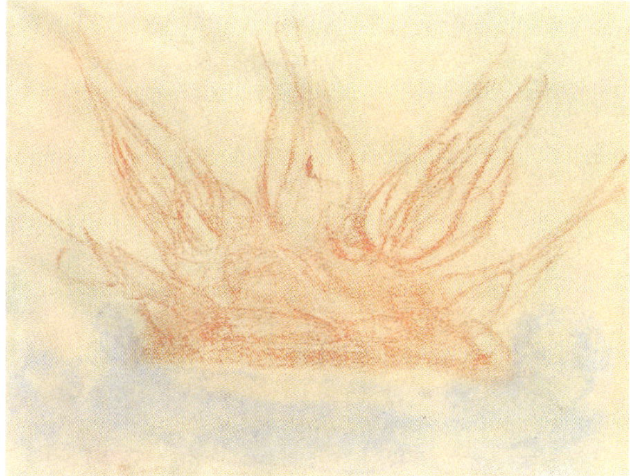

2

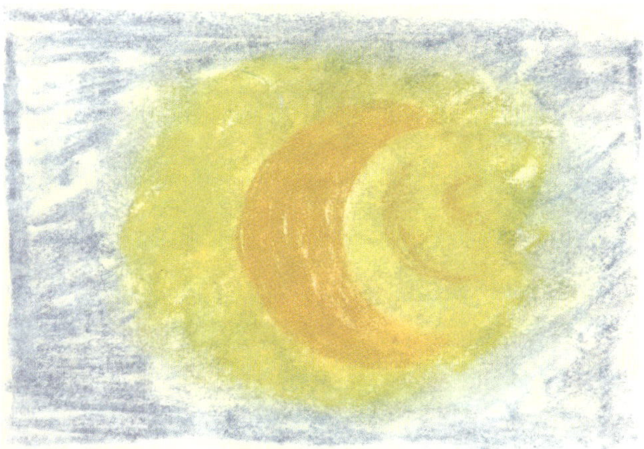

3

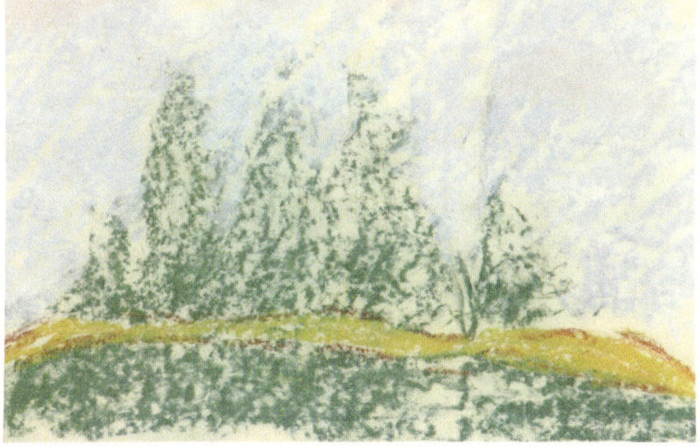

4

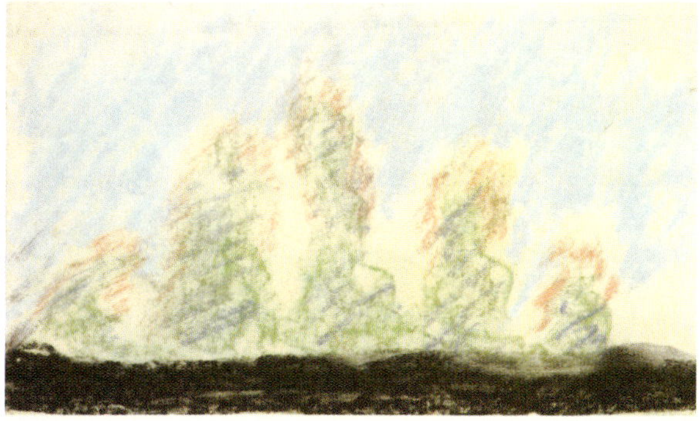

5

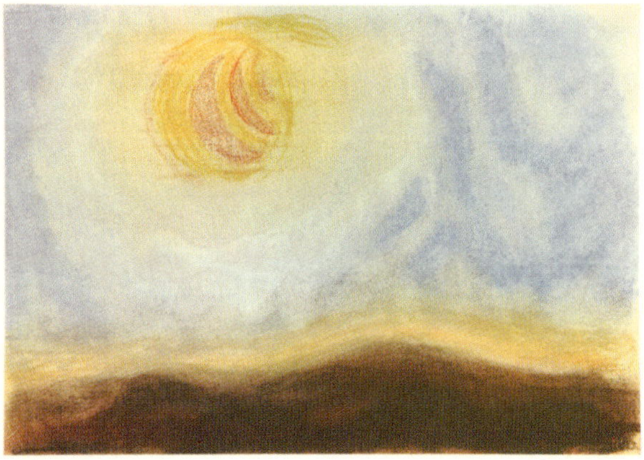

6

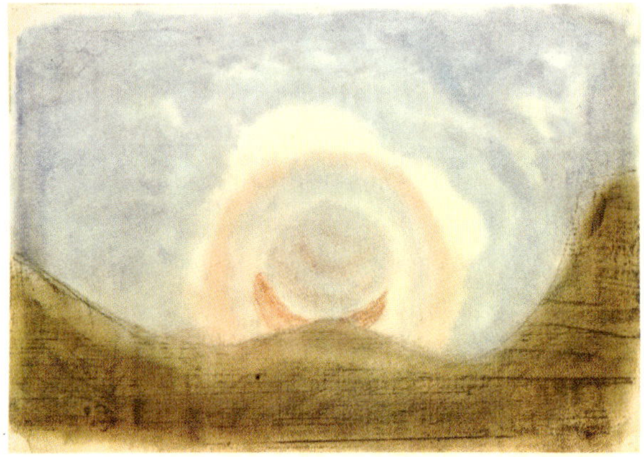

7

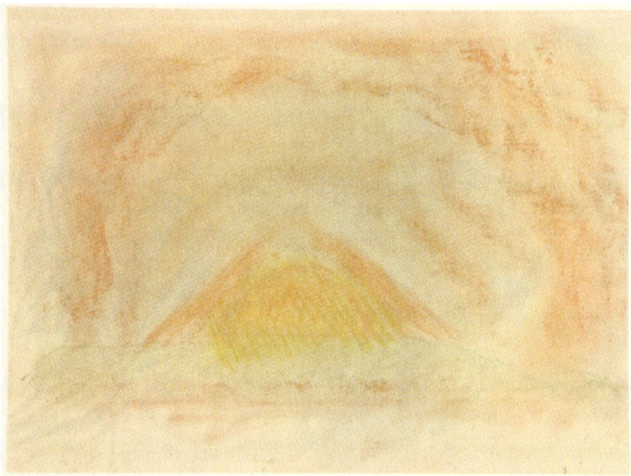

8

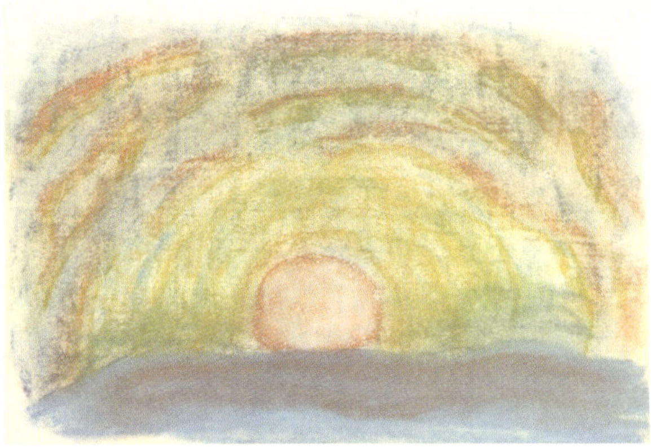

9

1. *Sunrise I*
2. *Sunset I*
3. *Shining Moon*
4. *Trees I*
5. *Trees II*
6. *Moonrise*
7. *Moonset*
8. *Sunrise II*
9. *Sunset II*

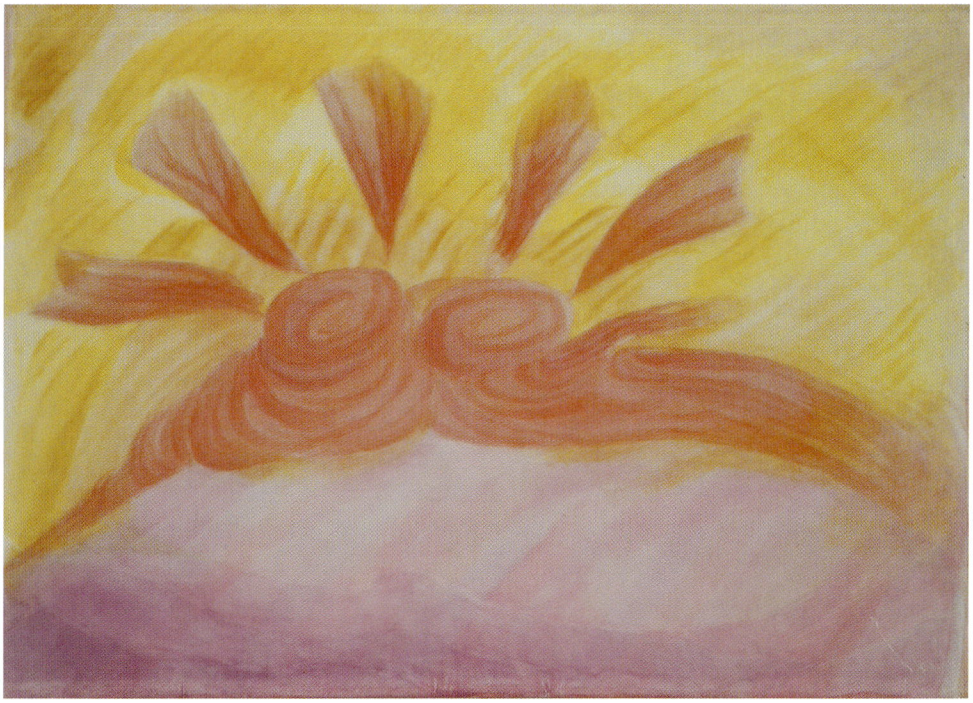

Sunrise I painted by Henni Geck. Watercolor on paper. 78 x 107.5 cm. Goetheanum Art Collection (Dornach). On loan from the owner and copyright holder: Humanus-Stiftung (Basel).

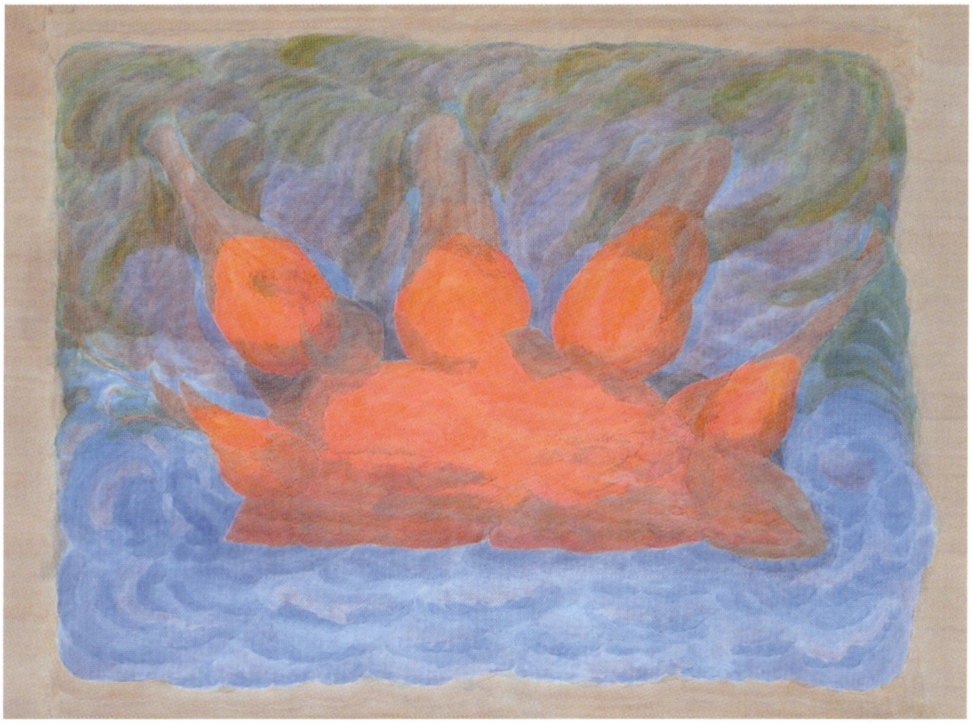

Sunset I painted by Henni Geck. Watercolor on paper. 78 x 113 cm. Goetheanum Art Collection (Dornach). On loan from the owner and copyright holder: Humanus-Stiftung (Basel).

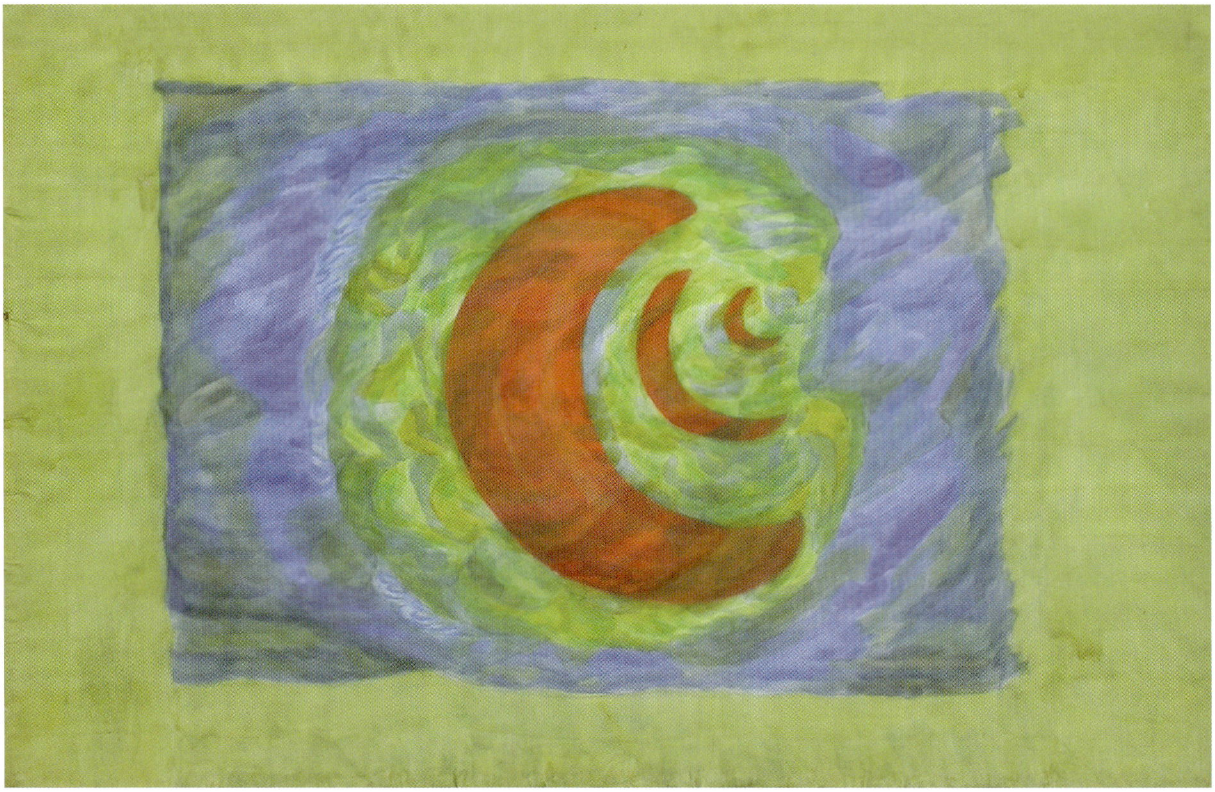

Shining Moon painted by Henni Geck. Watercolor on paper. 78 x 119 cm.
Goetheanum Art Collection (Dornach).
On loan from the owner and copyright holder: Humanus-Stiftung (Basel).

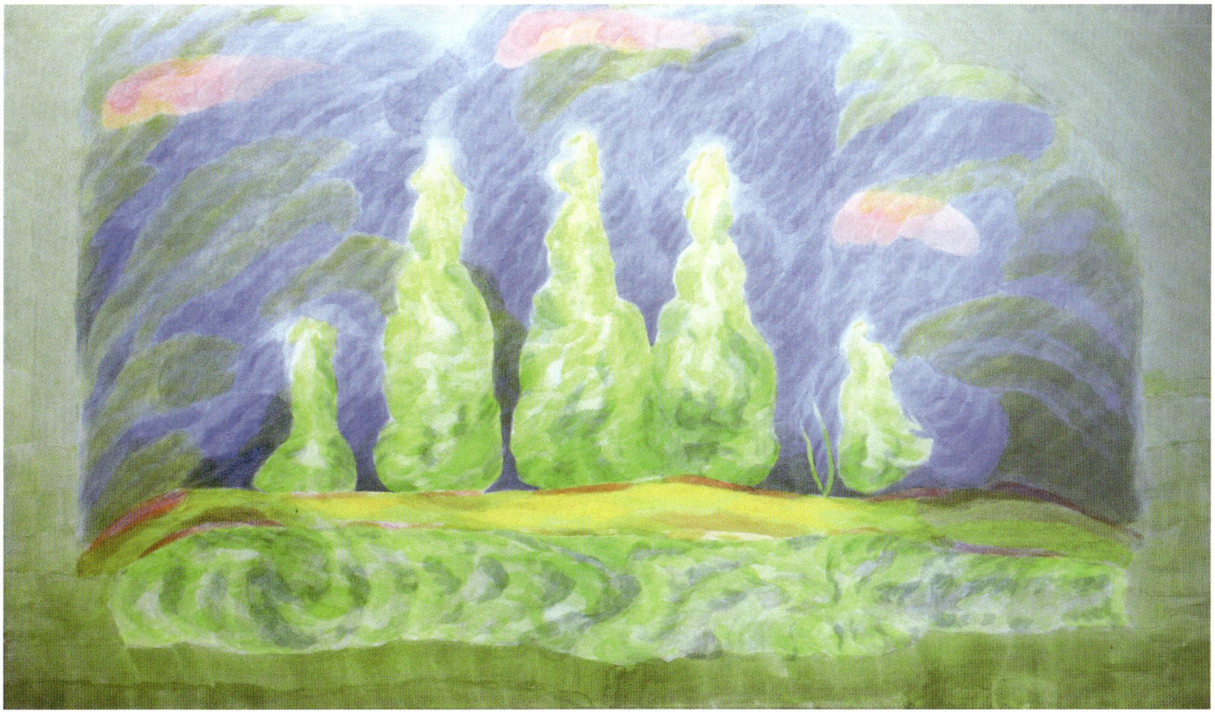

Trees I ("Summer Trees") painted by Henni Geck. Watercolor on paper. 78 x 131 cm. Goetheanum Art Collection (Dornach). On loan from the owner and copyright holder: Humanus-Stiftung (Basel). Photo: Peter Stebbing.

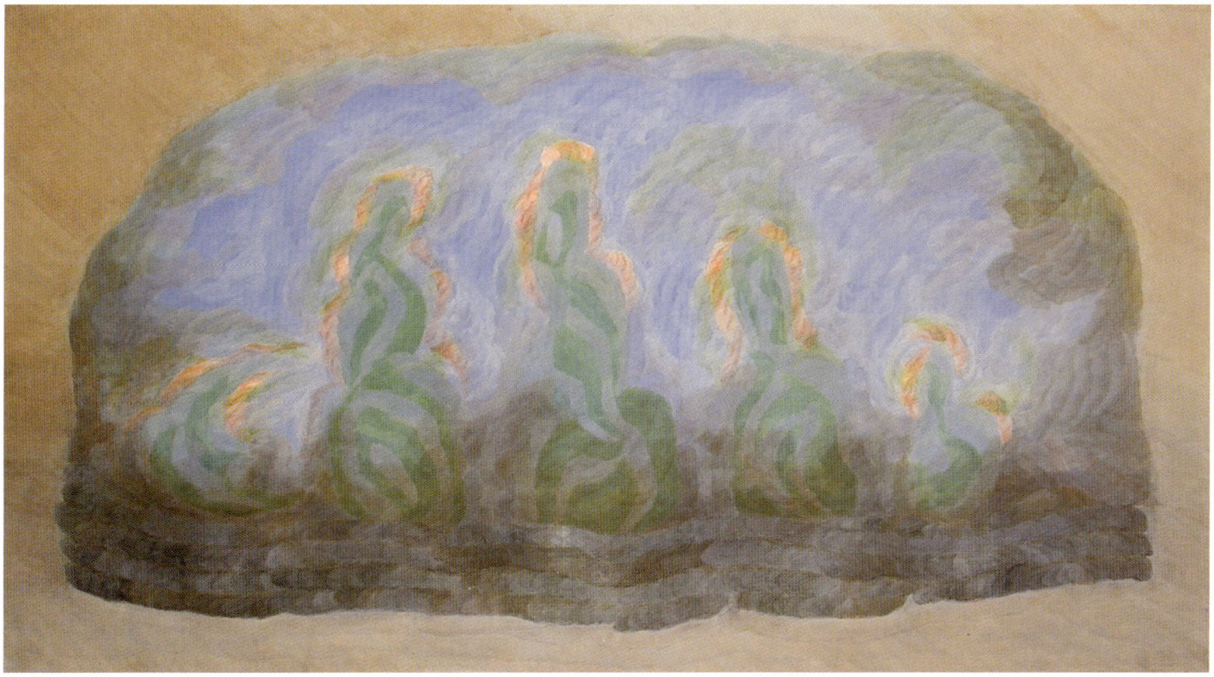

Trees II ("Blossoming or Fruiting Trees") painted by Henni Geck. Watercolor on paper. 74.5 x 132.5 cm. Privately Owned. Copyright: Humanus-Stiftung (Basel).

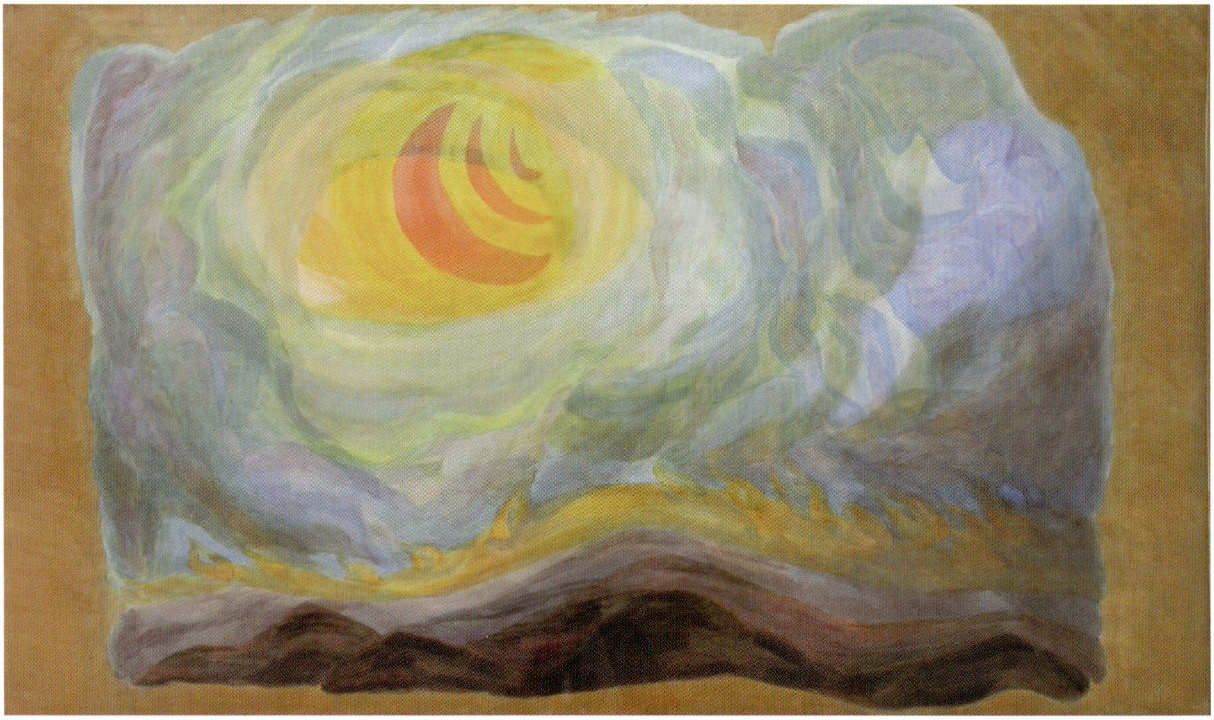

Moonrise painted by Henni Geck. Watercolor on paper. 77.5 x 128.5 cm. Goetheanum Art Collection (Dornach). On loan from the owner and copyright holder: Humanus-Stiftung (Basel).

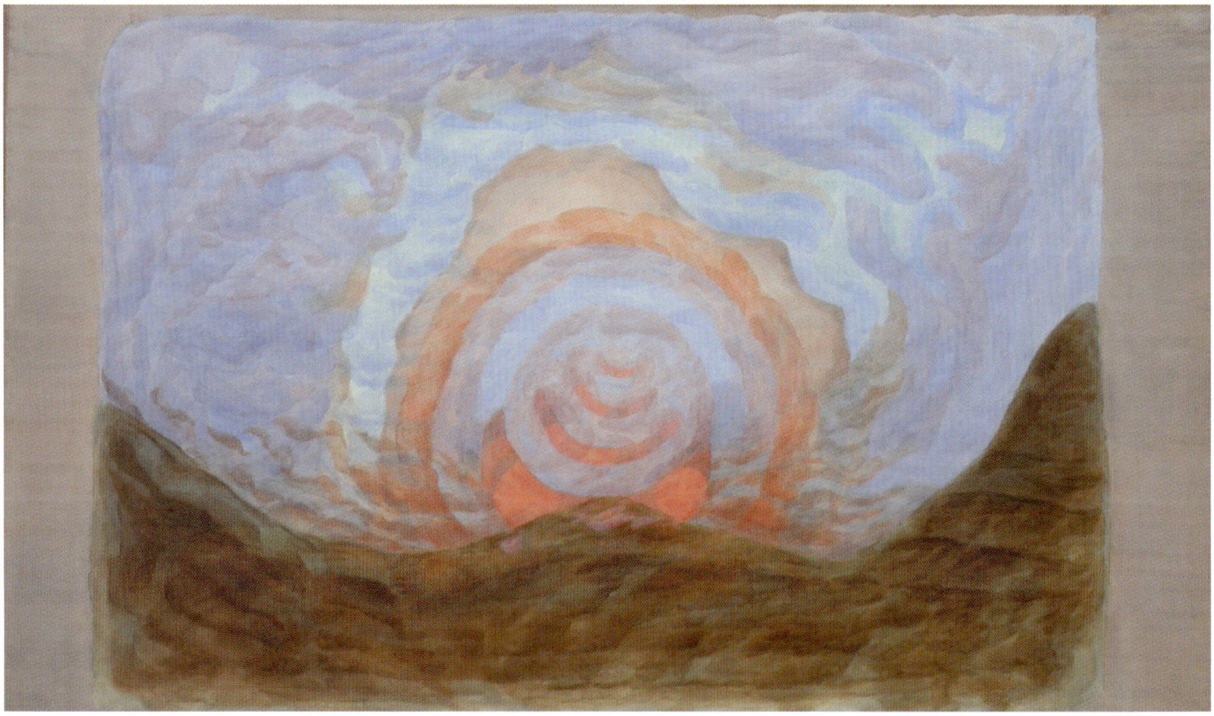

Moonset painted by Henni Geck. Watercolor on paper. 77.5 x 127 cm. Goetheanum Art Collection (Dornach). On loan from the owner and copyright holder: Humanus-Stiftung (Basel).

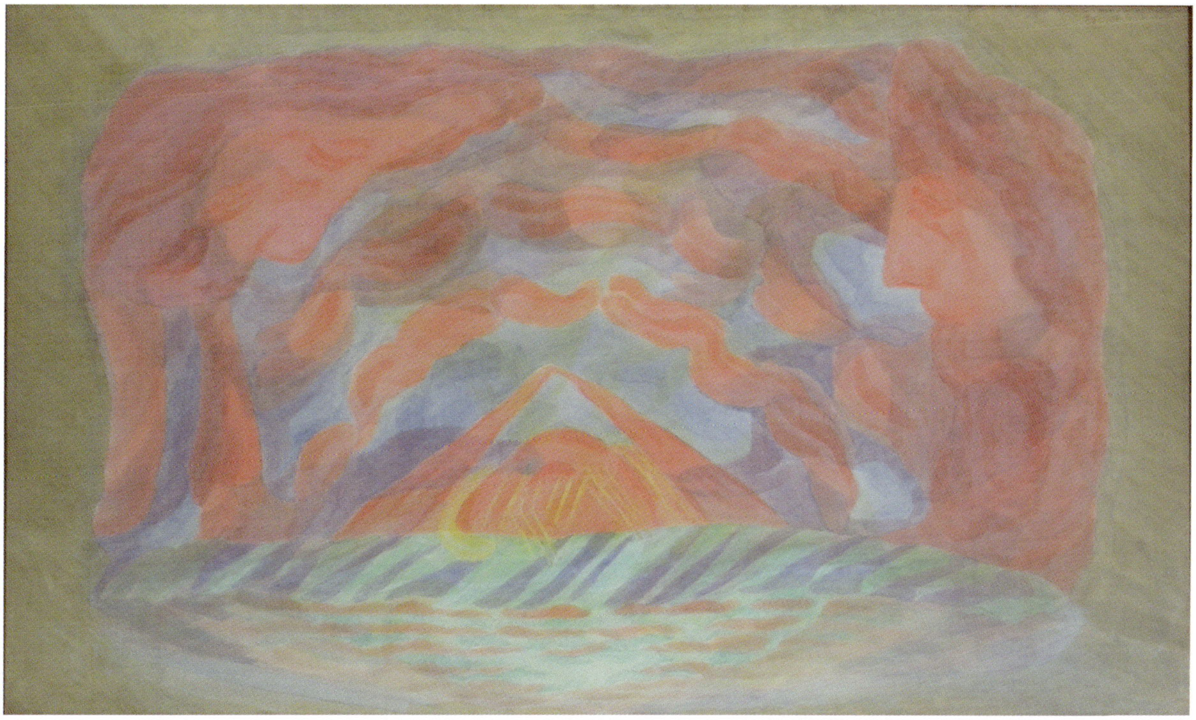

Sunrise II painted by Henni Geck. Watercolor on paper. 77.5 x 127 cm. Goetheanum Art Collection (Dornach). On loan from the owner and copyright holder: Humanus-Stiftung (Basel).

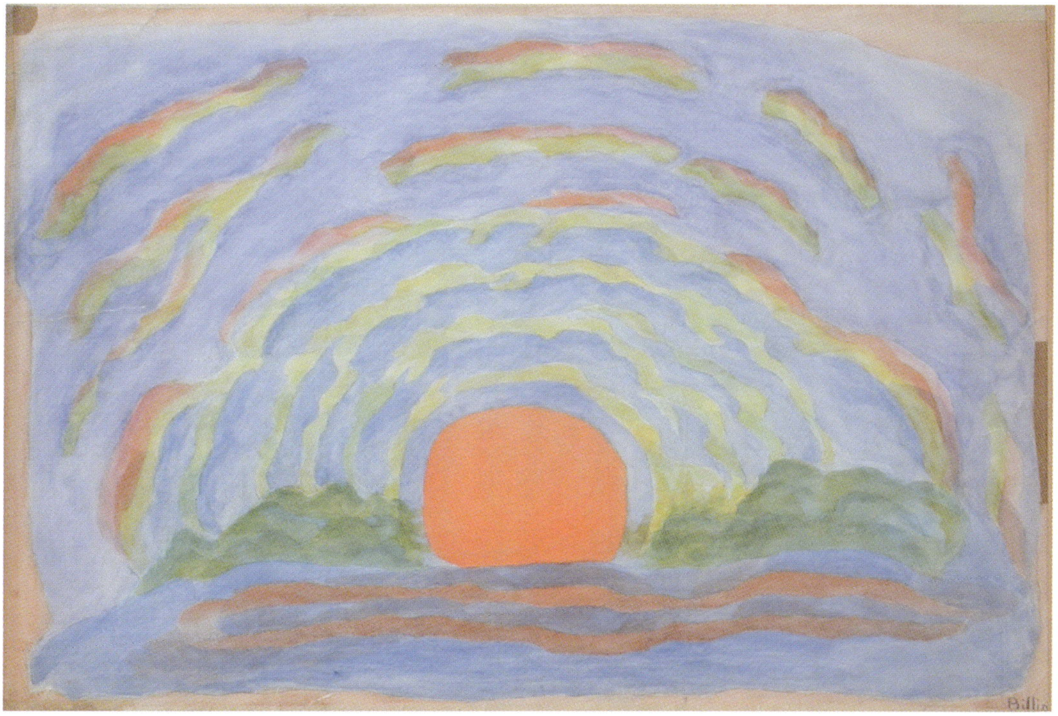

Sunset II painted by Fritz Billing. Watercolor on paper. 69 x 101 cm. (An early work from the year 1929). Privately owned. Copyright unknown. An example of this motif painted by Henni Geck is not available.

THE MOTIF SKETCHES OF RUDOLF STEINER

Their Origin and Task

Fritz Billing

This artistic and at the same time pedagogical oeuvre, ever more crucial for the comprehensive renewal of the art of painting (consisting of twenty-two motif sketches and five large-format watercolors), was entrusted to humanity during the final phase of Rudolf Steiner's life.

He gave it in the first instance as indispensable work and study material for the painting courses held at the Goetheanum by the painter Henni Geck from 1921 until 1929. It is at the same time a matter of an impulse of Rudolf Steiner that transcends anything of a personal nature.

The first sketch was made on May 25, 1922, three days before Whitsun.[35] Henni Geck, an academically trained painter, directed a specific question to Rudolf Steiner concerning a path, practicable also for students, leading step by step to the development of a style of painting commensurate with the Goetheanum, its spirit and its art impulses.

Just as specific was his immediate response in sketching a fiery sunrise in pastel, with the assignment of carrying out this sketch quite freely, yet with regard for its underlying lawfulness of color and form. This meant not "copying" it, but awakening to the inherent life latent within the sketch, employing fluid watercolors to which he attached special importance.

Over approximately eighteen months another twenty-one motif sketches followed in organic sequence, and this sequence is certainly to be taken into account in studying them. The motifs painted in this way by Henni Geck were then utilized for large-size program-posters at all artistic events at the Goetheanum, for which reason Rudolf Steiner included space for the lettering in five of the sketches and in two paintings. They were put up each time in a prominent place and shown illuminated during the intervals. Rudolf Steiner often referred to them, specifically in his lecture of June 29, 1923, in Dornach: "And if you take a look at what has been tried in the simple attempts of our program-posters, then you will see: there, even if it is only a beginning, the beginning has nonetheless been made,

---

35 Prior to this, Henni Geck had already held painting classes for about six months at the Goetheanum starting in late 1921.

to free colors from weight, to experience color as a self-sustaining element, to let colors themselves speak. If that succeeds, then over against the inartistic worldview of physics, which deadens all art, out of the free element of color, of tone, an art will be created that is once again free of weight."

When Rudolf Steiner had sketched one of his most beautiful motifs, *Light and Darkness (Lucifer and Ahriman)*, in pastel, he remarked, prompted by the admiration expressed at it: "But pastel is inartistic." – An utterance which shows how important the question of the medium was for him. Every motif was to be re-experienced and re-created out of the fluid medium of watercolor. He did not regard his motif sketches as works of art in themselves, but as objective "picture seeds" that leave individual creativity free while at the same time leading to a higher stage. They were not to be viewed as static in their imaginative character. As follows from his lecture "The Being of the Arts" (October 28, 1909, Berlin), it is not "Imagination" but "Intuition" that is the representative starting point for the activity of painting. In the sacrificial fire of Intuition, creativity is to be directed at the "how." Through union with the seraphic being of Intuition it will become possible to free the Imagination (still shackled to the material substance of the color in the "pastel sketch"!) from earthly weight, by appropriate artistic means.

This can only be attained by degrees, and in fact only by means of an active process of "repeating" the exercises at a higher stage, an on-going activity closely bound up with Rudolf Steiner's motif sketches. The same motif painted again and again at appropriate intervals in new ways yields the possibility of penetrating out of the color (by means of enhancement) to the archetype of the motif. In this way the well-known saying of Rudolf Steiner can eventually be converted into practice: "The motif, which until now has been the starting point in painting, must become the result in the painting of the future!"[36]

With such a change of focus from the semblance to the actual ethos (or distinguishing character) of a motif, a new impulse will be realized for the future of painting.

To this transformation of the activity of painting in living and working with the motif sketches, if it happens in the right way, there will be added a new kind of "seeing." Significantly, this is to come about in consequence of activating the sense of sight connected

---

[36] See Hilde Boos-Hamburger on p. 72 of this volume (in "The Struggle for the Underlying Principles of a New Spiritualized Painting Impulse").

with Imagination by means of the "I"-sense identified with Intuition.[37] In this way, both sense qualities interpenetrate in the act of seeing, complementing each other. Only such a sense of sight strengthened by the "I"-sense will ultimately be capable of mastering the polarity of forces of Lucifer and Ahriman which arises with such immediacy for the painter.

Rudolf Steiner had to make considerable demands precisely in the field of painting. This is by reason of the much greater possibilities of straying to the "luciferic" or the "ahrimanic" side, as compared with other arts.[38] Here we touch upon the central task of his series of motif sketches: to reconcile polarities and achieve harmonious balance.

From these and other points of view a great deal could be said about each single motif sketch, as well as, for example, about their relationship to the lectures of Rudolf Steiner, which would, however, exceed the limits of this exposition.

An overview of the sequence of motifs sketched by Rudolf Steiner allows us to distinguish three groupings within the whole series. This magnificent rhythm, which as a creative principle has found its expression in many of the cultural institutions of humanity, is reflected in that the 1st group of motif sketches starts out from Nature as a source of revelation; the 2nd group presents relationships within body, soul and spirit; and the 3rd group is concerned with the spiritual communion of the human being and humanity.

The following may be said as regards the first motif sketch:

In 1924 in his address to the young people in Arnheim, Rudolf Steiner pointed to the fact that since the end of the Dark Age, of "Kali Yuga," the sunrise in Nature has become no longer glowing, but flaming.

If one observes the sketch with this in mind, it becomes directly evident that in its form and gesture it corresponds to this new spiritual reality enunciated by him on a later occasion. Thus even if for Rudolf Steiner (the artist and researcher in one person) the purely artistic aspect was the primary criterion, the sketch nonetheless also proved itself "true" for the seer. It may perhaps be said that a style of painting corresponding to the spirit of our time could not have proceeded more consistently than from this sunrise sketch.

The painter should "listen in" on it, should "read" from it something of that wonderful law of all genesis incorporated in the rhythm of tension and resolution, in- and out-breathing, coming-into-being and passing-away.

---

[37] See Rudolf Steiner's lecture of August 8, 1920, in Dornach.

[38] See *Secrets of the Threshold*, Lecture VI, August 29, 1913 (GA 147).

Those who experience the drama of concentration and raying-out which, as the main polarity, so clearly balance each other in this motif, will feel themselves drawn into the activity of color itself. The birth of form out of the color as a basic phenomenon becomes direct experience. (See *Sunrise I* by Henni Geck, p. 99, as well as the pastel sketch by Rudolf Steiner on p. 97).

Rudolf Steiner once declared: "Color has the yearning to become the human being." His twenty-two motif sketches can be viewed as stages on a path corresponding to this goal. Starting out from the sun as the fount of color and proceeding via the polarity of Lucifer and Ahriman, they culminate in the final sketch, the *Three Kings Motif*, in which color becomes one with the human form.

According to notes and verbal reports of Henni Geck, Rudolf Steiner himself painted into her first attempts at both the *Elemental Beings* and *The Three Kings*, adding a few concise indications which he had not yet given in the actual sketches.

It can make a deep impression on reading, for example, in a straightforward note, that on the morning of December 25, 1923, at 9 o'clock – one hour before the refounding of the General Anthroposophical Society – Rudolf Steiner took brush in hand in order to paint something into Henni Geck's watercolor of the concluding motif of his series of sketches, *The Three Kings* (originally given as a pastel sketch eleven days earlier on December 14, 1923).

From January 17 to August 8, 1924, Rudolf Steiner painted five large-size watercolors as the culmination of his three-year collaboration with Henni Geck. On the one hand the intention was to provide an incentive to painting also without a motif sketch, and on the other hand to achieve an intensification of color.

Henni Geck painted each of these watercolors separately, at the same time as Rudolf Steiner, out of a spirit of free participation in, and direct experience of what arose objectively from his hand.

In the case of the first transitional motif from the sketches in pastel to these watercolor paintings, the so-called *Moon-Rider*, Rudolf Steiner had Henni Geck carry out in watercolor the color-beginning he had initially sketched in pastel, before developing the motif out of this himself. The four other watercolors then followed.

When, on viewing his watercolor *Easter* (*Three Crosses*), some people marveled at the strong, luminous colors of this painting, Rudolf Steiner responded by saying that he would need thirty years in order to be able truly to paint out of the color. – An utterance which shows, among other things, what unimaginable possibilities of development for the future lie contained within this new way of painting.

Fritz Billing notes in conclusion that freely created versions of the motif sketches of Rudolf Steiner painted by Henni Geck were exhibited publicly for the first time in the *Kunsthalle* [Art Gallery] in Berne in the spring of 1931.

Published on the occasion of the centennial of Rudolf Steiner's birth in 1961, by Fritz Billing, Atelier "Farbentor," Dornach, Switzerland.

THE WORK IN PAINTING AT THE GOETHEANUM WITH HENNI GECK

Clara Bosshardt

With this contribution I should like to discharge a debt of thanks which I feel I owe to Henni Geck.

I was able, when I first came to Dornach, to join the Painting School at the Goetheanum, which she directed at that time. I was thus privileged to learn and assimilate with her help what Rudolf Steiner had given the world in regard to a new art of painting commensurate with our age, the age of the consciousness soul.

Henni Geck was a strict teacher and in everything having to do with the subject of painting, unconditionally objective. As uncompromisingly as she placed her earlier painting training in the service of the new, she conducted herself in other matters as well. She viewed her task as that of imparting a thorough training in the new way of painting, and for the sake of this aim she brought everything to bear. She did not want simply to "give painting lessons." From the beginning she required of her students that they themselves aspire after this thorough training and place enough time for it at their disposal, i.e., enough time to work through the whole course of sketch-motifs given by Rudolf Steiner.

This course of training signified for her a life-task entrusted to her, in regard to which she had taken upon herself a binding commitment. Hence, she did not consider it right simply to place the sketches, expressly given and committed to her by Rudolf Steiner as a course of training, at the disposal of just anyone who wished it, not even of the professional painters working at the Goetheanum. She directed such people to the cupola sketches, given by Rudolf Steiner, which could provide them with a wealth of indications. But in this respect she was seriously misunderstood, as though she were refusing for petty or personal reasons.

More than once, Henni Geck told me how the sketches were given to her for the Painting School by Rudolf Steiner. She had come to Dornach to carve on the first Goetheanum. But being a trained painter, she was asked by members of the Anthroposophical Society for painting lessons. She consulted with Rudolf Steiner about this. He indicated his agreement and even placed a room at her disposal. However, this work proved unsatisfying to her, so that she again sought Rudolf Steiner's advice. Each person, she said, remained all too stuck in their own personal concerns. She asked whether there was not an objective course of training, similar to that given for eurythmy. At that Rudolf Steiner took a scrap of paper lying to hand and with a red crayon, made two concentrations and, proceeding from them, five rays. He let some cool red arise from below and placed yellow between the red rays, saying: "Try starting with something like that!" In this way the first sketch arose, a sunrise.

Fräulein Geck then immediately transposed this sketch into watercolor. Again and again she emphasized that Rudolf Steiner had not viewed his sketches as being works of art, also not as examples to be copied. Far rather, they were to set a theme to be worked out in the course of painting them; not once, but over and over again in quite different moods and strengths of color, not copying, but recreating them anew each time.

On his next visit to the studio, Rudolf Steiner expressed his satisfaction with the beginning that had been made, and at once gave a second sketch, a sunset. The build-up was similar to that of the first sketch, but as a new step, blue was added, the first passive color.

In this way gradually all twenty-two sketches arose, and then the five pictures were added, carried out in watercolors by Rudolf Steiner himself:

1. *The Moon-Rider (The Dream-Song of Olaf Åsteson)* 98.5 x 65.5 cm
   January 17–19, 1924.
2. *New Life (Mother and Child)* 100 x 66.5 cm
   February 15–29, 1924.
3. *Easter (Three Crosses)* 99.3 x 67 cm
   April 7/19, 1924.
4. *Archetypal Plant* 101 x 67 cm
   May/June 1924.
5. *Archetypal Human Being (Archetypal Animal)* 77 x 132 cm
   July/August 1924

At festival times these often hung as program-posters for performances in the Carpentry Building.

Whoever had the good fortune of working right through the course of training given in the pastel sketches, could experience nothing more magnificent in terms of method. Metamorphosis and enhancement in Goethe's sense are their mainstay.

Right from the start, with such a way of painting it is a matter of understanding a fundamental fact. Rudolf Steiner says: "The medium of painting is the surface." To most people it would seem, as it did to me, that it ought to be "the color," yet it is "the surface." What is meant by this? It may be said that what is meant is what some modern painters have struggled with, namely color-perspective. This signifies nothing other than that the painter should renounce the three-dimensional effects of physical space and enter into the two-dimensional picture plane. It can also be expressed by saying: the painter has to come to terms with the etheric world and its laws. This world is two-dimensional, like the surface (and depends on overcoming the third dimension). A duality involved in painting is that of color and form. Both are to be brought to a unity on the surface. To come to a full experience of this in painting and make it one's own is not as simple as it might seem. Yet this alone can help us understand in practical terms what Rudolf Steiner elaborated in his color lectures concerning the new art of painting.

A list of the individual training sketches follows:

From *Mitteilungen aus der Anthroposophischen Arbeit in Deutschland,* Nr. 75, Ostern 1966.

Nine "Nature Moods"

		(Height precedes width)
1.	Sunrise I	16 x 21 cm
2.	Sunset I	19 x 23.5 cm
3.	Shining Moon	17.5 x 24.5 cm
4.	Trees I ("Summer Trees")	18.5 x 27 cm
5.	Trees II ("Blossoming or Fruiting Trees")	16 x 27 cm
6.	Moonrise	21 x 29.5 cm
7.	Moonset	25 x 34.5 cm
8.	Sunrise II	27 x 36 cm
9.	Sunset II	22 x 31 cm

The "Motif Sketches"

(Thirteen training sketches and one color-beginning)

10.	Group Souls (The Human Being)	46.7 x 30.5 cm
11.	Light and Darkness (Lucifer and Ahriman)	61 x 47.5 cm
12.	The Seer in the Midst of Marianus and Gabrilein	55 x 74.5 cm
13.	Distance and Life Come into Being ("Archangel Looking at Planetary States")	67.5 x 65.3 cm
14.	The Threefold Human Being	71 x 52.5 cm
15.	The Human Being in the Spirit	74.2 x 49 cm
16.	The Spirit in the Human Being	99 x 59.5 cm
	*	
17.	St. John's Imagination ("Reddish Figure with Sun and Moon")	72 x 55 cm
18.	Druid Stones	89 x 73 cm
19.	The Human Being in Relation to the Planets	91.5 x 68 cm
20.	Elemental Beings	71.5 x 64 cm
21.	Adam Kadmon in Early Lemuria	101 x 70 cm
22.	Three Kings Motif	67 x 52 cm
23.	The Moon-Rider (color-beginning)	86.5 x 66 cm

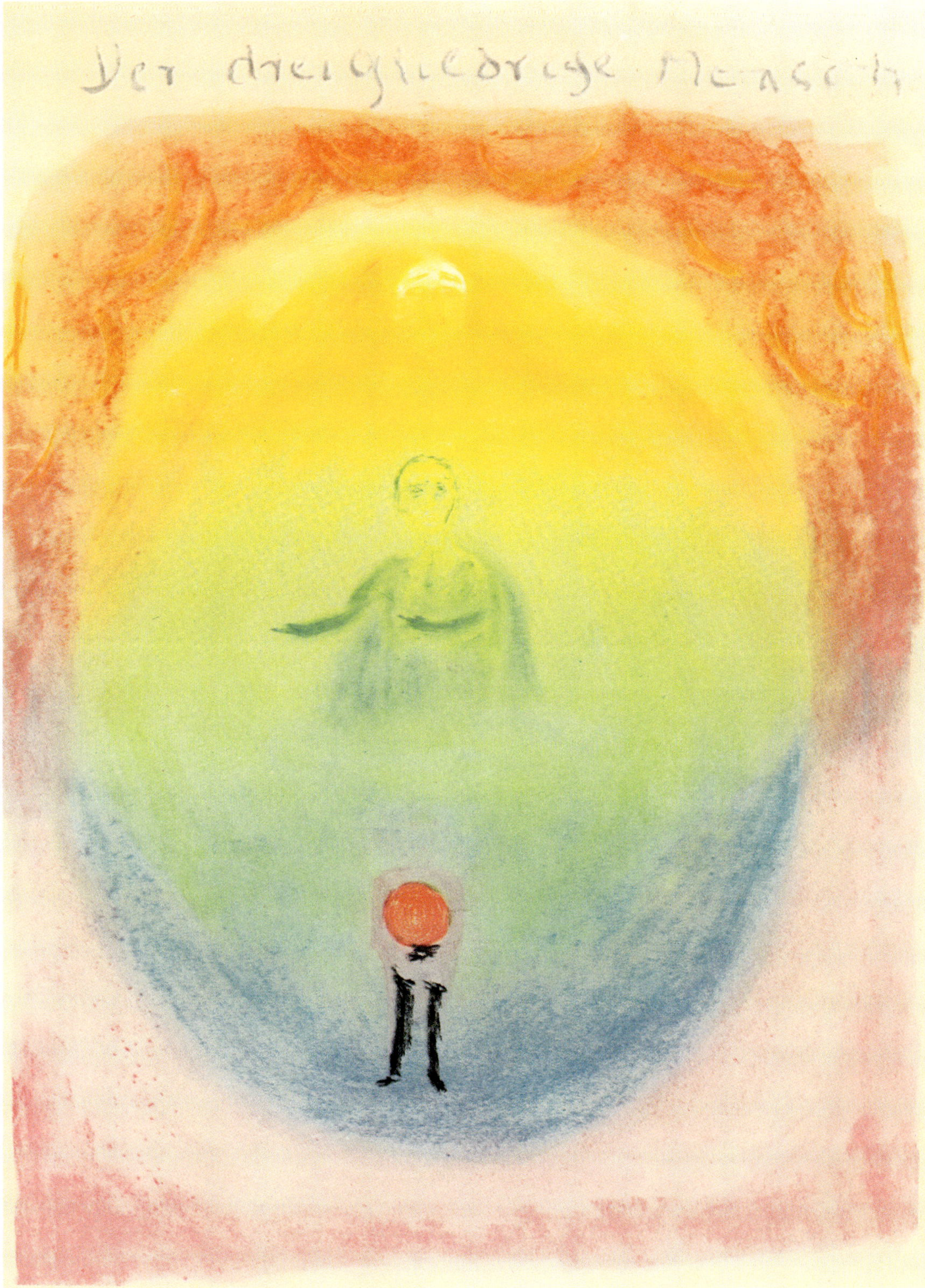

The Threefold Human Being by Rudolf Steiner. Pastel sketch.
Rudolf Steiner Archive (Dornach)

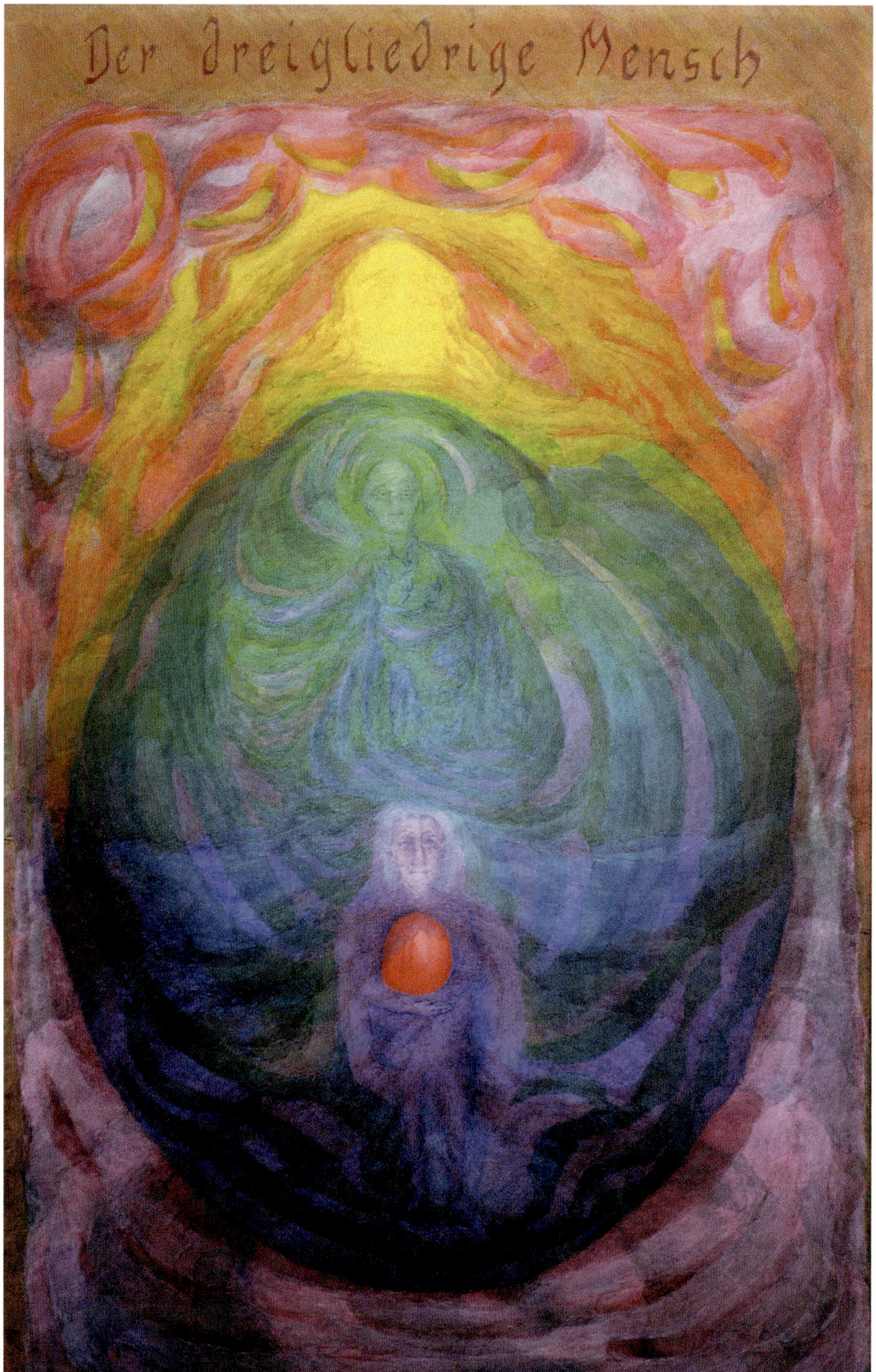

The Threefold Human Being painted by Henni Geck.
Watercolor on paper. 127.5 x 78 cm. Goetheanum Art Collection (Dornach).
Loaned by the owner and copyright holder: Humanus-Stiftung (Basel).

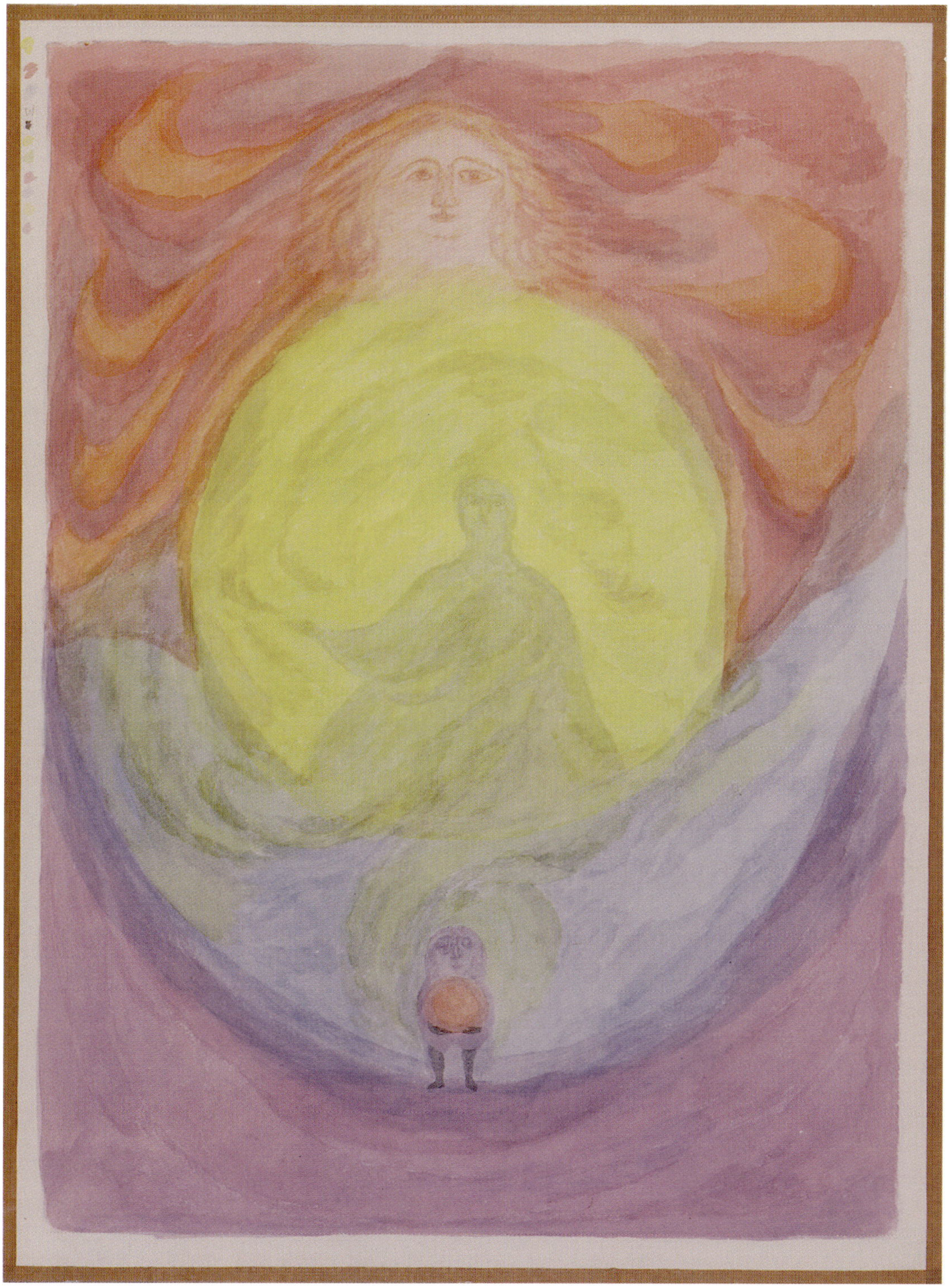

The Threefold Human Being painted by Gerard Wagner.
Watercolor on paper. 71 x 53 cm. Copyright: Elisabeth and Gerard Wagner Verein (Arlesheim).
Gerard Wagner (1906–1999) studied from 1928–29 with Henni Geck in Dornach
before her school temporarily closed.

The "Nature Mood" Sketches painted by *Elisabeth und Gerard Wagner*
(Included here as further examples of Rudolf Steiner's sketch-motifs transposed into watercolor.)

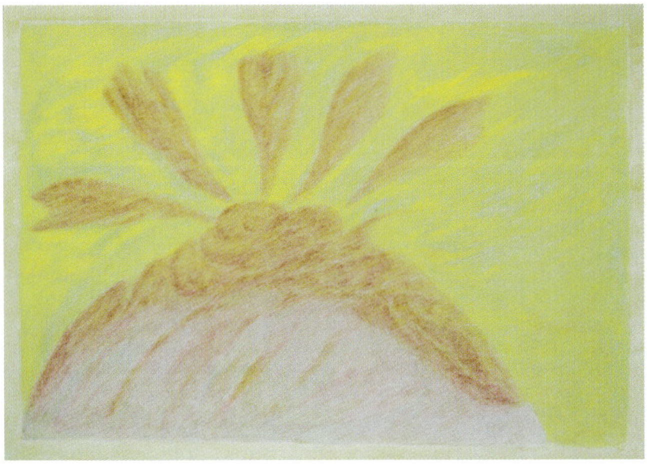

1

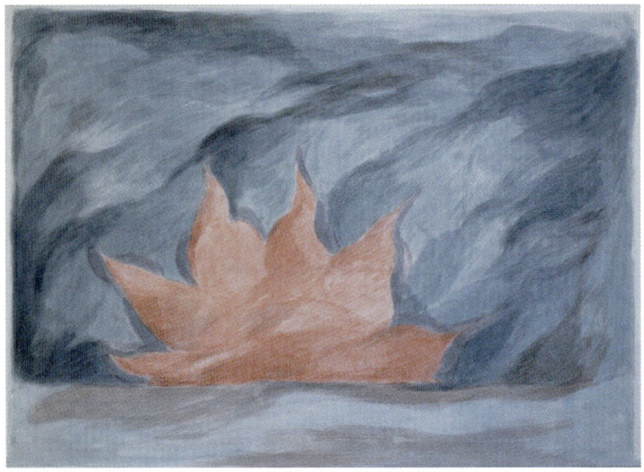

2

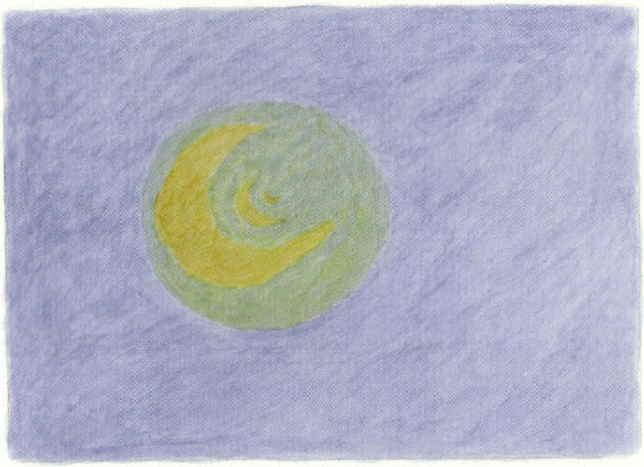

3

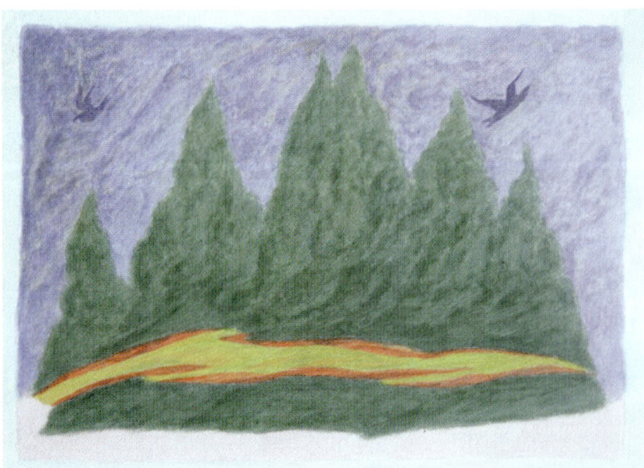

4

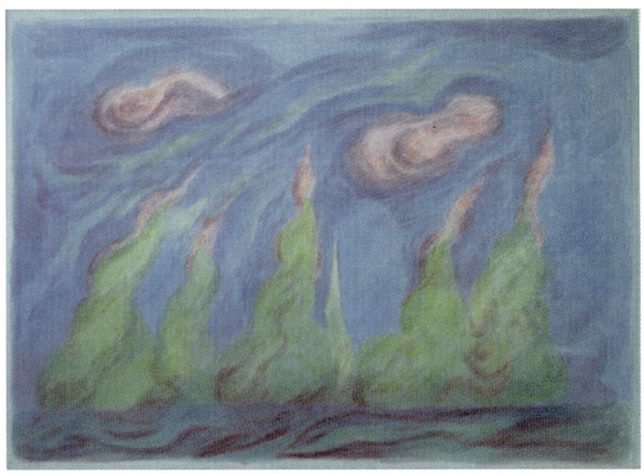

5

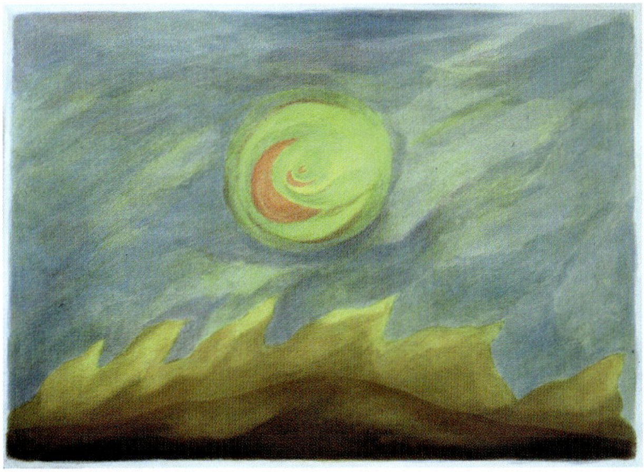

6

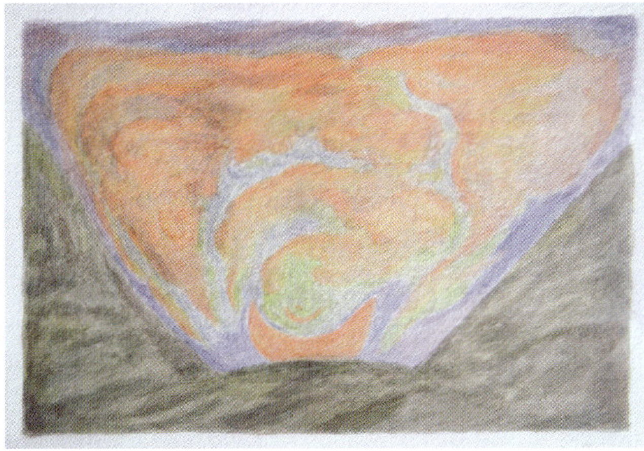

7

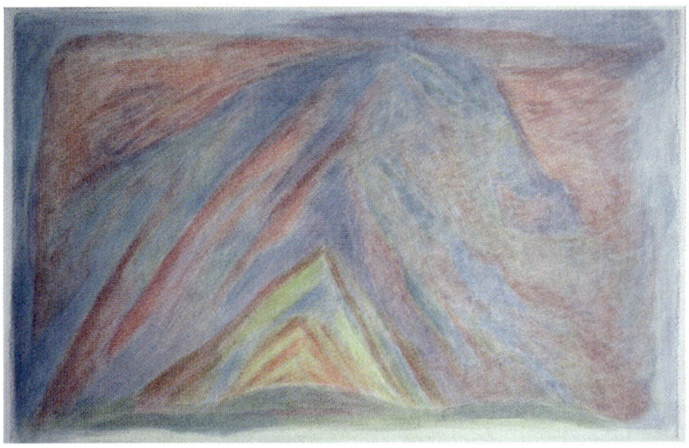

8

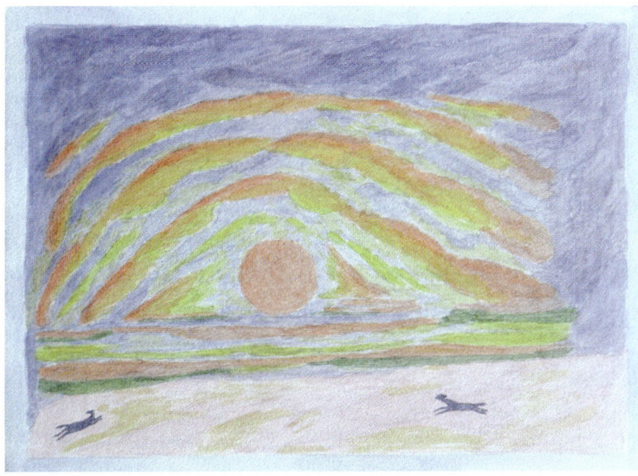

9

The nine "Nature Mood" sketches painted by Gerard Wagner are reproduced courtesy of the Elisabeth and Gerard Wagner Verein (Arlesheim).

On Studying in Henni Geck's Painting School

In 1928 I was admitted by Henni Geck into her painting school. The classes took place at that time in Rudolf Steiner's Studio (*Hochatelier*) in the Carpentry Building, where the great wax and plasticine model of the sculptural group, *The Representative of Humanity,* stood. On the walls all around hung the originals of the training and motif sketches. – A new art of sculpture and a new art of painting. Here the whole mood of the teacher still lived, and the earnestness of his manner of working.

Henni Geck had been present when all the sketches were made. Following an indication of Rudolf Steiner, we were directed to transpose the motifs, which are given in pastel, into watercolor. In doing so, we had to pay careful attention to the forms and their mutual relationships of balance, down to the smallest detail. Henni Geck always gave us the color sequence. After nine months – as the result of tragic circumstances – the classes ceased in this form. Later the sketches came to be hung in the Goetheanum, where they were accessible to students and those interested. But that brief time of instruction became of lasting value for all later years.

I had only painted the first three motifs: the Sunrise, Sunset and Shining Moon. By means of careful observation, while attempting to live into the colors, lines and forms of these models, something transpired within one: a tremendous interest arose that could be expressed more or less in the words: "Why, those are organisms." One experienced something in connection with these formations, of which one had to say to oneself: "They are 'exact', as though without anything accidental or arbitrary in their creation. They do not depict any objects of nature – but the details of their forms and movements are so mutually adapted to each other, carry and determine each other, as otherwise only the members of a living organism do, where every detail is necessarily linked to the whole. They do not depict – they *live.*"

This was something like a permanent feeling, which was only gradually to become more conscious in the course of the following decades.

— *Gerard Wagner*

From *Gerard Wagner: Die Kunst der Farbe.* Verlag Freies Geistesleben. Stuttgart 1980.

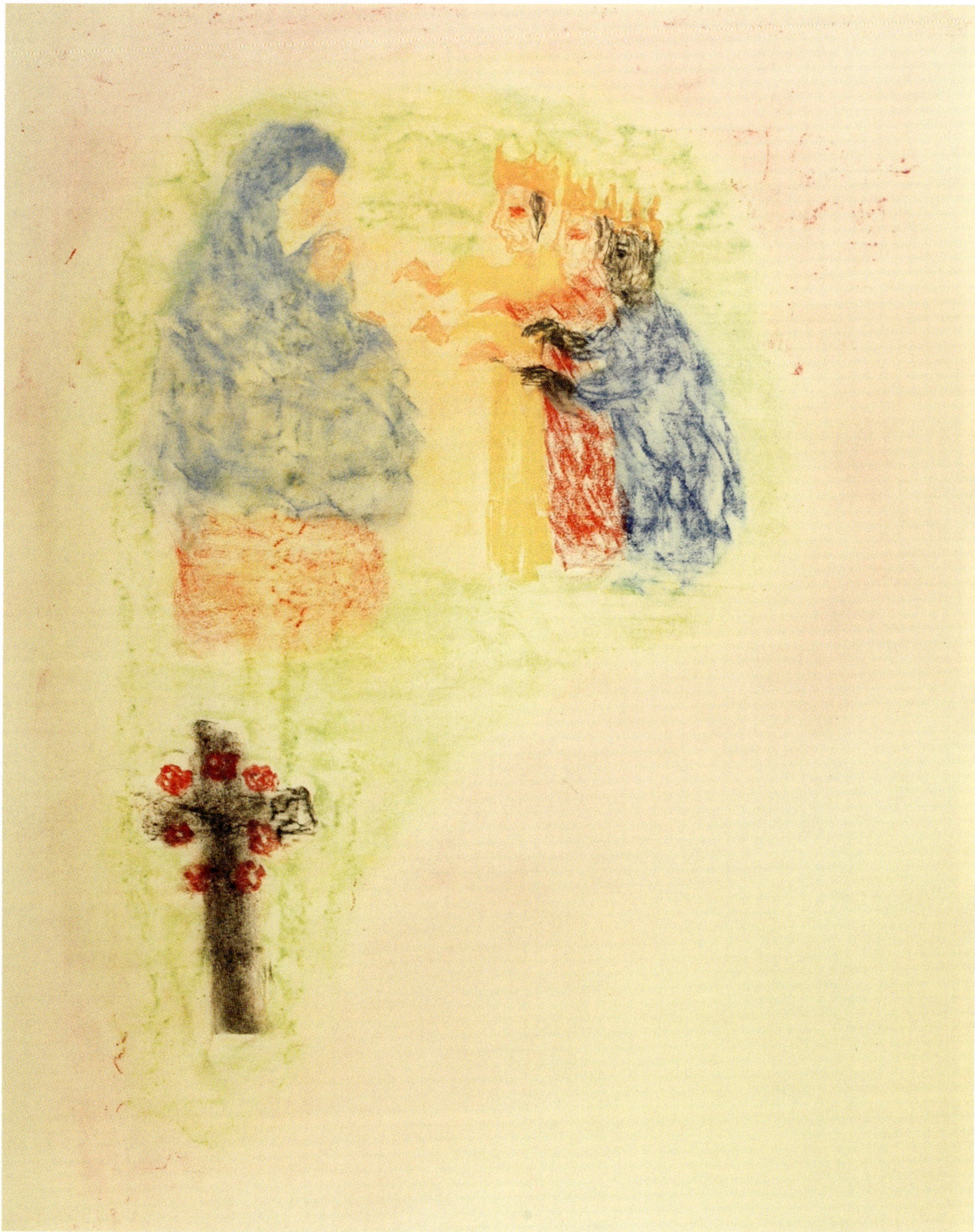

The Three Kings Motif by Rudolf Steiner.
Pastel sketch. 67 x 52 cm. Rudolf Steiner Archive (Dornach).

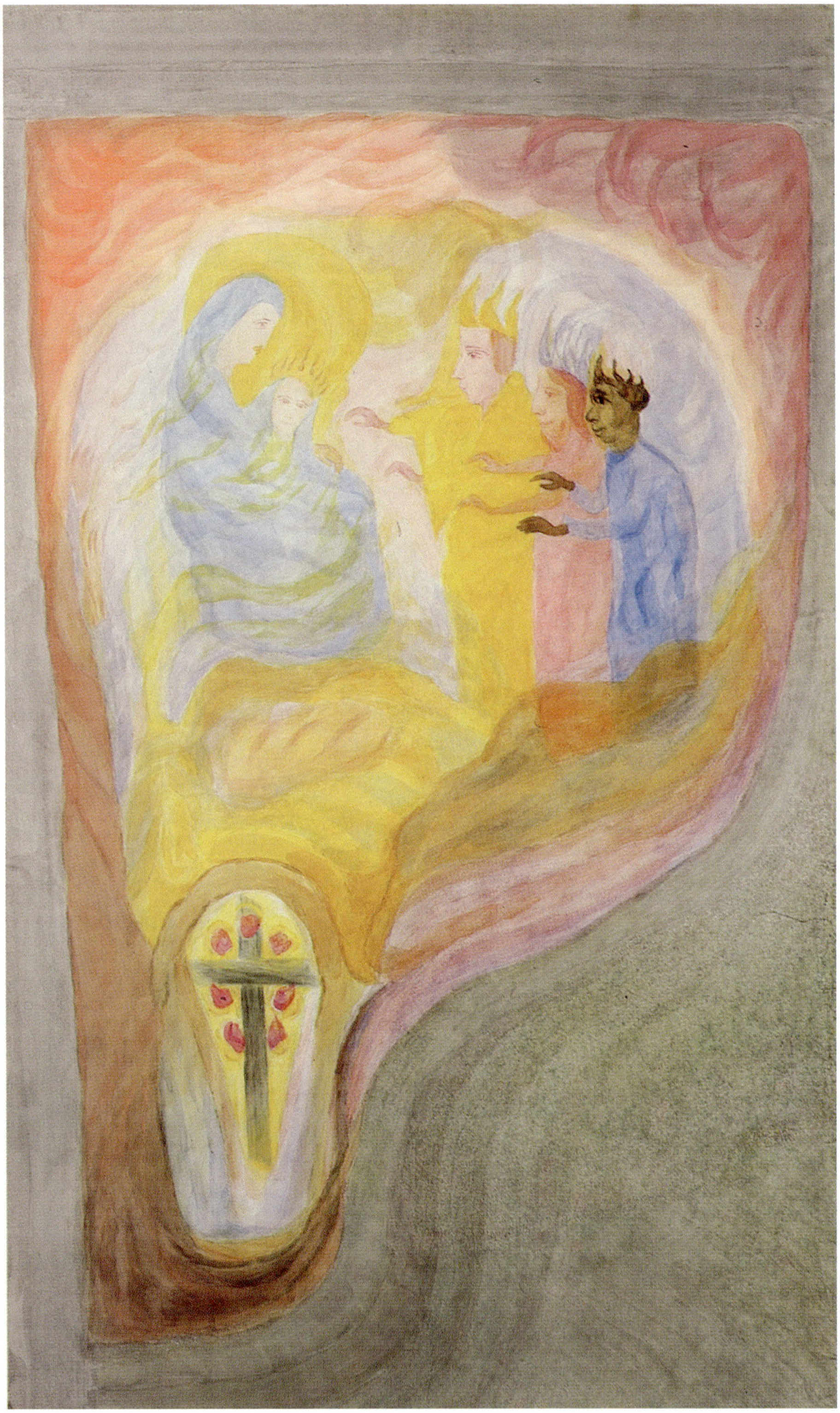

The Three Kings Motif painted by Henni Geck.
Goetheanum Art Collection (Dornach).
Humanus-Stiftung (Basel).

About Henni Geck

1884–1951

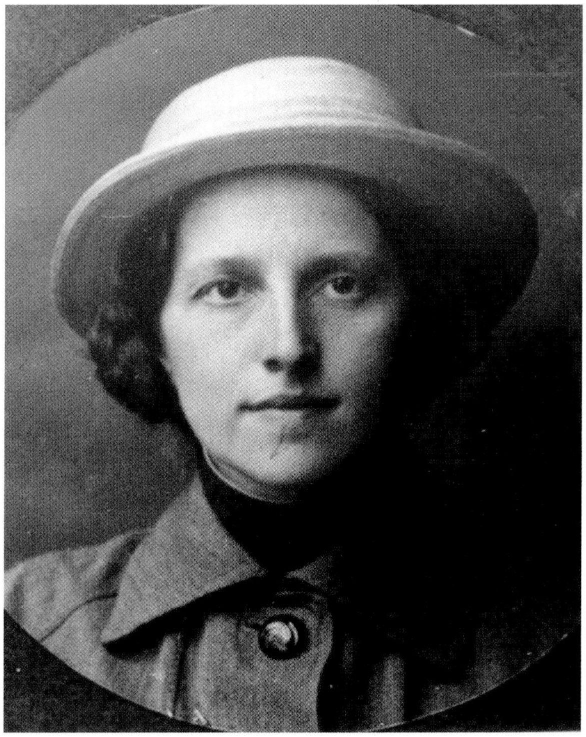

Henni Geck (born Berta Henriette Geck) was the youngest of five children of an industrialist in Altena, Westphalia. Two of her siblings died at an early age. She also lost her mother so early that she retained no memory of her. She had no strong bond with her family or with her contemporaries. Already during her childhood years she began to suffer from goiter, which accompanied her throughout her life. She told me once, that as a young girl she often sat whole nights on her bed struggling for breath, without anyone among her relatives knowing anything about it. Such experiences in youth contribute to forming a person's soul-disposition. Coming to terms with difficulties on her own, personal reserve and dogged perseverance were features of Henni Geck's character. Early on she separated from her family and went her own way. Around the turn of the century she began studying painting in Berlin. There, as well as at the academies in Düsseldorf and Munich, she acquired for herself a thorough artistic training (studying with such painters as *Lewin Funke, Hans Balutschek, Lovis Corinth,* and especially *Martin Brandenburg*). Her particular interest was portrait painting. In 1907 she became acquainted with anthroposophy in Berlin and joined the Theosophical Society. She belonged to the circle of Rudolf Steiner's closest pupils. She had a part in decorating the so-called "Art Room" in Berlin. In Munich she participated in the Mystery Plays, taking a group part.

In 1914 Rudolf Steiner called her to the Goetheanum in Dornach, where she then took up permanent residence. At first she was active as a carver on the first Goetheanum building. Rudolf Steiner, who valued her capacities and reliability, made her a co-worker on the "Group Statue" of the *Representative of Humanity*. She carved the being called "Cosmic Humor" on the upper left and other parts of the background. When after the completion of the second Goetheanum the "Group" was to be taken from the Carpentry Workshop into the new building, the dismantling and re-assembling of this enormous sculpture was entrusted to her.

When Henni Geck came to Dornach she sacrificed her painting activity and took up the work that had to be done. For seven years she wielded a carving tool. This could be seen in her hands for the rest of her life. However, the impulse to paint broke through again in 1921. She began to paint on her own, alongside the carving work. This was now no longer the old way of painting. She had in the meantime not only assimilated spiritual scientific knowledge, but permeated her whole being with the new artistic impulses. She showed Rudolf Steiner her paintings and he recognized in them the seeds of the new. At this point something uncommonly significant and rare came about: A trained and accomplished artist at the level of contemporary art, developed in her will forces, (at the same age as Goethe when he undertook his Italian journey), began a painting training once again, this time with the foremost spiritual teacher of our time. In this way the possibility was given for an impulse needed for the progressive development of humanity in art to be taken up by one artist, and thereby reach future generations of painters. In the three years remaining until his illness, the training path arose, leading to artistic work in painting out of the spirit of anthroposophy. This is contained in the pastel sketches and watercolors given by Rudolf Steiner to Henni Geck for her painting school. She was the first to fully traverse this path and make it her own. Everything further painted by her is a fruit of this path. She was an outstanding teacher. She first taught in the large studio in the Carpentry Building that stood at her disposal on Rudolf Steiner's instructions, and then later in her *Atelierhaus zum Farbentor* (Color-Portal Studio). A considerable number of her students received decisive help from her and bear the greatest gratitude toward her.

In Henni Geck there lived the certainty that what had been given her by Rudolf Steiner was not merely something personal, but objectively valid. And in the awareness of her responsibility toward her contemporaries and posterity, she looked after the sketches entrusted to her. In this respect she was struck by the harshest blow of her life: In 1929 the administration and care of the sketches was withdrawn from her and the right to continue her work at the Goetheanum taken away. She never entirely recovered from this. But with iron strength of will and unshakeable self-confidence – from now on thrown back upon herself – she carried on her destiny-alotted task. Three seven-year periods were still granted her to work. Twice she presented her pictures to the outside world, at the beginning and in the middle of the thirties with an exhibition in Bern and in Basel. Then came years of increasingly dire financial straits. A time will come when it will hardly be comprehensible, that one of the most significant bearers of an anthroposophical impulse had to endure such bitter privation. At last it seemed as though the pressure would yield, new students applied, new possibilities emerged – then destiny intervened: in the second week of September 1950 Henni Geck slipped and fell in her apartment, breaking the left thigh bone. When after a six-month, pain-filled hospital stay she was able to return to her house, full of plans for the future, the unexpected happened; in the absence of any illness, her soul loosened itself eight days later and laid the body aside.

– *Ernst Marti*

From *Mitteilungen aus der Anthroposophischen Arbeit in Deutschland,* 1951.

Recollections of the Teacher

(Some Personal Experiences and Impressions on Meeting Henni Geck)

In 1949, for the first time after the War, students from Germany were once again permitted to enter Switzerland and work as stage-hands at festival-performances of *Faust* at the Goetheanum in Dornach. I was there and was able, as a result of this opportunity, to get to know various individual artists who had collaborated in building the first Goetheanum. Thus I obtained access, through the agency of *Frau* Boos-Hamburger, to a room in which many original sketches and drawings of Rudolf Steiner were exhibited; I could draw and paint there at any time, and move freely among the various course participants and copyists devoutly painting there. One day, as I faithfully copied, color-veil for color-veil, the large watercolor by Rudolf Steiner entitled *Easter*, an elderly, gray-haired lady came up to me and began in a suppressed undertone, but still persistently and clearly, to criticize my work. – How I came simply to copy these pictures of Rudolf Steiner without having done the exercises and followed the necessary training path. Such presumption and such daubing.... It was Henni Geck, the painter, about whom I had already heard that she had worked together with Rudolf Steiner, that she knew and was capable of a great deal; also that she was difficult. – Exactly the reverse of *Frau* Boos-Hamburger, who, with Austrian charm, was always full of praise and approval and encouragement.

From that moment on Henni Geck interested me more than anyone else: she had other ideas and had high expectations in painting and art! – We got into conversation, and she invited me to the next exhibition of her pictures in the *Atelierhaus "Farbentor."*

Only after some weeks had gone by did I discover the announcement of an exhibition in the form of a handwritten poster in the *Speisehaus* ("Canteen") of the Goetheanum. Thus, apprehensively, I finally entered the reclusive-looking building at the time indicated. [See photo on p. 94]. In subdued light, was a high-ceilinged studio space painted a golden-ochre, with large pictures on easels and on the walls. Broad, untreated wooden frames enhanced the tone of these works. A cool stillness pervaded the room, which only gradually warmed up for the eye and the mind. Then only did the unexpected experience begin to emerge from the colors of these paintings: In rich shadings and differentiations, glowing depths disclosed themselves, drew the viewer's soul-eye into strange, unknown spaces that were not disconcerting, yet unusual, establishing new trust. It must have been a similar experience for the remaining visitors, as no one spoke very loudly. Reverential quiet and devotion. Henni

Geck came, like a visitor herself, checked the lighting in the room and quietly regulated the Venetian blinds of the large skylight window; the external light was not to disturb the inner luminosity of the colors.

After various conversations with Henni Geck, in which she pointed out the importance of a step-by-step approach to practicing the sketches of Rudolf Steiner, and stressed the significance of the motifs for painting of the future, we came to the mutual decision to embark on a course once more.[39] She made the effort to get the necessary papers from the local authorities in Dornach and wrote joyfully in a letter: "It has become a certainty for me that it has to happen, since it has come about..."

A new little beginners' painting course met, occasionally enlarged by means of "guest students" who had already practiced their "training path" for many years in the holidays or at conference times. The hand-written schedule regulated our period of study from the first day:

"Color-Portal Studio" Dornach
Painting School

mainly on the basis of the training course given in the form of
sketches by Rudolf Steiner for Henni Geck's painting classes

Three-Year Training Course
from June 1st 1950

Painting Classes:

Monday	9.30 – 11.30 and 2 – 4	
Tuesday	9.30 – 12.30	5 – 7 Reading of art lectures (14 days)
Wednesday	9.30 – 11.30 and 2 – 4	
Thursday	9.30 – 12.30	
Friday	9.30 – 11-30 and 2 – 4	
Saturday	9.30 – 12.30	

Short blocks in portrait painting, poster design,
"black and white" and free composition.
The students' work will be returned after completion of the
training. A graduation-diploma qualifies the individual to
work on the basis of the sketches as a freelance artist or to teach.
Annual fees: Fr. 700.-- (payable quarterly)
Register with the director: Henni Geck

---

[39] It would appear that there had been a pause in Henni Geck's teaching activity, presumably for lack of students in the difficult postwar period.

„Atelierhaus Farbentor" Dornach

Malschule

vorwiegend auf Grund vom Skizzen-Lehrgang
Rudolf Steiners für Henni Gecks Malunterricht

Dreijähriger Ausbildungskursus
ab 1. Juni 1950

Malstunden:

Montag	½10 – ½12	und 2 – 4	
Dienstag	½10 – ½1		5 – 7 Lesen von Kunstvorträgen (14tägig)
Mittwoch	½10 – ½12	und 2 – 4	
Donnerstag	½10 – ½1		
Freitag	½10 – ½12	und 2 – 4	
Samstag	½10 – ½1		

Kleine Epochen zum Studium von Porträt, Plakatentwürfen, „Schwarz-Weiss" und freien Kompositionen.

Die Schülerarbeiten werden nach Absolvierung der Ausbildung zurückgegeben. Ein Abschluss-Diplom berechtigt, auf Grund der Skizzen freischöpferisch oder lehrend zu arbeiten.

Jahrespreis: Fr. 700. (¼. jährlich zahlbar)

Anmeldung an die Leitung: Henni Geck

Henni Geck instructed us thoroughly in stretching the paper (which could not then be done as quickly and effortlessly with gummed tape as now). She obtained good marten-hair brushes from Basel, and in this way the first painting class was already carefully prepared on the previous day. The first exercises went extraordinarily slowly and demanded considerable effort. The "other" way of looking and discovering was an unknown one, a new activity that stirred us inwardly. Thus our beautiful white painting surfaces were already quite worn out in places from correcting and washing out. Only a few delicate colored shapes arose. The experience of painting is an inner process of creation. The continual alternation between looking within and without, experiencing and reflecting, changed us in the course of carrying out the exercises and led to new observations.

Henni Geck spoke little about details in the picture, attempting rather to assist us in finding the expression, the gesture within the surface. The colors had to be kept transparent and translucent. Her practiced eye saw not only shades of densification, but also unconsciousness and lack of expressiveness in the smallest passage.

The time for practicing began punctually with the striking of the Dornach clock-tower. During breaks we sat in the garden, while our pictures dried, and talked among ourselves, often with Henni Geck as well, for instance about the construction period of the first Goetheanum, about which she could tell stories in great detail.

No one other than Fritz Billing, who had lived with his wife for many years already in the *"Farbentor"*and was a life-long loyal student, assistant and companion of Henni Geck, saw and knew *how* Henni Geck herself painted. We only heard in the lower studio the regular pacing to and fro above us. Henni Geck painted for months on one picture. She followed a strict build-up in creating the motif and handled the veils of color very deliberately.

On special holidays and during conferences at the Goetheanum, the *Farbentor* was opened for visitors to the exhibition held there. Now supervision of the exhibition rooms and regulation of the light was transferred to us as well. When we removed the sand-colored curtains, which otherwise covered the pictures to protect them from the light, there arose for us again and again, new, deeply moving moments of concentration on this picture-world. It may be mentioned further, how strangely it moved us when we unpacked pictures from large cases made of beaten zinc plates. They dated from the time when war threatened and Henni Geck had evacuated a large number of her works to the Swiss interior. Among them were those paintings which Rudolf Steiner had seen, or which he had painted into. – How Henni Geck lived in the awareness of her great responsibility in regard to the task she had received!

At that time, with the restoration of the sketches by Julius Hebing, the pain and powerlessness regarding the task she had taken on, broke through yet again. In a letter, she characterized her purpose, her most important life-task, as being "to develop painting further on the basis of the twenty-three sketches, for the benefit of a wide circle of artistically striving people as well as the whole of humanity." This self-sacrificing work did not unfortunately lead to the intended writing down of her recollections of meeting Rudolf Steiner in the year 1906; also not to a detailed report concerning the indications given her regarding the sketches; nor the method of painting.

— *Walther Roggenkamp*

From a longer article on the life and work of Henni Geck entitled *"Henni Geck: Malerisches Gestalten aus Bildkeimen,"* in the periodical *Die Drei,* July/August 1989, published by Verlag Freies Geistesleben.

Thoughts on Method

(In the Sense of Henni Geck)

On the question as to why the painting student does not proceed from his own creative resources alone, but works from a given motif, I should like to single out a few aspects.

Everyone practicing anything at all knows how difficult it is to learn two things at once; the learning process requires a succession in time, even if the acquired capacities come into play simultaneously. The painting student stands initially before two tasks: the choice of content and the form it is to take. It would not be required of any student of music that he also compose the works which he practices in training his technique, hearing and musicality. If the "what" is first of all given, then the one who practices can concentrate fully on the "how."

At academies it is common even today to train perception, exactitude, technique and perseverance, and to get to know certain inherent laws, all on the basis of a particular object. The training sketches of Rudolf Steiner likewise aim to develop the required capacities. But since they present unfinished models, they demand of the painting student not only a correction by means of an exact comparison with them, but above all a testing of his own inner feeling for color and form that evolves at the same time. It is a matter therefore, not of copying, which can after all be achieved with a certain soulless facility, but rather of a way of working, the main effect of which is a capacity for extended seeing and creating. The finished picture is only an end-result of the actual process.

– Bettina Roder

From a longer article on the work with Rudolf Steiner's training sketches entitled *"Bildgestaltung – Selbsterkenntnis"* in the periodical *Die Drei,* July/August 1989, published by Verlag Freies Geistesleben.

Henni Geck's Quest

The sketches given by Rudolf Steiner to Henni Geck were intended in the first instance as material for instruction, and she had all her students paint them. However, she also saw them as a gift to those who were thus trained as painters, who would then, in recreating them, transmit them to humanity in general. Henni Geck painted all of the sketch motifs herself several times, corresponding to her own development, with ever increasing artistry, and never in terms of mere mechanical repetition. Her painter's eye came again and again on the track of new secrets, which she brought to light with her ingenious brush strokes. She created besides, pictures on the basis of self-chosen motifs, but the work with the sketches was a sacred bequest to her. In this way an extensive world of the most splendid work arose in luminous, pure colors, a life-work of rare beauty and significance.

When Rudolf Steiner made the first sketch, certainly neither the painting teacher nor her students could have foreseen that it was to become the starting point for works that stand alone and unrivaled.

To strive for personal renown was far from Henni Geck's nature. What gave meaning to her tireless efforts was a hope and an eager anticipation she cherished within her, and which others only suspected in confidential moments.

This hope found expression in words spoken on one occasion by Dr. Friedrich Rittelmeyer (1872–1938)[40] to one of her students. When Henni Geck heard of the conversation years later, a blissful joy shone from her eyes and showed on her earnest features. Dr. Rittelmeyer had said: "I visualize to myself how in the future, in the sacristies of the Christian Community, in the conference rooms of our schools, in the branches, in the clinics, these tremendously effective pictures will pour out their salutary blessing. Indeed, you (Henni Geck's student) will have to work toward this; it will be of the most far-reaching significance."

Year after year, since these words were spoken, Henni Geck's work has grown, becoming richer and nobler. She had to overcome many obstacles, taking heavy sacrifices upon herself with straight-forward matter-of-factness. Everything personal had to take second place to

---

[40] Dr. Friedrich Rittelmeyer was the co-founder of the movement for religious renewal known as the Christian Community.

the task, the impulse, she had been permitted to receive from Dr. Steiner, her revered teacher, in order to pass it on to present and future generations.

– I. St.-E.
(Ingrid Stinzing-Eriksson)

From *Blätter für Anthroposophie,* 1951, p. 37.

MARGARITA VOLOSCHIN

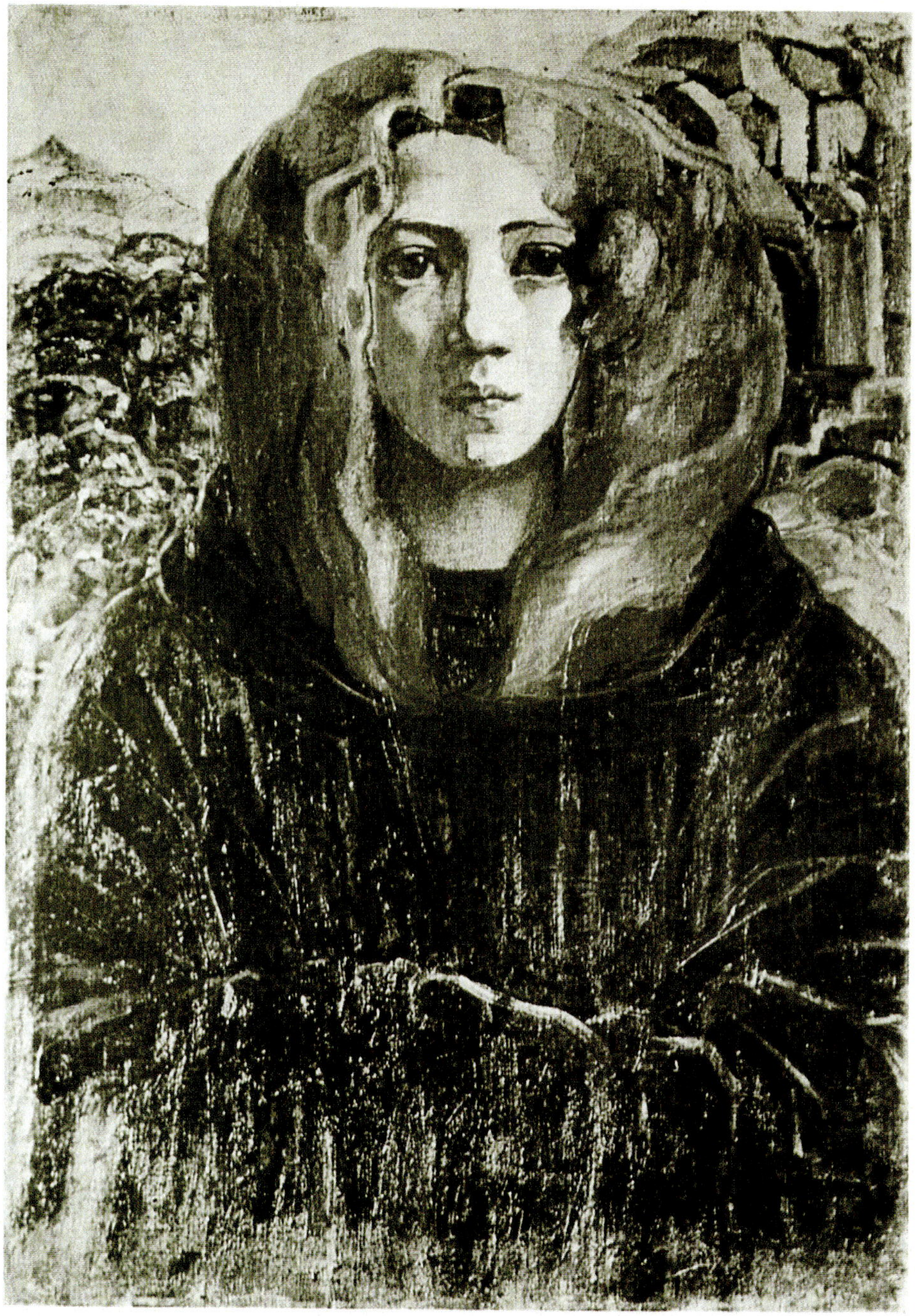

Margarita Voloschin
Self-Portrait
1905

Oil on canvas. Pensa State Gallery (Russia). Copyright: Rosemarie Wermbter (Stuttgart).

Self-Portrait

In Zurich, as I could find no model, I began to paint a self-portrait. My face was reflected in the second glass of a three-sided mirror so that, as a result of the double mirroring, the two sides should not be exchanged. I painted myself with flowing hair so that it formed a sculptural, rose-gold mass on both sides of the face. Each of these surfaces, composed mosaic-like in color and form, were reminiscent of a pearl oyster. The face I painted in bluish, cold-rose and warm-rose tones. Behind the head, the surfaces were set forth in the same manner, forming an architecture. With great intensity and as though gazing out from eternity itself, the eyes looked out. Later this picture was bought by the directors of a museum in Moscow; to which city it was finally sent, I could not find out in the chaos of the revolution. What amazes me today is the fact that the architecture in the background and the treatment of its surfaces reminds one, in every respect, of the sculptural forms of the Goetheanum that was built twenty years later.[41]

—*Margarita Voloschin*

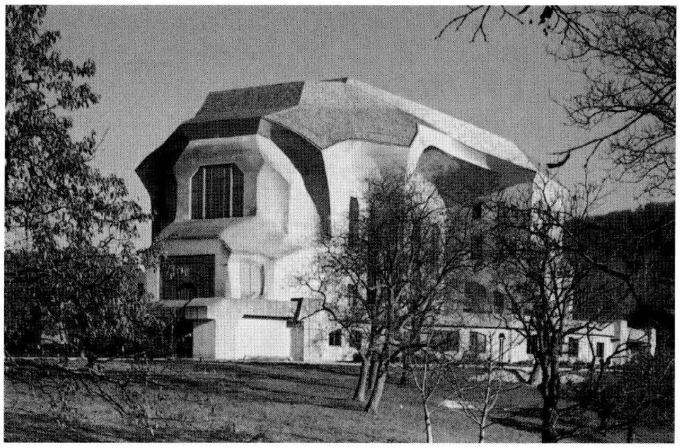

[41] I.e., the sculptural forms of the second Goetheanum, built between December 1924 and September 1928. The passage quoted is excerpted from Margarita Voloschin's autobiographical work *Die Grüne Schlange* (The Green Snake), published by Verlag Freies Geistesleben, Stuttgart 1997. Later in the same chapter, Margarita Voloschin describes her first meeting with Rudolf Steiner. But it is clear that the self-portrait painting arose before this meeting took place. Elsewhere she describes how the shapes of a double-domed building reminiscent of the first Goetheanum (built between September 1913 and October 1920) were originally to be seen on the left side of the picture, but were painted over.

MEMORY-PICTURES FROM A TIME OF INTENSIVE WORK

Margarita Voloschin

In April of the year 1914, I saw the Dornach *Bau*[42] for the first time, toward evening. The two cupolas had not yet been covered with slate, but only overlaid with fresh wood, and they radiated a golden light through the blossoming cherry trees. The day's work was over; the workmen from the *Bau* streamed toward me down the hill. At the gate of the grounds a group of young artists in light-colored work-shirts greeted me. The joyous light in their eyes attracted my attention.

I knew what was intended with the *Bau*. Like a sun-seed, it had been implanted in the earth-sphere "that the earth too might sometime become a Sun." – "Soon," I thought, "I shall see the forms that, in material substance, manifest the forces of the Word through which the world was created. But am I myself yet capable of inwardly experiencing these forms directly? – Do I still love too much the repose and perfection of the antique? – Will my soul be able to resonate with the new? – Such a thing cannot be forced."

My apprehensions vanished, however, when I caught sight of the *Bau* still full of scaffolding, when I beheld the mighty forms of the different architraves, capitals and bases. These sculptural forms in wood, which stood there like rocks in the entrance hall of the *Bau*, and in the neighboring sheds, were something quite new to me, and yet of kindred origin.

Crystalline surfaces fashioned organic forms. One form flowed out of another and led to the next. One form vouched for the other, completing and perfecting it. The tripartite windows formed a unity. The steps of the stairways, spreading out like watery circles, rose before one in an inviting manner. It was as though in manifold gestures a being were disclosing its love, which encompassed and pervaded everything in a living metamorphosis. Here the soul breathed freedom.

The next morning, even from a distance, I heard the tapping of hundreds of hammers and mallets. "It is coming into being," was the exhilarating feeling. And can there be a greater good fortune than to participate in the coming into existence of a God-willed work? Is not the experience of Paradise itself a participation in a God-willed creation, in which the cosmic body and the human body are still one? I believe that those who, in those months in Dornach, were able to participate in the work, will agree with me when I say that the

---

[42] The first Goetheanum building in Dornach, Switzerland.

sheer enthusiasm which filled us at that time was akin to that paradisaical experience. And if later the mood changed, it was because each of us brought with us, from the world, dead thoughts, illusory feelings and lack of courage. Besides this, out in the world itself, the destructive forces had unleashed the fury of the World War, and the work in Dornach had to be continued under this tragic sign.

When I came to the *Bau* that first morning, I was given, like all the other artists, a gouge and a mallet. I was assigned a capital and was shown how I was to carve.

Soon I heard the hammering around me gradually die away. Dr. Steiner came into the hall. He seemed to me younger and fresher than I had seen him previously in lectures and consultations. In Dornach, on account of the mud on the Goetheanum grounds, he wore high boots, which recalled the time of Goethe. I was told that on the previous day he had himself begun to carve. He climbed onto a crate in front of a capital and began to work. We stood behind him. I could see his profile and his hands. For a long time he carved in silence. His face was concentrated and jubilant as though inwardly he were listening in on something beautiful. It was like a dialogue with the wood. Cautiously and unfalteringly he took away the wood in layers, as though seeing exactly the limits of the form hidden within it, and as though only wanting to free it from the superfluous material.

Then he said something like the following: "In sculpture, one must feel the planes, one must be mindful of the planes in space, just as the plants in their growth follow the direction of the planes in space. In sculpture the edges must arise only as an outcome, as boundaries; they do not need to be pre-determined. One has to be curious about the edge; that helps one a great deal."

When I greeted Dr. Steiner soon after, he asked how these forms pleased me.

Each time Dr. Steiner greeted one, and one met his affirmative glance, it was as though this moment were anticipated out of the future. One had the feeling: the one whom Dr. Steiner is greeting there, who is permitted to greet him, is in fact not yet fully present. One answered with a solemn promise to be fully present someday. That glance, in which lived the highest victory, spoke at the same time of the whole gravity of a world tragedy, in fact a world catastrophe. It was as though, through this countenance, as if woven of light, the black of the cross shimmered through. One knew that this prodigious life had gone through death. The love which one met in this glance was akin to death. Each time one was torn out of time – for this reason one had to be strong and matter-of-fact, in order to be able to answer objectively – and on this occasion I could not do so. My reply was inept, too reserved, so that he could not possibly infer from it how much I loved these forms already. Thus he said:

"You will take to them. I would like you to learn to understand this building with its single axis of symmetry. Here for the first time a building with a single axis of symmetry has been attempted."

The next time Dr. Steiner made a correction on one of the architraves, he said the form being worked on was too bombastic, it had too much of a pot belly. The forms in the building, he asserted, are not taken from nature, although some people will seek in them for a similarity to natural forms. True art, however, has nothing to do with imitating nature. From nature the artist can learn the laws according to which she creates her forms, however, the artist must not remain at the stage of an apprentice, but must create from the sources out of which nature herself creates. "Naturalism is inartistic," he said, and suddenly turning to me, he asked, "Do you not believe that?"

"Oh yes I do," I replied, asking myself afterwards if, as a matter of fact, I was as finished with naturalism as I thought I was. Naturalism certainly did not satisfy me, still less the theosophical-symbolic pictures, head-oriented or visionary creations. Cubism, which treated what is living like something dead, seemed to me demonic, futurism arbitrary. I loved the ancient art of mosaics and the Russian icons, but did not know what language the spirit active in the present required.

Thus I had come to Dornach full of anticipation.

In the small wax model, on the large cupola, Dr. Steiner had applied the color curves. Some painters had already received their sketches for the large cupola from him and were working in studio-like rooms in the *Bau*. I was to paint in the small cupola, as I found out.

"You must be patient," Dr. Steiner told me several times, "and carve a while longer. I also must wait until it comes to me."

In our unspiritual age everyone thinks that cleverness and talent alone suffice for being able to produce a work of art at any time. But anyone who has to place something actually effective into the world reckons with the laws of the spiritual world. And just as fruit needs a definite time in which to ripen, so the soul that has put its question to the spiritual world needs time in order to receive the answer. To ask questions of the spiritual world and wait reverently for the answer, as though waiting for grace, does not mean being passive. In Dornach, we could daily observe with what energy and perseverance Dr. Steiner sought for various new technical procedures, trying things out again and again, overcoming the greatest obstacles.

Once, in these early days, I visited the studio of a painter who was working on his studies for the painting in the large cupola. Dr. Steiner came to him and they spoke about various things in connection with the plant colors, with which the painting was to be carried out, and which were produced according to his instructions. These colors have a quite different effect from the mineral colors; they are luminous and create an etheric space. As far as I now remember, the ground and the painting medium were spoken of: wax, cellulose, various resins were to protect the fine plant pigment and keep it vivid, as in the plant blossoms. I stood to one side and, without taking part in the conversation, I thought of the historical moment we were experiencing, when an initiate was fructifying with his knowledge the various realms of life, even into the technical details. "Why are you standing apart so devoutly, saying nothing?" Dr. Steiner asked me jestingly. "I understand too little of organic chemistry," I replied in embarrassment. If I had at that time only understood the hint: take an interest, set to work, study, seek. With an attitude of passive piety and *ignorabimus,* he could certainly have started none of his cultural work.

With the outbreak of the war, that painter [Hermann Linde] had to go to Germany, and I received the assignment of working out a sketch given to him. (Later on, however, he was able to take over the work again himself). It was the motif of the blue eye and the red ear. (See page 143.)

From this picture, one can learn how the law of inversion,[43] which Dr. Steiner again and again pointed out to us, was also carried out by him in terms of color. We see on the one side a blue as the center [the large eye], which, through chromatic tones [ochre], becomes red on the periphery; on the other side a red as the center [the large ear], which leads via transitions [dull ivy-green], to a blue circumference. The strength of the composition rests on the contrasts, on the struggle, between cool and warm. At that time I remained unaware of this painting language. I asked about the representational content; what kind of beings were depicted here, what Hierarchies?

"Those are the thoughts of the Second Hierarchy," was the answer. I asked whether one might increase the number of these forms, seven on each side, through shadow repetitions, so that they unite with the background.

"You can do that very well," replied Dr. Steiner, "because the etheric world is like a mirror-image; there one being can appear as a multiplicity."

I asked how I should paint. "I would like you to remain quite free," he replied. – Of a small study, Dr. Steiner said he would like it carried out like that in the cupola, because here the space and the form had been rendered purely by means of the color. "It is living, not

---

[43] (The German word *Umstülpung* used here implies a reversal of inside and outside).

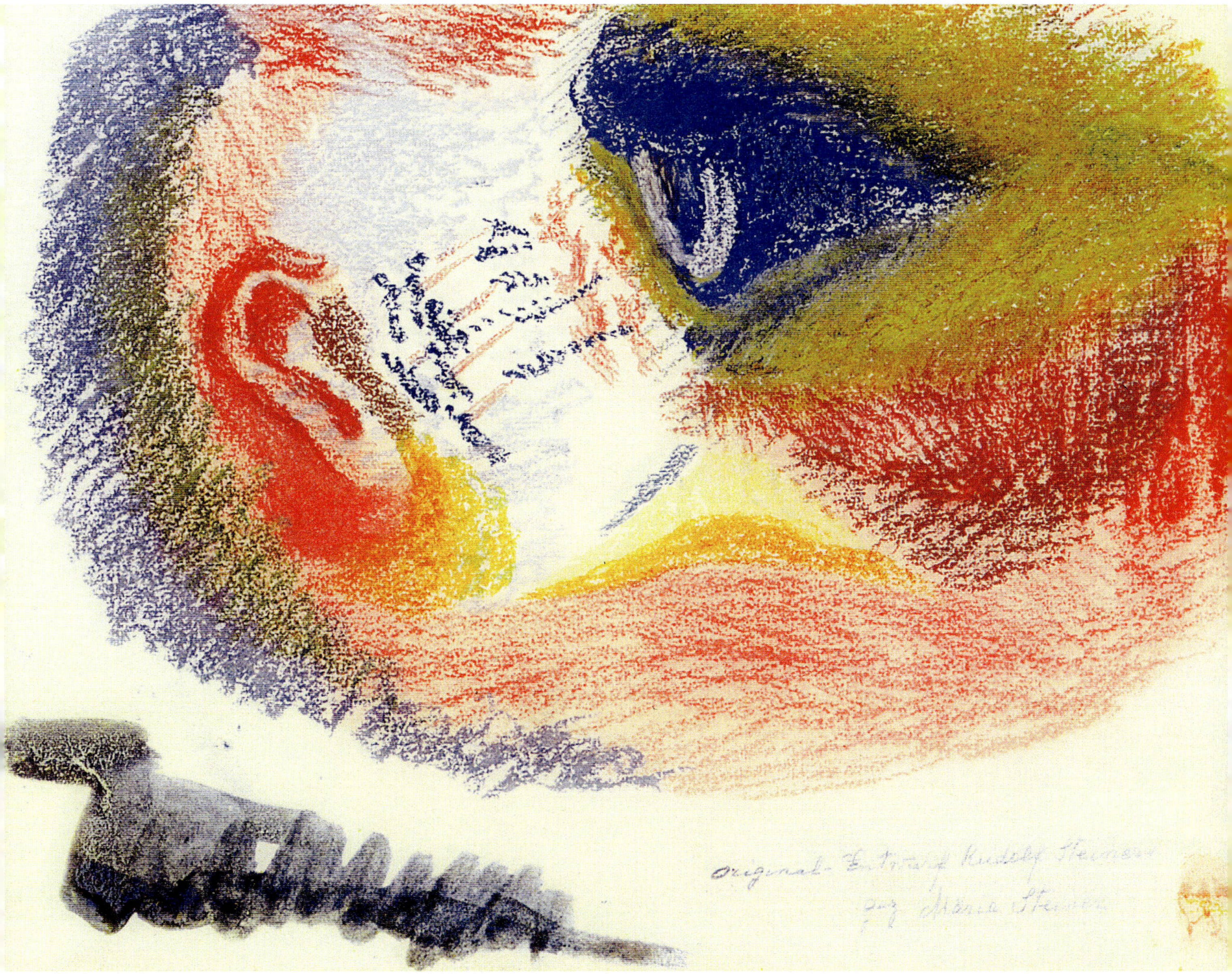

The Senses Arise, Eye and Ear Come into Being.
Oil crayon sketch by Rudolf Steiner for the large cupola of the first Goetheanum. 26 x 35 cm.
Rudolf Steiner Archive (Dornach).

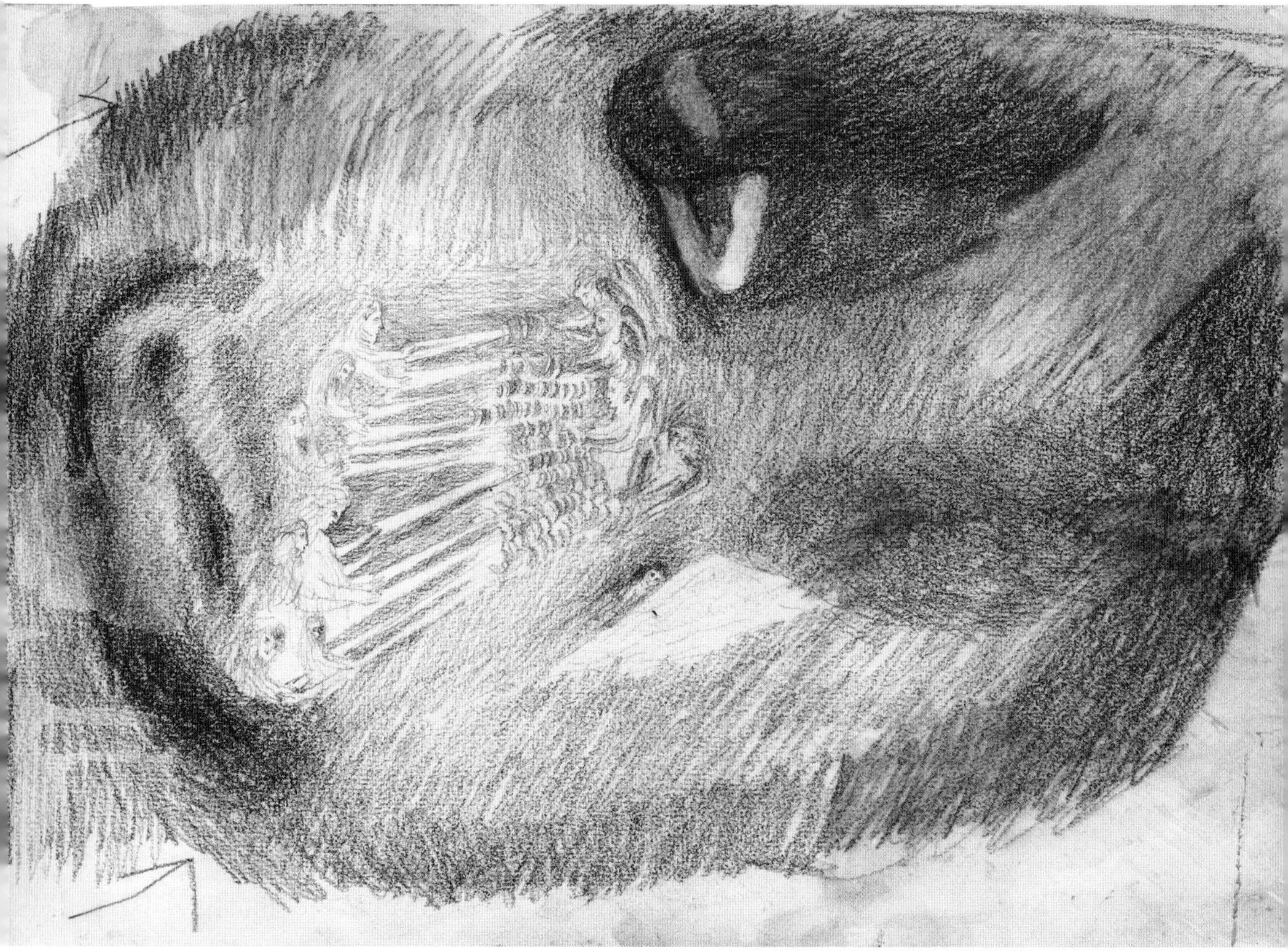

The Senses Arise, Eye and Ear Come into Being.
Pencil drawing by Rudolf Steiner.
Rudolf Steiner Archive (Dornach).

rigid." It interested me, what place chiaroscuro, shadows, would have in the painting we were striving for. He said, "Darkness, should not be employed as shadow, in order to reproduce sculptural form, but only to mediate a soul-impression; for example, of something like a spring, something that distinguishes itself for the feelings as being deep."

"How is it in this respect with portraiture?" I asked, "since portraiture so much depends on form?" "Portraiture," he replied, "stands quite on the borderland of painting – it is an ahrimanic art."

In the autumn, the artists received their sketches for the small cupola.

Dr. Steiner brought me a little sheet of paper. An Egyptian priest sat upon a blue crystalline seat within a formation that consisted of two transparent, intersecting triangles, one rose-violet, the other blue-violet. Above him was a rose-colored angel, overshadowed by a fiery archangel. Aside from a small black-and-white drawing, the same motif was indicated in colored crayon. (See page 146.)

When I measured the size of the figures as they were to be painted in the cupola, I found that the wings of my angel and the outspread arms of my archangel extended far into my neighbor's territory. I communicated my predicament to Dr. Steiner. "That does not matter," he said. "In the spiritual world things do not stand side by side, they interpenetrate. In painting, too, the forms can interweave; the colors should be transparent, should have depth."

Five, then six of us composed our individual sketches into a whole, in a small model of the cupola. Aside from this, we each worked in our own studio on the forms of our compositions in their anticipated size. We painted in plant colors on wood panels, which were duly primed. Dr. Steiner attached great importance to a white luminous ground, which was to act as a source of light, and to a transparent painting medium. The colors were not to be applied thickly at one time. They had to acquire their strength through many superimposed veils, one upon the other, which gave them depth and luminosity. For one who had previously painted only in oil with opaque colors, this technique meant a considerable adjustment.

"Painting must not have the effect of being a surface only, it must create a space, so that the walls are annulled," Dr. Steiner said.

On one occasion, probably to encourage me, Dr. Steiner praised my Egyptian who, over life-size, sat upon his throne. I then asked him what he found good about it. He showed me a place around the mouth that was painted, mosaic-like, in definite, transparent surfaces. From colored surfaces placed side by side and superimposed one upon the other, the form was to result; it should come into being out of the inner gesture of the color.

"Line in painting is a lie," said Dr. Steiner.

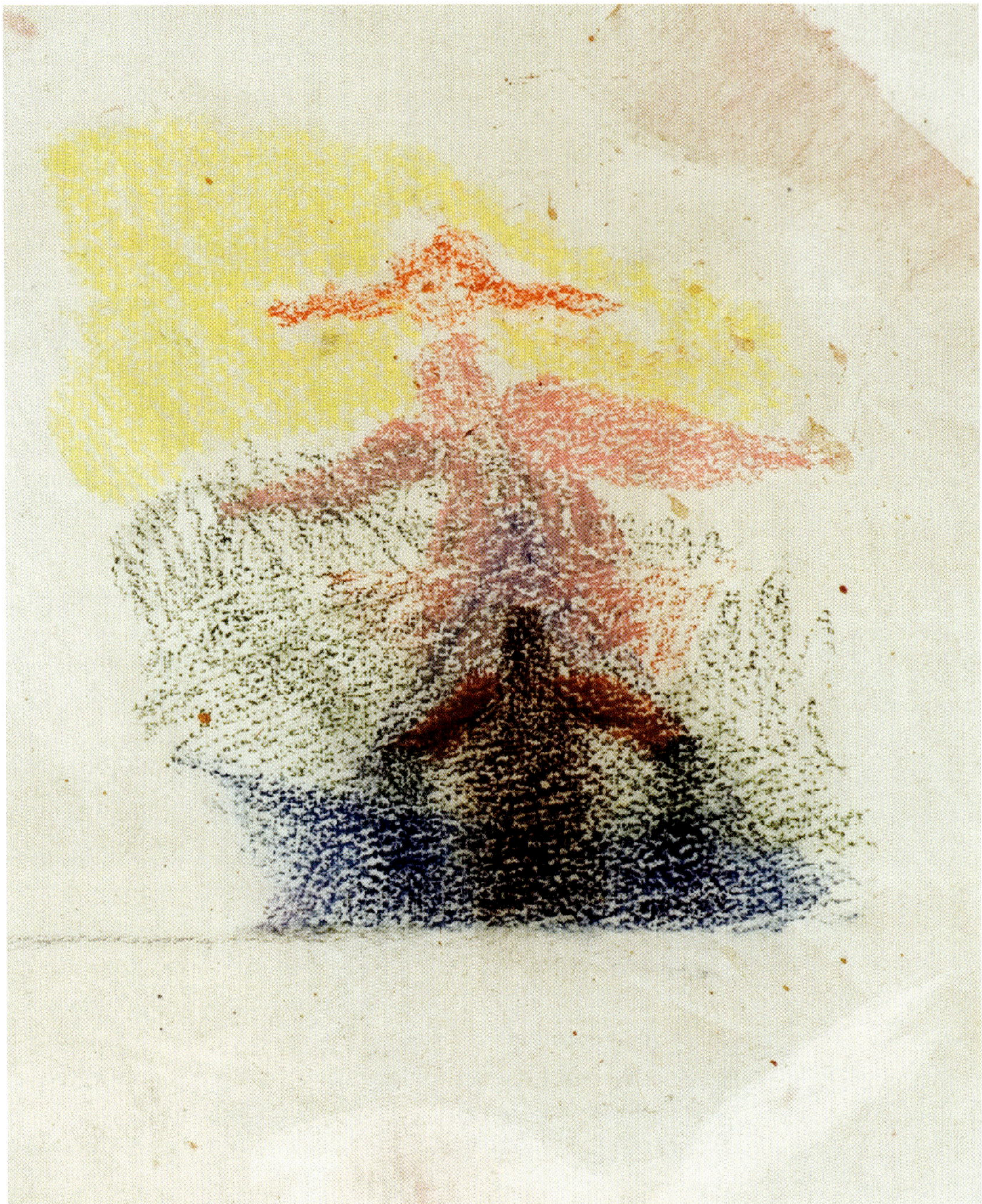

The Egyptian Initiate.
Oil crayon sketch by Rudolf Steiner for the small cupola of the first Goetheanum.
Rudolf Steiner Archive (Dornach).

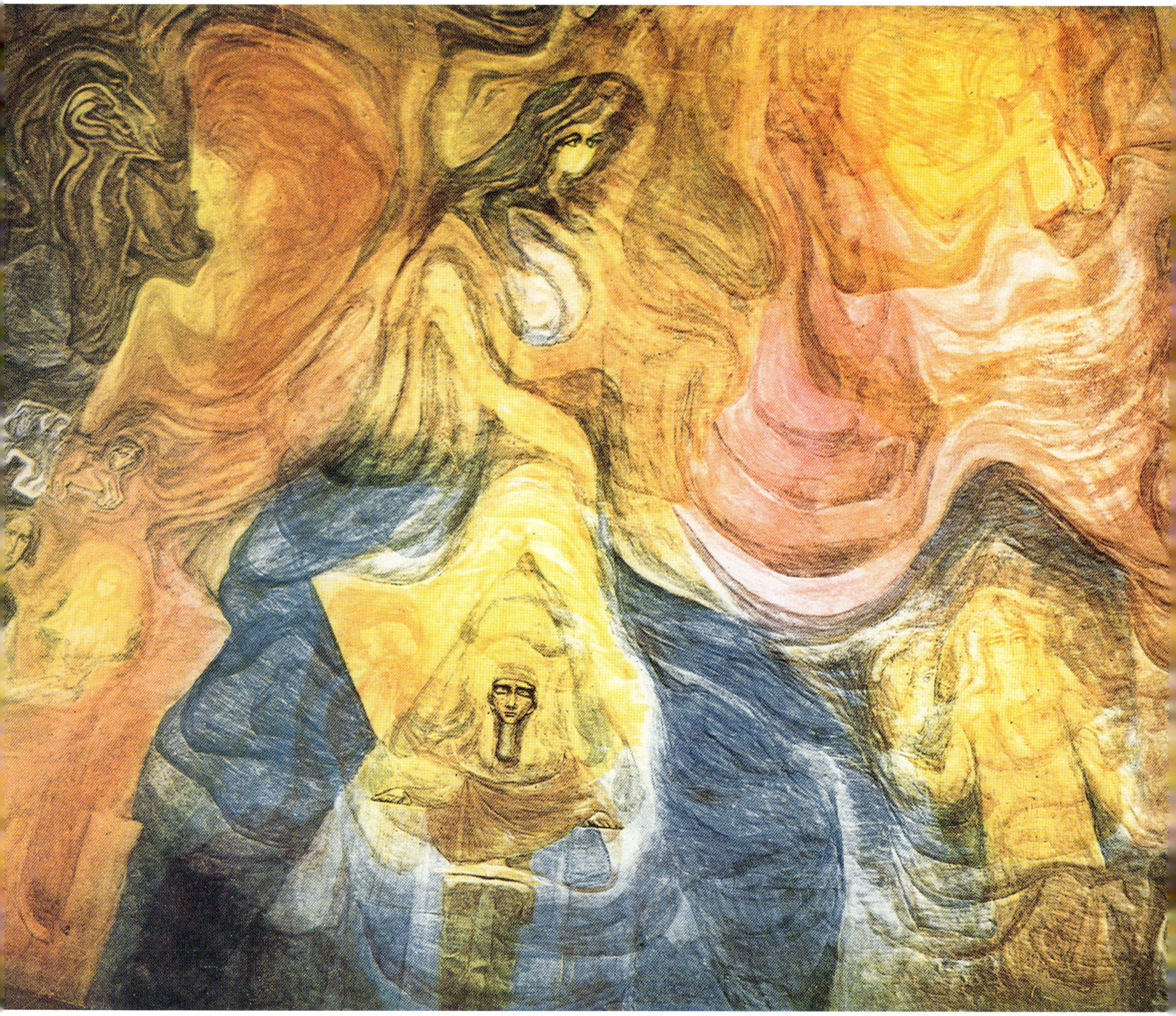

The Egyptian Initiate by Margarita Voloschin. Plant colors. 1917. Over life-size, this motif formed part of the painting on the south side of the small cupola of the first Goetheanum, painted by Rudolf Steiner. (This early color photograph gives at best an approximation of the colors of the original.) Rudolf Steiner Archive (Dornach).

He spoke of line as of an abstraction, as of something that kills. I believe I heard him say, although I cannot now repeat it exactly, that for the dead, who perceive painting, line acts as a hindrance.

The small cupola rested upon twelve columns. Before each column stood a great seat or throne. On each side of the stage area there were six different thrones, carved out of wood in geometrical forms. Above in the cupola, over each column, within a form resembling the thrones, a figure was to be painted, overshadowed by geniuses.

Next to the Egyptian composition, which corresponded to the fourth column, toward the west, a yellow Athene tamed a serpent. Above her was Apollo with the lyre, hovered over by a genius, while further toward the west on a red ground, was the figure of Death and above him a blue Faust. He held a book in which the small word "ICH" ("I") had a peculiar effect in being the only lettering in either cupola. An angel led a child toward Faust, who reached toward him from the corner where the small cupola of the stage area and the large cupola of the auditorium bordered on each other. To the east of the Egyptian, two giant winged figures were to be seen turned toward each other, the red Lucifer and the dark Ahriman (whose color should have the effect of horn, as Dr. Steiner said). Between and beneath them an initiate was holding up a luminous child in one hand. Still further to the east stood the Slavic human being, he himself a pale rose, with a dark doppelgänger who split off from him like a shadow. The Slav gazed upward toward a manifestation of the Rose Cross. (Since I was to paint the Slav, Dr. Steiner said to me: "You should not represent him as anguished and sentimental, but joyful over the future and strong.") In the open space between Ahriman and a blue genius, above the Slav, one saw a strange red winged-horse with multiple legs and a human face. As the culminating central motif in the east, the great, light-filled figure of Christ was represented. With the left hand he pointed upward, and out of his heart, like a red flame, the redeemed Lucifer rose aloft into the green easterly heaven. The right hand, pointing downward, rayed out a force which fettered Ahriman to the earth as though with chains. In the background were to be seen the three crosses.

That was the task we were faced with. At long last, after months of work in the model cupola, when our figures stood peacefully side by side in "beautiful harmony," without fighting each other (yet without furthering each other), Dr. Steiner painted in this model cupola the great colored curves. Out of a narrow violet wave from the west came a glowing red one, out of it an orange dividing itself and a yellow wave, which, in the east passed over into the green of the eastern heaven of the central composition. (See schematic illustration on p. 149).

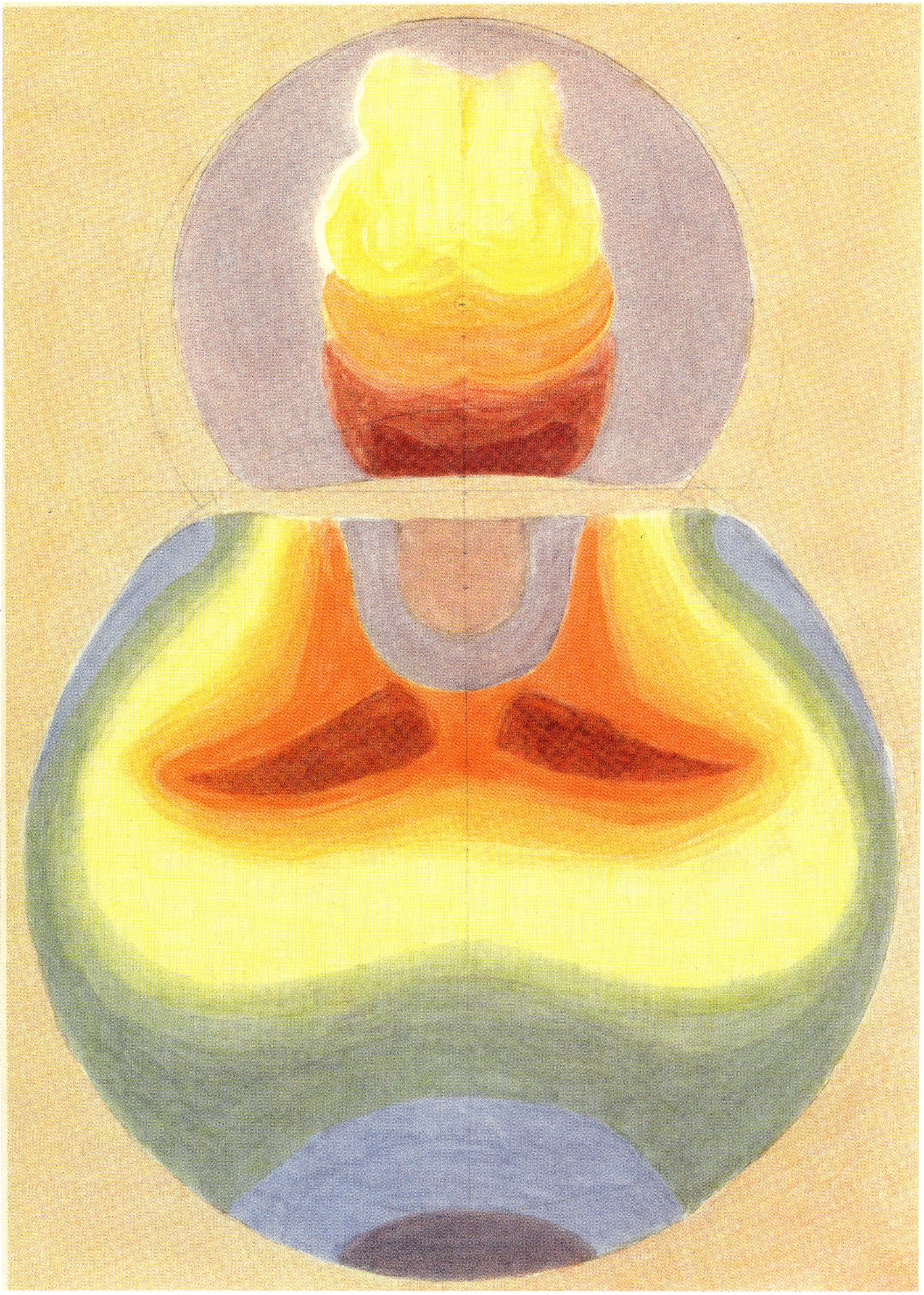

An illustration of the colored backgrounds of the two cupolas of the first Goetheanum, carried out in watercolor according to indications of Rudolf Steiner by Hilde Boos-Hamburger.

The effect of these colors was warm and dignified, as dignified as the entire wooden sculpture of the small cupola itself. These colors demanded that our paintings also be imbued with glowing life, weaving activity and movement.

But still more than our helplessness in painting, the rigidity of our thoughts impeded us, the past attaching to us, the incapacity to create out of the living spiritual stream. The eurythmy in which we were able to participate, the dynamic forms of the building which surrounded us, the lectures of Dr. Steiner which also dealt with painting and the world of creative color, these could only come alive in us in the course of time. At that time, we still had no proper basis for asking Dr. Steiner about painting problems. And to clothe in concepts what should work through the color contradicted his artistic ethos; therefore he said little to us about our work in personal conversations.

I despaired of our accomplishments. "The work comes with the work," he said consolingly. He asked one of us, whether we were also really inwardly occupied with our painting, whether we thought a great deal about it?

Certainly I thought a great deal about it, but in the wrong way. "How can I paint an angel or an archangel having never seen one?" I thought. "I don't know what they look like." I wanted to have a clear vision in front of me, which I could then paint. It was a case of transferring naturalism to another realm. I wanted to stand before the spiritual world with the passive attitude of a naturalistic painter. I was not aware of the fact that the heirarchical beings, who are active within and around us, are able to reveal themselves precisely by means of the intuitive activity of painting.

To work out of a dreamlike, visionary state of subdued consciousness is not the way to the new painting, but rather an awakening in feeling and willing. "If you were able to bring your heart to rest, then you would see what is in you," Dr. Steiner said to a painter. The heart of human beings who no longer feel pain and happiness on their own account, but for whom feelings are harbingers of spiritual facts, becomes an organ for the new art of painting. When the light of day-consciousness penetrates the darkness of the world of will, human beings experience by means of color, now imbued with being in their own soul, the color in nature as imbued with being as well. Darkness lightened to blue, light dimmed to red, proclaims to them in the kingdoms of nature the "becoming of things, the deeds of the gods." "Art is related to death," Dr. Steiner once told us, "like death it takes away maya and reveals true 'being'." Released from the weight of matter, from what has become, into the realm of the living-becoming, color works to redeem the dead world through the art of painting. In transferring things from their existence in three-dimensional space onto the surface, it grants them a new existence in a new space. In this space the "inner" of the human being manifests as the "outer." The external world, however, becomes ensouled, becomes inner experience. Time becomes space. The spiritual light of Lucifer and the heavy darkness of Ahriman become color in Christ.

"Color is the revenge of the gods against Lucifer," Dr. Steiner said to me on one occasion, during a conversation about my work with regard to the healing power of painting. It was only later that the meaning of these words became comprehensible to me. The Lightbearer, who locks up his light in the glow of passion, in a wealth of shades of feeling within the isolated experiences of the human heart, is purged by means of the objective experience of color and offered up to the world. Thus when, out of the cosmic circumference, the Christ-Spirit enters into the heart which has been brought to rest, the Spirit of Separateness (Lucifer) is freed from his imprisonment in the world and becomes pure Holy Spirit. For this reason color can have a healing and redeeming effect. (This is why sentimental, luciferic people often have an antipathy to strong colors.)

Once someone told Dr. Steiner about a conversation I had had with a Russian shepherd. When this shepherd heard that I painted, he said:

"I understand little, and can find few words, but the words that come to me I will say: Christ wishes to give His Image. He came in order to give His Image, not to take. Only for the Turks and Tartars is it forgivable not to know this. But we Christians must know that since He lived on the earth, *everything* – a stone, a cloud, a flower is His Image. And when Luke the Evangelist painted the Child with the Mother, the Child wanted it done. And the woman after all only held out a handkerchief, a simple piece of canvas, but He gave His Image. So must you offer your soul and pray that God may recognize His Image in your picture, that your work may be counted among His works."

When I was able to speak with Dr. Steiner several weeks later, he said to me: "When the man spoke to you about Veronica, he answered you from the heart." (Dr. Steiner drew an arrow that started from a point.) "I, however, answered you out of the cosmos." (He drew arrows directed from the periphery to the point.) "And you stand in the middle and cannot yet unite the two answers." Whereupon he instructed me to be more active in my own work.

"If the real experience of color is not cultivated in our age, and the mechanistic theories concerning the nature of color continue to live in humankind, children will come into the world who no longer possess an organ for perceiving color. Life reveals itself through color. But humanity will no longer be capable of seeing color, just as it is no longer capable of seeing the elemental spirits weaving in nature. The world will be gray," Dr. Steiner said.

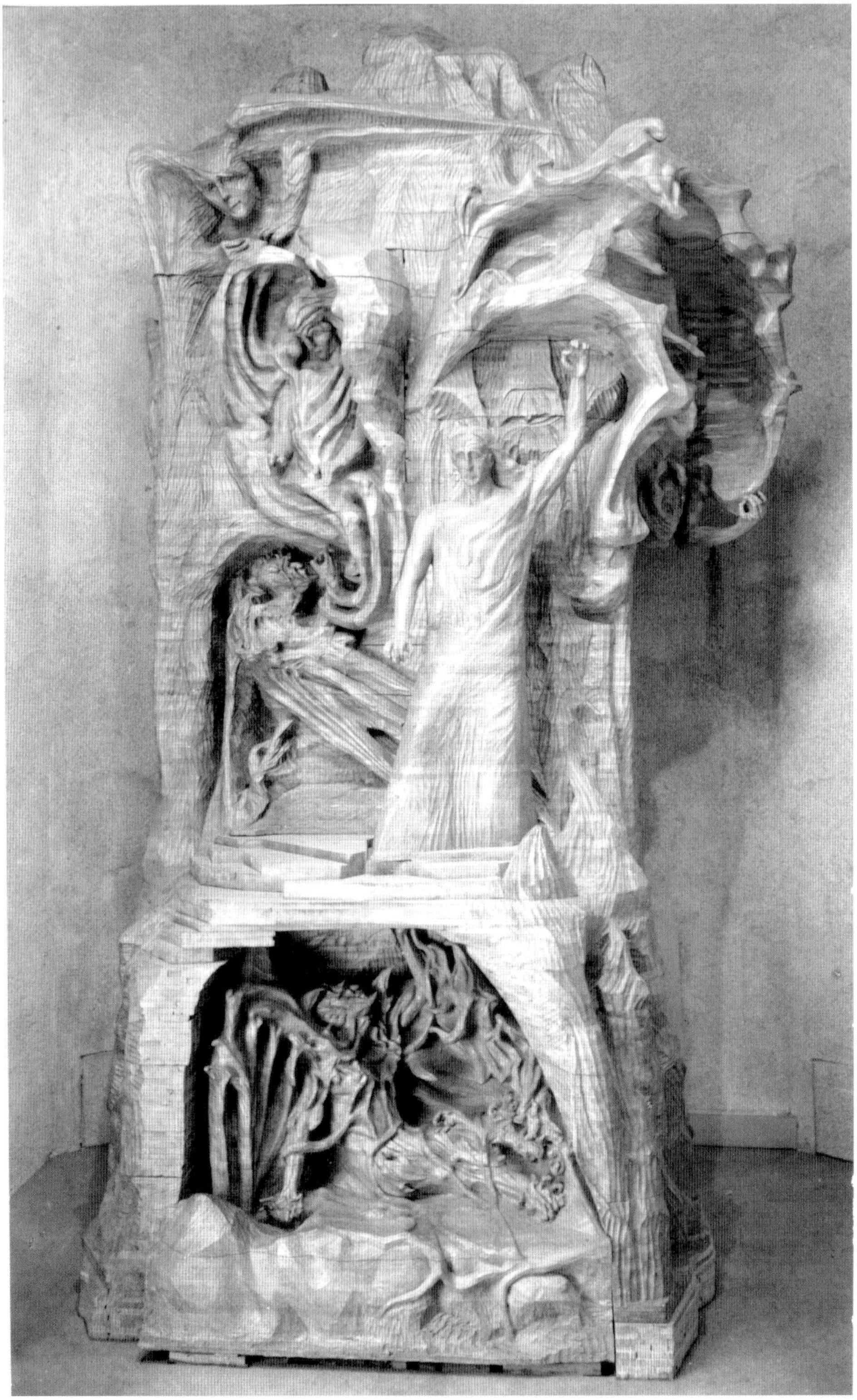

Rudolf Steiner's "Group Statue" of *The Representative of Humanity* with Lucifer and Ahriman, carved of laminated elm-wood. (Now to be seen in a special room in the second Goetheanum.)

Once I complained to him that my intellect was disturbing me in painting. "Intellect," he said, "has nothing to do with painting. If I have a lecture to give, I also do not know beforehand what I shall say. I only hold fast the mood out of which I am to speak." Another time he said, "In the eye the power of cosmic thinking lives, which is not impaired by human thinking. Painting should make this cosmic thinking manifest."

Once, after visiting an exhibition of modern art, Dr. Steiner said, "Non-representational painting is a protest against naturalism, but strictly speaking it is absurd. If one truly penetrates into the world of color, one comes to beings. We do not need to look for the lion first in the physical world; we find his archetype in the realm where colors exert their influence."

How different is what Dr. Steiner meant with the words "painting out of the color" from what many have made of it in playing around with the color and producing accidental figures – as with telling fortunes from coffee grounds, – these pictures, often mediumistic, often deriving from the physiological experience of their own bodies are designated as "painting out of the color." The greatest alertness, the greatest energetic determination and concentration are demanded by painting out of the color, of which Dr. Steiner says: "It demands of us another state of consciousness, another ego force, than that which we possess today. And above all, also great technical ability." When Rudolf Steiner himself painted in the small cupola, he is said to have remarked that he would have needed to work for thirty years in painting in order really to paint as he wanted.

I myself did not see these paintings. In the year 1917 I returned to Russia with the intention of coming back after a few months, when the others had finished with their work, and together with them harmoniously coordinating the whole. A year before my departure, when one of our Russian friends went to Russia, Dr. Steiner said to me: "In Russia one will not be able to work. In Russia one will only be able to experience chaos and Kamaloka." I forgot these words and remembered them only later, when I actually experienced that chaos, that hell and that impossibility to work. There, for six years I was able to study the demonic cubism, which treated the living like the dead, not only on canvas but in life itself. There, one could see where the materialistic worldview uncompromisingly leads. There, one could not look for support anymore in the spirituality of the old culture – one could only look up spiritually to that building worthy of the human being in Dornach, in the organic forms of which the human social ideal was expressed.

When I was at last let out after six years, on the day I received a visa for entering Switzerland, the Goetheanum burned down.

So I never saw the first *Bau* completed.

The reproductions that have been made of the paintings of the small cupola give an idea of the life, of the strong movement that held sway in them, of the tremendous distances and spaces that were opened up through the colors; of the chaos, in the beautiful Greek sense of the word, of growing and coming into being. These figures are not beautiful by virtue of a flattering luciferic beauty, but through an earnest truth, through the living gesture of the spirit, through a strong, free characterization.

When I saw in the Carpentry Building the posters for eurythmy performances painted by Dr. Steiner, or carried out from his sketches by *Frl.* Geck, I could only take note for the moment, that here it is a matter of an entirely different kind of painting from any that had ever existed in human civilization up till now. Everything having to do with what is earthly and three-dimensional, with perspective, with the sculptural element in Western art, but also everything having to do with the flat surfaces and linear qualities of the East, was here annulled. The glow of color creates a new space. One breathes a lighter air in looking at these pictures, which have nothing to do with memory-pictures, with what has already come into existence, and which yet remain completely true to the earth in its essential being.

When in the year 1923, after a long time, I was able to see the Christ statue again in Dr. Steiner's studio, I felt, "It is eternity itself which strides through time – it is that Being which takes everything upon Itself." Not only earnestness and strength, but sorrow also I saw in this countenance. I asked Dr. Steiner whether the lines of pain were expressed in the central figure of the painting of the small cupola as well. "Pain? I only wished to portray love," he answered. "This figure need not be taken as dogma. That is how I see Him."

The last words I heard from Dr. Steiner were:

> "Christ must be sought in our age in all realms, even in painting."

Rudolf Steiner has given us the path to a new Christian painting. Like the doctors, the teachers, the actors and other workers in various fields of art and science, painters have also received from him a legacy, a task. Not only through the comprehensive worldview of anthroposophy is art stimulated, but also through specific indications for the painter. Already by means of the technique of color-veiling, the painter holds the balance between the dark, heavy Ahriman and the volatile Lucifer, and creates through the power of color a definite and yet not rigid form. Thus handicraft itself again becomes hallowed.

One who, through a long period of soul-culture, no longer considers as dogma but as experience what Dr. Steiner has said in his color lectures about "lustre" and "image" colors, will see in this turning of lustre into image and of image into lustre, a priestly, redeeming act for the earth – a transformation...

A translation of *Erinnerungsbilder aus arbeitsreicher Zeit* by Margarita Voloschin, in *Rudolf Steiner: Zwölf Entwürfe für die Malerei der grossen Kuppel des ersten Goetheanum.* Philosophisch-anthroposophischer Verlag 1930.

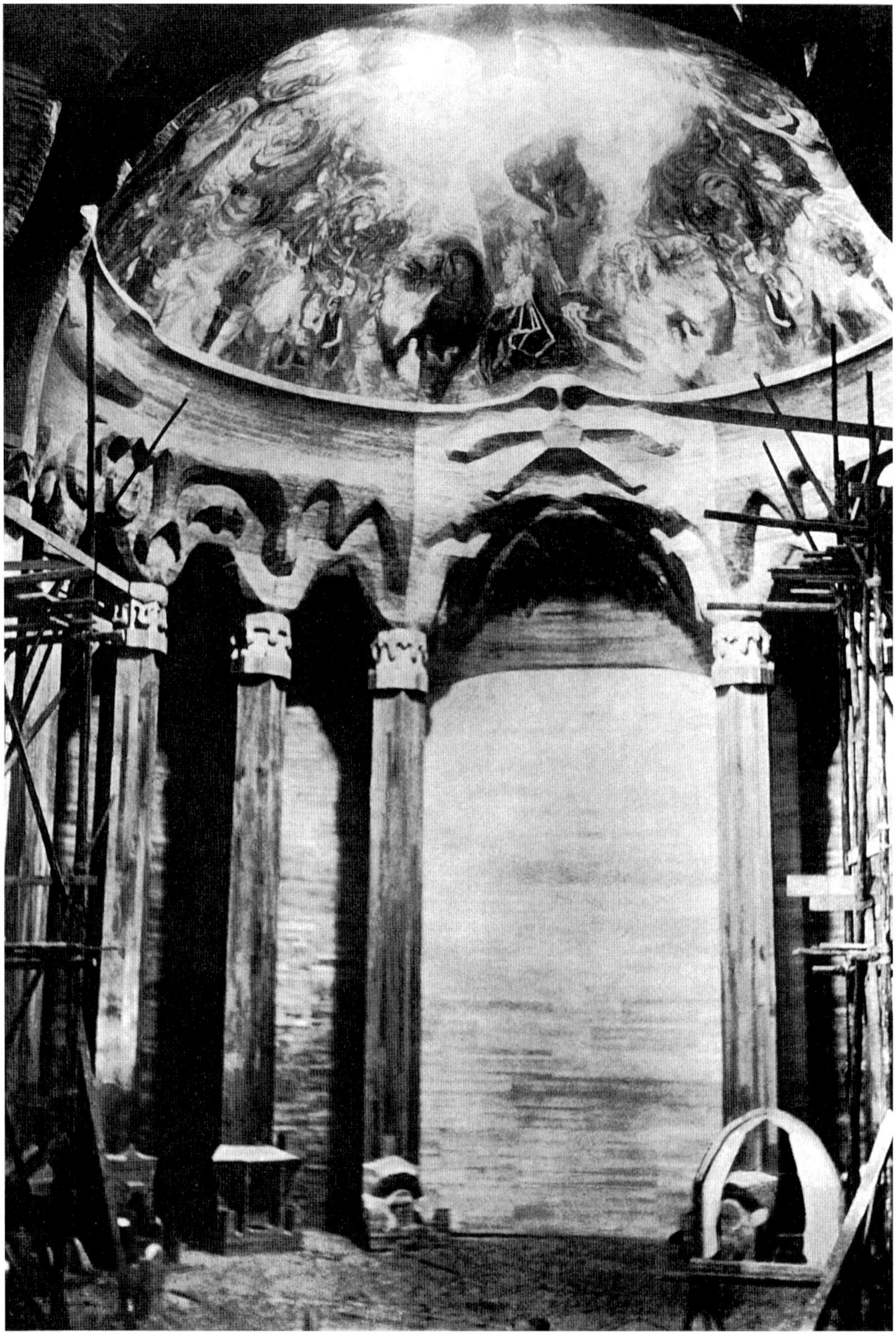

The small cupola of the first Goetheanum. (The "Group Statue" was to have stood in the central niche at the back of the stage.) Dokumentation am Goetheanum-Bildarchiv.

HOW RUDOLF STEINER HIMSELF PAINTED IN THE SMALL CUPOLA

Luise Clason

An eye-witness account of how Rudolf Steiner painted on more than half of the small cupola of the first Goetheanum by one of the six artists entrusted with the motifs for the cupola above the stage. These were: Margarita Voloschin, Luise Clason, Arild Rosenkrantz, Jeanne-Marie Bruinier, Ella Dyubanjuk, and Mieta Waller.

> *It was always a great event to watch Dr. Steiner paint, it was so different to what one was used to with other painters. Sometimes he came up only for a quarter or half hour, going straight to the surface he had painted the day before. He would dip the brush in the color and make a huge color curve over the entire painted surface. On the following days he would return ever again and set yet new layers of color in curves across each other. Surface by surface the whole sea of color was brought into movement. The picture surface receded and a three-dimensional space arose, filled with majestic flowing color which surged and ebbed, disappearing only to re-emerge elsewhere. Within this color flow hovered beings never before seen with the physical eye. Their eyes looked at us, speaking of mysteries which waited to be revealed to understanding human beings.... When we once again came into daylight after our work on the cupola we had to rub our eyes. Such a different world received us. We loved the world up there and could only be removed by force when the scaffolding was to be dismantled and the boards taken from beneath our feet. A lost paradise ... even Dr. Steiner sensed our mood; at the first meeting below he said emphatically, "Yes, it has now passed! One part of the work – indeed, a major part itself!" Today, the only thing that remains of this world is a memory.*[44]

[44] The first Goetheanum building in Dornach, Switzerland, was destroyed by fire on the night of December 31, 1922/January 1, 1923.

Translated by Christl Hoffmann from "Some Recollections of the Years of the Painting in the Small Cupola of the First Goetheanum Building" in *Mitteilungen der Allgemeinen Anthroposophischen Gesellschaft,* June 1950. Published in *The Language of Color in the First Goetheanum,* Walter Keller Verlag, Dornach, Switzerland 1987 (p. 134–135).

About Margarita Voloschin
1882–1973

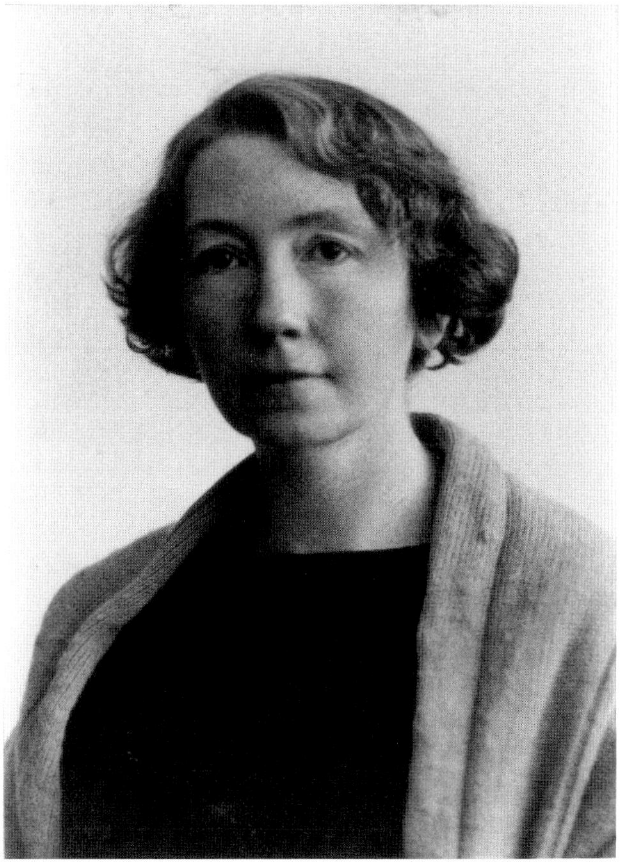

Dokumentation am Goetheanum-Bildarchiv.

Margarita Voloschin's reputation as a painter extended far beyond anthroposophical circles. She was also active as a writer. Born in Moscow on January 31, 1882, she was the first child of Wassily Michailovitch Sabaschnikov, a businessman, and his wife Margarita Alexievna Andreyeva. Her father was from Siberia, while her mother came from a distinguished Moscow family. As a child she grew up in a very well-to-do family of diverse cultural interests. Two of her father's brothers founded an internationally known publishing house. From her childhood on, it counted as a certainty that she would become a painter. She began painting lessons before passing her school-leaving examinations, studying later with such well-known Russian Impressionist painters as *Ilya Repin* (1844–1930), *Abram Archipov* (1862–1930) and *Konstantin Korovin* (1861–1939), among others.

However, Margarita Sabaschnikova did not want only to be instructed in painting. She wanted to know what mission painting and art in general has in the social life of human beings. This question did not let go of her and preoccupied her so much that she sought an answer from the revered Leo Tolstoy. He advised her to become a farmer's wife, since if she only painted, it would be "as though she were to sit in a high tower and let things down with a cord, which were not needed down below at all." In spite of this devastating remark, she continued to paint and made considerable progress. When, as a twenty-one-year-old, she showed pictures for the first time in an exhibition, she became famous overnight, received commissions, and museums bought her paintings. (Some can still be seen today in Moscow, Astrachan, Pensa, Koktebel and other places).

The question concerning painting had by now widened to the more troubling one as to the meaning of life. A first decisive answer came after hearing a lecture by Rudolf Steiner in Zurich in 1905. Her question to Rudolf Steiner was: "How can one come to knowledge of the spiritual world in full possession of one's waking consciousness, and without losing the ground from under one's feet?" A few weeks later, she attended a lecture cycle in Berlin, which Rudolf Steiner held for a small circle of listeners.

Her further path in life led her first of all to St. Petersburg, where she came into the circle of the Russian symbolists under the leadership of Vyatscheslav Ivanov. There she got to know the poet and painter Maximilian Voloschin, whom she married in 1906.

In the following years Margarita Voloschin accompanied Rudolf Steiner on many lecture tours, and increasingly took on the role of a mediator between Anthroposophy and Russianness. She acted as interpreter, translated (among other books, *An Outline of Esoteric Science* by Rudolf Steiner), delivered verbal and written reports to her friends in Moscow, and was involved in the founding of the Russian Anthroposophical Society on September 20, 1913.

An early pupil of Lory Maier-Smits, the first eurythmist, Margarita Voloschin stood onstage as a eurythmist for the first time in the Mystery Dramas in Munich in 1913. In Dornach, during the building of the first Goetheanum, she was a carver before being assigned by Rudolf Steiner to paint two of the seven motifs of the small cupola: the "Egyptian

Initiate" and the "Slavic Human Being." Here she experienced an answer to the question concerning the meaning of art.

After the preliminary completion of her work she traveled, as she supposed, for only a short time to Moscow, and got entangled there in the chaos of the revolution. In the beginning it was still possible for her to give painting courses for workers, and the anthroposophical work could be continued in spite of the most adverse conditions.[45] But gradually all possibility of doing anything worthwhile was taken from her by the daily terror, the chaos, the fight against hunger, cold and sickness. After five and a half horrifying years, she received permission to leave the country on the basis of a lung disease.

After brief stopovers in Holland and in Switzerland, she found a temporary residence with her friend Lory Maier-Smits in Einsingen, near Ulm, until she finally settled in Stuttgart in 1924. While living in the humblest conditions – usually only one room – she painted her large-format pictures. She created nearly all the altar pictures for new congregations of the expanding Christian Community. At seminars in Stuttgart she was invited to talk about the first Goetheanum and Rudolf Steiner. She gave painting courses, conducted anthroposophical study-groups and wrote articles. She earned her livelihood mainly through painting portraits. Otherwise, she liked to devote herself to motifs from fairy tales and legends. Her chief works, however, dealt with religious themes, often conceived in unusual and quite original ways. Until the end of her life, she prevailed in her search for a Christian art of painting.

– *Rosemarie Wermbter*

Excerpted from an account of the life of Margarita Voloschin-Sabaschnikov in *Anthroposophie im 20. Jahrhundert,* Verlag am Goetheanum 2003.

---

[45] At one point, circumstances led to her being commissioned to paint a portrait of Lenin, which was accepted and hung in a government building in St. Petersburg (from her autobiography *Die Grüne Schlange*).

ASSYA TURGENIEFF

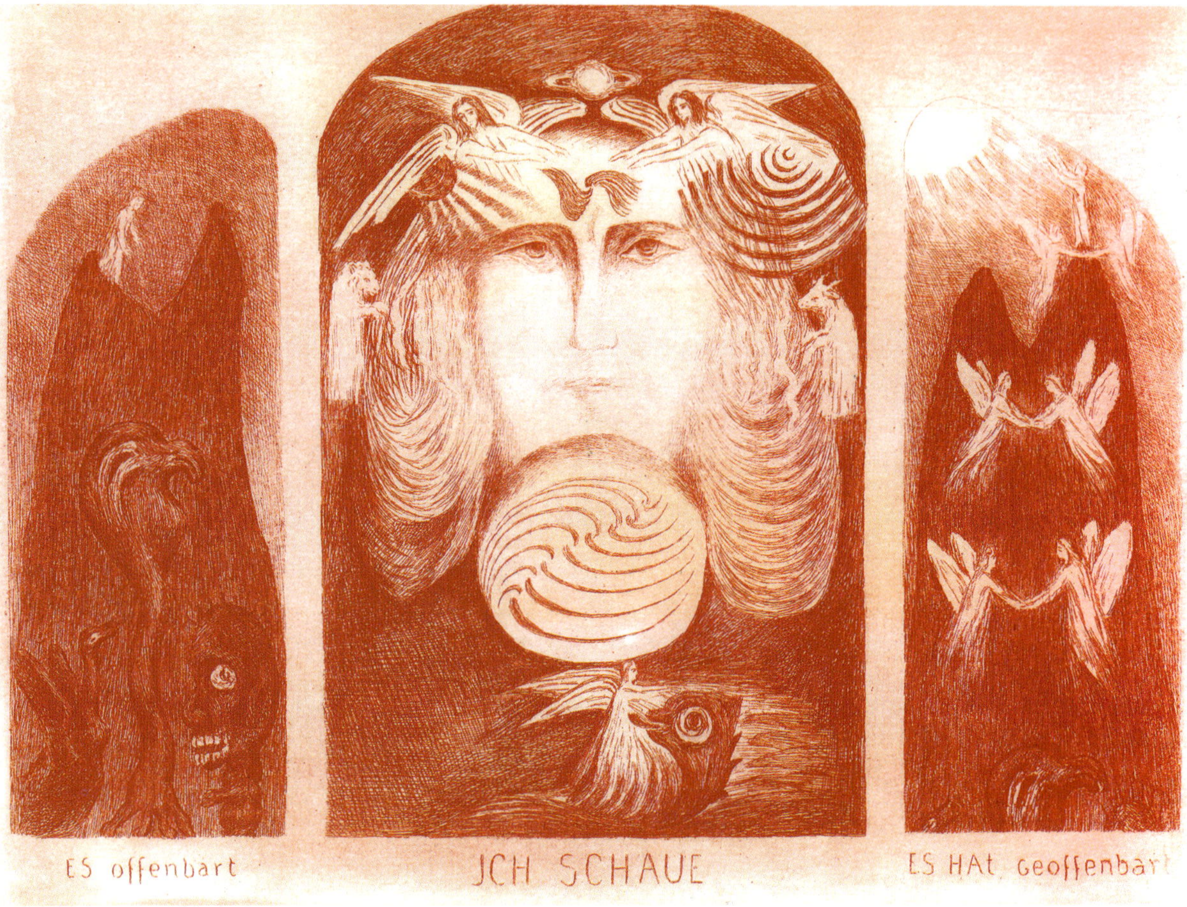

It reveals *I behold* *It has revealed*

Etching by Assya Turgenieff, made between 1918 and 1922, after Rudolf Steiner's Sketch for the Red Window of the first Goetheanum. Rudolf Steiner Archive.

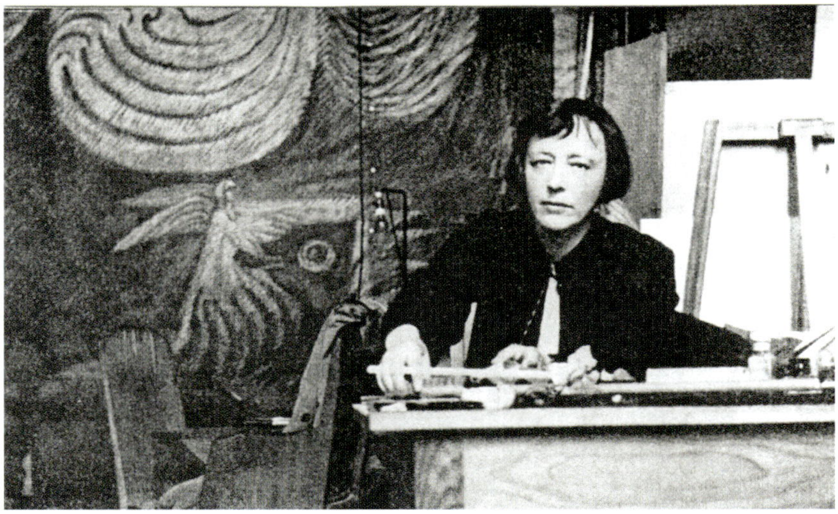

Assya Turgenieff in the Glass House Studio, c. 1940. In the background is her 1:1 preliminary drawing for the Red Window of the second Goetheanum. Rudolf Steiner Archive.

WORKING ON "LIGHT AND DARK"

Assya Turgenieff

At this time, in 1917, I was able to take up my work, broken off years before, in giving artistic form to the medium of "light and dark." Since my childhood this world had appeared to me mysterious, full of questions that I did not know how to formulate. It mediated the surrounding world to me, but the play of light and dark was most beautiful when conjured up out of its own element, in airy space: in towering cloud-formations, in translucent pictures that arose in negative relief. One sensed a world of living being behind all this. In the end, my studies in the art of etching in Brussels had been a disappointment. It linked "light and dark" with sculptural form and deadened it as a result. Or it completely negated this as was the case in modern painting. My teacher, the eighty-year-old *Auguste Danse,* took me, an eighteen-year-old girl, into his house and studio in Brussels. He was well known, particularly for his excellent etchings of famous paintings, but also through his beautiful portraits and landscapes. Thus he gave support to my abilities in doing a few things in this direction, which were then accepted for exhibition. But this was not the path to the kind of art that I envisioned. The acquired proficiency in working from nature only stood in my way.

I now attempted some drawings in which the shading was laid in *one* direction, independent of the form, and yet allowing a third dimension to arise. The result was not bad, but it did not satisfy me. Would Dr. Steiner help me to come to a new means of expression out of "light and dark," free of the externally perceptible play of light and shadow? Perhaps I could, in order to free myself from what is given by the senses, take a few of my own inner experiences as a point of departure? By this means I could also retain my contact with Dr. Steiner, for since Bugayev's[46] departure, I had not wanted to take advantage of him with my visits in the same way as before.

Dr. Steiner complied with my unspoken wish in an open and friendly manner, and from this arose a three-year collaboration in search of an artistic language in "light and dark," which became for me an inexhaustible source of ever new discoveries. Only after many years did it become clear to me why the world of light and shadow appeared so enigmatic, bringing everything into appearance, concealing itself behind its own reflection. Following this path

---

[46] Boris Nikolayevitch Bugayev, whose pen name was Andrei Belyi, a prominent Russian poet, novelist and essayist, and the husband of Assya Turgenieff. He had recently returned to Russia.

single-mindedly, one can arrive at a form of artistic expression which is capable of awakening the creative element free of mental images.

In my book devoted to the Goetheanum windows,[47] I have written down, at Marie Steiner's request, the most important aspects of this work with Dr. Steiner.

So as a matter of destiny, the world of light and dark became for me an essential, life-filled world that connects one by definition with what is spiritual. I was also helped in this regard by my later work on the translucent glass windows of the second Goetheanum.

Translated from: Assya Turgenieff, *Erinnerungen an Rudolf Steiner und die Arbeit am ersten Goetheanum,* Verlag Freies Geistesleben, Stuttgart 1993 (p. 89–90).

[47] *Rudolf Steiners Entwürfe für die Glasfenster des Goetheanums,* Dornach 1961.

RECOLLECTIONS OF THE BEGINNING OF STUDIES IN LIGHT AND DARK

Assya Turgenieff

No matter how imperfectly it turns out, it is incumbent on anyone to whom it was granted to witness the development of Rudolf Steiner's work in light-and-dark drawing, to convey what has been retained in memory.

A concerted effort is required to press such recollections into words. Little more will be possible here than to indicate the mood and circumstances in which utterances were made. As the content of memory, they cannot lay claim to literal accuracy. Every artistically striving person will have experienced the necessity of returning to the elementary questions of one's studies again and again, of concerning oneself repeatedly with the fundamentals, testing oneself with regard to them and learning new things in doing so. This prompts me to record seemingly self-evident statements. May they be taken in the sense in which they were given: not as theory or dogma, but rather as indications and characterizations with which feeling is to come to terms in putting them into practice. Only then can they reveal their meaning and prove beneficial.

Not until 1916 did circumstances bring it about that I approached Dr. Steiner with my "light-dark" problems, first of all in the mute form of a few drawings that I showed him. An ability acquired earlier on had been almost completely forgotten. Thus, to my satisfaction, these work-sheets turned out to be quite unsophisticated.

To start with – a figure. Dr. Steiner measured it with his hand and said (these conversations are not given word-for-word, but only as a rough summary of what I was able to grasp and retain): "There are over eight heads in the human height. I have nothing against it, if one does not reckon with the naturalistic proportions. Only it must be inwardly justified and artistically motivated, in terms of the whole." Did he mean that the non-naturalistic is harder to achieve than the naturalistic? How should one go about seeking *this* kind of lawfulness?

He was pleased with the head of a Madonna: "There nothing is thought out, no thought is contained in it. But did you make this light on the veil consciously?"

Fortunately it was conscious; but why was I to place the main importance on this light? And what does it mean, to work "consciously" and "without thoughts"?

In the case of a motif of the "Good Shepherd," Dr. Steiner praised the attempt to imbue the whole figure with inner light.

"It is very important," he said, "that an auric light be sensed throughout the body. That is connected with the spiritual impulses which now have to intervene, with the *after-death* impulses, which humanity must, however, conquer consciously. Spirituality up to now has been tied to the head-organization. This the human being brought from *prenatal* life. This light shines from the East, from Asia. A lofty tradition, a knowledge of it has been extant on Mount Athos until today (1917). From these impulses the art of the Middle Ages produced its saints with spiritualized heads, with the halo around the head and heavy, clumsy bodies. Take a look at my 'Kabiri.' Out of their own forces, human beings would only become such monsters. They first acquire their true human nature by means of what is cosmic and spiritual. The new 'after death' impulses must, however, be actively recognized.

Then again, this head-aura looks as though it were made of straw; that would have to be done differently."

There was a question here. But an answer came about only after a lengthy search.

As time went by, Dr. Steiner took a look at still other drawings and wrote underneath them: *A vision — An experience — A daydream —*

"Why do you not like that one?" he asked. "It is important precisely in our time, to draw people's attention to the fact that artistic impulses really can come out of the spiritual world. And even if it has not taken place here in full consciousness, there nonetheless lives in it a higher wisdom than what you are capable of in your ordinary consciousness. For Plato the word 'dreaming' meant a soul-state that is higher than everyday consciousness."

In addition, I showed Dr. Steiner a "Madonna of the Steps," as he called it.

"The Child is quite Russian," he thought. "But this aura is like wire. I will show you what kind of shading to use."

And with strokes this way and that in all directions he drew the picture again on a sheet of paper. (See page 169.) The orderly auric circle around the Child was now bent out of shape. That also corresponded to my feeling, yet I had not allowed myself such freedom.

"Like this it is artistically true," he replied. "The important thing for me is that in this shading an *intensive* effect is arrived at; by that I mean that it *shines* from *within outwards*; that is what I am looking for, in contrast to what is extensive, lit from outside." Nevertheless, when the drawing was finished, Dr. Steiner looked at it for a long time and said, somewhat disappointed, that this way of drawing was not yet the right one. He did not yet know how one could render spiritual light impressions artistically. He wanted to think it over.

Thus for the time being I did not pursue this manner of hatching further. There remained the sense of a distant goal: the "intensive," the "shining from within outwards."

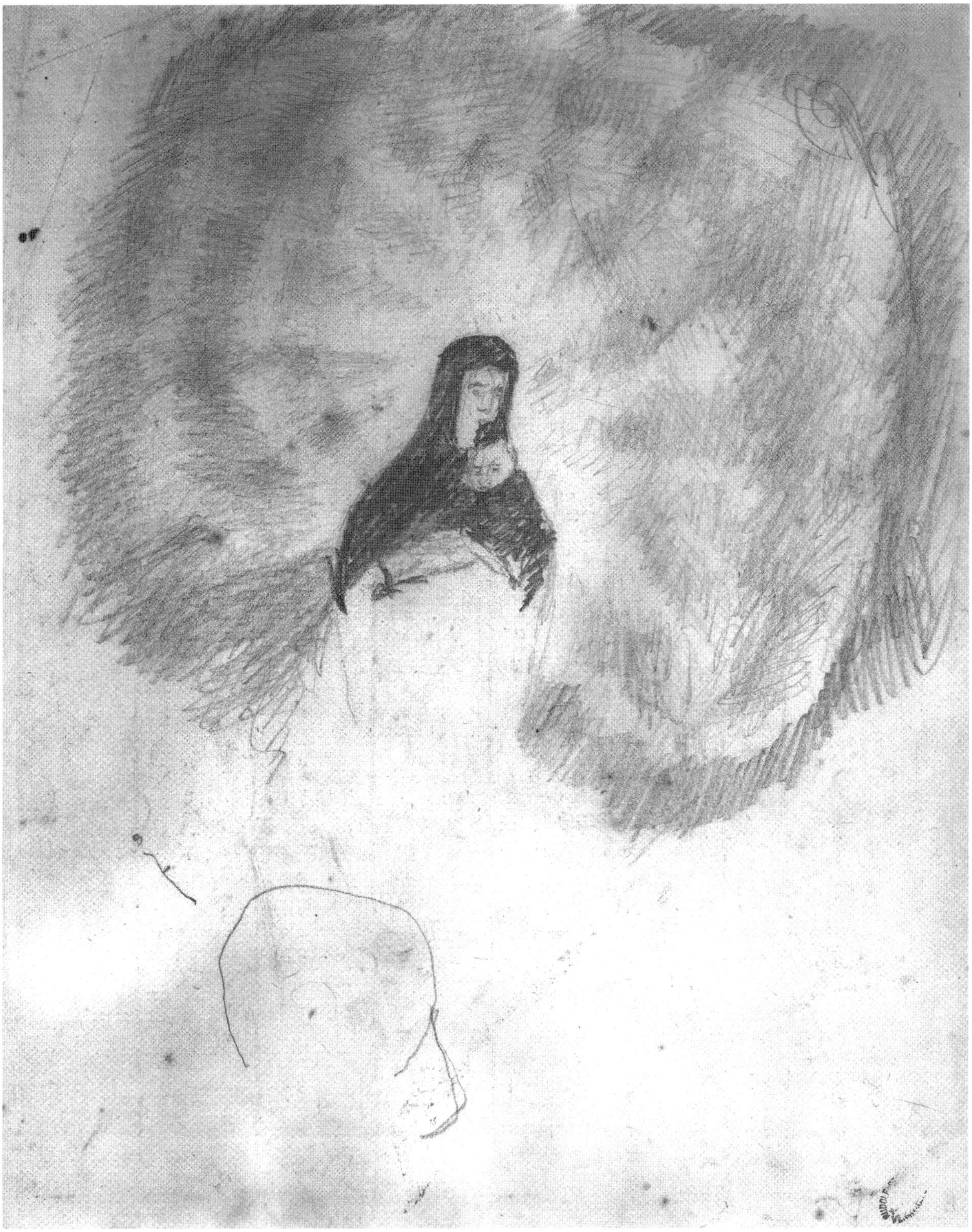

Madonna of the Steps by Rudolf Steiner (light/dark study).
Rudolf Steiner Archive (Dornach).

In the expectation of receiving new tasks, I again and again brought my drawings to Dr. Steiner; among others, the image of a child in bright light, lying on straw. This time I used the straw intentionally to strengthen the glow of light. But again it did not please: "You do not need to make this straw so naturalistic. You could make use of it to bring out etheric, cloud-like currents, so that one does not really know what it is. Study the color movements in the painting of the small cupola. What is around things, what is between things, what leads into the etheric, that one should look for."

And Dr. Steiner drew soft forms flowing into each other, with the direction of the strokes accompanying the forms, more or less in the following manner:

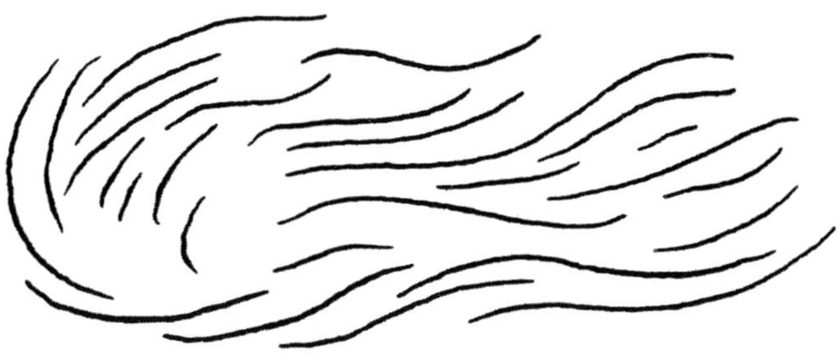

"What lies between things..." – These words bore an image of the future in them, an image not visible for one's consciousness, which only feeling could cautiously approach. Should one already now make it a field of work? Is the simplest artistic feeling supposed to serve as a suitable path to it? – Already for the second time Dr. Steiner showed me, in transforming my pictures, how the meagre inspiration conferred on them had to yield to straightforward artistic feeling.

Roughly at this time – it was the end of January 1918 – I met Dr. Steiner with a drawing block in his hand, and as he so often liked to do, he stopped to show me what he had just been working on. It was a drawing of the Kabiri, which he had previously sculpted for the *Faust* performances. (See page 82.)

"Photographs of sculptures are always an atrocity," he said. "I have sought here to render the sculptural in terms of drawing."

It only became clear to him later that in this sketch he had actually found a new path as regards drawing.

Around this time between 1917 and 1918, several opportunities presented themselves in which I could speak with Rudolf Steiner about artistic questions. I should like to mention a few things from these conversations here.

With reference to illustrative art Dr. Steiner once told me that works the content of which take place purely in the realm of the soul, as for example the *Chymical Wedding*,[48] are only to be rendered by means of color. On the other hand, the technique of black-and-white is suitable for works that appeal to what is spiritual, thus to what is of the nature of thought. He would have liked to have seen his *Philosophy of Spiritual Activity* illustrated in black-and-white. Black-and-white is appropriate also for the images of the apocalypse.

Several attempts at compositions that I brought him caused him to remark that it is good to use such symbolic motifs as the four apocalyptic beasts: one has to do that, but one should not approach the symbolic directly, but disperse it within the picture, conceal it, as he did for instance with the four animals in the drawing of the Red Window.[49]

"The intellect is a 'bad dog' when it comes to the artistic," he said another time. "Certainly you must have had a thought, an idea. But you must then leave it behind you, forget it and only work out of feeling. You may never know beforehand how the picture, or the composition will look when it is finished. First you make a figure, concentrating on it wholly; then comes the second figure, and then you watch how it relates to the first, and so on, till finally you have a composition. You must wait for the composition, never visualize or determine it beforehand."

Once again one stood dumbfounded at such words, only able to listen in on them inwardly. Yet the composition of his pictures was so completely lawful, so enigmatically and consistently built up.

Once during our carving work at the Goetheanum, which he often came to see in order to give advice and make corrections, Dr. Steiner told us about an exhibition of paintings he had just seen in Germany. Some of what he said, I remember: "The Impressionists have certainly had their say in the history of art. In terms of color, in *plein air* painting they have created something new, only it was not enough: they excluded the human being, and so this direction in art could not develop further and had to disintegrate and come to nothing. The Expressionists rely only on themselves; they do away with the world and in this way become

---

[48] *The Chymical Wedding of Christian Rosencreutz* by Johann Valentin Andreae (1586–1654), a theologian.

[49] Of the first Goetheanum.

in the end completely unresourceful, completely abstract. Finally they are only able to draw lines and geometric figures. They come into a region within themselves where mathematizing has its seat. There, however, is Ahriman. The Expressionists do sometimes gain insight into what is spiritual; but it is a matter of fragments only, of moments. In a mere moment, however, there is nothing artistic. An anthroposophical style will lie right *in between* these two directions."

In a conversation about poetry he said, among other things: "What I value in poets, no matter how imperfect they are, is when they have the insight and the courage to take their stand on spiritual-scientific ground. For there will not be a second Goethe. The spiritual world has no interest in that at all, except perhaps with younger peoples, where the language is not fully developed, as with the Russians. But the spiritual world has the greatest interest in bringing it about that there are spiritual scientists. It is working on that. And from this, new impulses will come into all artistic life."

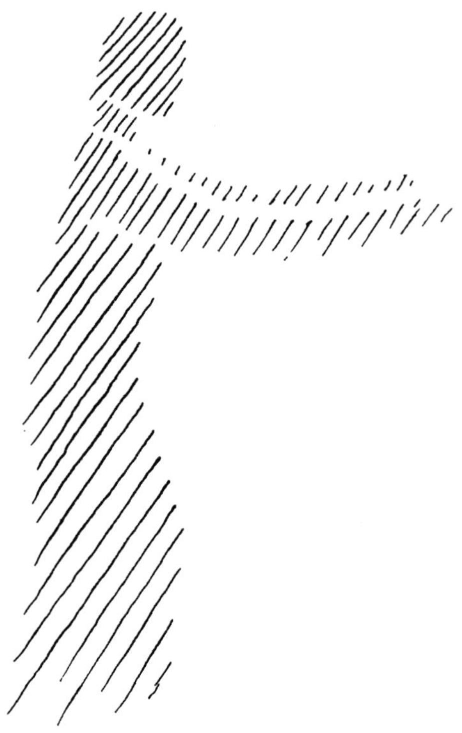

Soon after Dr. Steiner indicated for me the diagonal-stroke way of working, I saw a drawing he made for Miss Maryon. Much became clear to me from this barely suggested sketch. Since it got lost, I can only reproduce it from memory here. It showed a woman inclining herself towards a group of children. Only a shadow, but the whole figure and movement were already there. And yet one had the feeling: the figure can change, incline lower, stretch her hands further out. It left the viewer free. It also left the artist complete freedom to change it and look for the form up to the point where the whole picture is completed. A prescribed contour would not have permitted this. It can also be reckoned as one of the first experiences to be made with this method: a contour drawn in advance is felt as enslavement. Artists who begin by fixing their picture in contours, eliminate the purely artistic from the outset, weakening their own activity. By searching for the form without making contours, they have the possibility, until the picture is finished, of creating their work in the element of becoming, in the process of arising.[50]

"You have to make a surface and direct your whole feeling, your attention to it, and then to the next surface," Dr. Steiner often told us in carving the architraves in the Goetheanum, "and await expectantly, with curiosity, what sort of boundary arises between the two surfaces. You should never determine it in advance."

In transposing it, this statement can just as well be applied to drawing. Renouncing the fixing of boundaries by means of line brings with it an element of the unexpected that approaches one while working, an "unknown" that calls for greater vigilance and inner activity. It brings with it – assuming one actually comes to the point of working in the sense of this method – a liberation from the disturbing intellectual mental image that would nail everything down. It frees one from everything head-oriented, and concentrates awareness on an activity within feeling itself, which experiences the contrasts of cold and warm, light and heavy, and out of this inner touching, shapes the forms – not imagining them beforehand, but directly creating them.

"Only in your heads are you sentimental," Dr. Steiner said to us eurythmists; "the heart knows what is right."

But the heart has above all to do with the rhythmic system. A kind of rhythm, a rhythmic lawfulness, into which one comes with the hatching technique, makes it possible to incorporate the rhythmic element as the bearer of life into visual art.

"In the stroke lives the 'I', the character. It has to be varied as far as possible, since it has the task of characterizing."

One only needs to test for oneself, how much richer the shadings are, when carried out by means of hatching, and how positive it is for creativity itself when it is limited to one direction.

So as to be given more definite tasks for diagonal hatching, I brought two further drawings

---

[50] Elsewhere the author quotes Rudolf Steiner, though not verbatim, as saying:
– *"Forms must be felt – not invented."*
– *"The means of approach to the world of forms is not in the head, it is in the region of the thorax."*
and:
– *"The mathematical-geometric should be carried over into organic-living form."* (From an article entitled "Zu acht Skizzen von Rudolf Steiner" by Assya Turgenieff in the periodical *Die Drei*, Stuttgart, ca. 1960.)

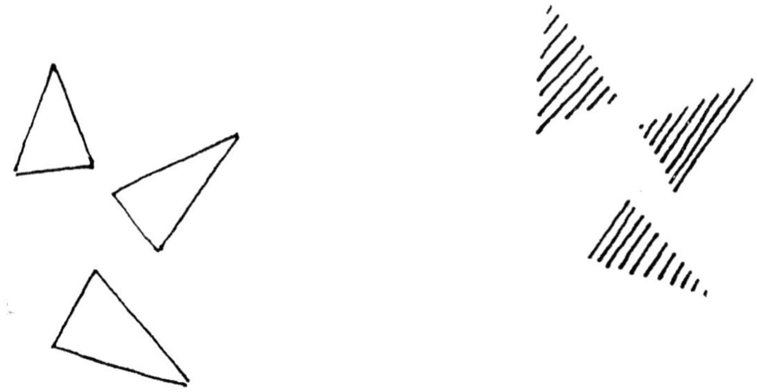

to Dr. Steiner. The first: two large heads; the second: a figure on a dark background. He then spoke about the handling of the stroke and clarified it by means of small drawings.

"The strokes may never go along with the form – they must have nothing to do with the form. You can see how, in your case, the strokes bend themselves to the plastic forms even if only very slightly. [See the upper examples on p. 175.] Those are errors. One has to hatch quite independent of the form. Consequently, one has never to make curved strokes, otherwise in the end one comes to outline after all; and outline is a lie in the realm of art. You can quite well make use of line in building up a drawing – but no more than an architect makes use of a scaffold in building a house. When the house is finished, the scaffolding is gone. Thus you must not start from line, and when the drawing is completed, every trace of anything like a contour must disappear.

The strokes must be quite clearly visible, free and characteristic [See the illustration on page 175.] But there has to be character in the strokes themselves, as varied as possible; it is a matter of making them as varied as possible: laid on lightly, solidly, closely or more widely apart, and so on. That results in what is artistic. If you want to gradually darken a surface, shall we say, then if you cannot solve it any other way, you can intersect your strokes, but quite obliquely – never at right-angles. But try to achieve it by narrowing the strokes, laying new strokes between the strokes, so that the direction of the strokes remains always the same. With that you free drawing from line; because line is never beautiful when it comes to the artistic."

In order to become clearer about it, I showed him a eurythmy-form during a eurythmy rehearsal, which he had just drawn. Here everything was line, and yet it was artistically beautiful.

"You only think it's beautiful," he replied. "It is only beautiful, however, when run through in space. That means in time." "A line is artistically justified," he added, "only in caricature; for caricature is purely intellectual. Only in this art is the intellect, and with it line as well, really in place."[51]

A liberation from the intellectual life of ideas bound to our ordinary consciousness demands, however, a further intensification of consciousness, a training only to be attained through work. "Art comes from ability" (*"Kunst kommt von Können"*) was a favorite saying of Dr. Steiner. "Fifty times you will need to paint the picture, then it will be right," he said, to encourage a painter who actually possessed considerable artistry and ability. "You must go through a eurythmy-form also fifty times, until it becomes as instinctively familiar to you as when you lift a spoon to your mouth; only then are you free for the artistic," was his advice to eurythmists.

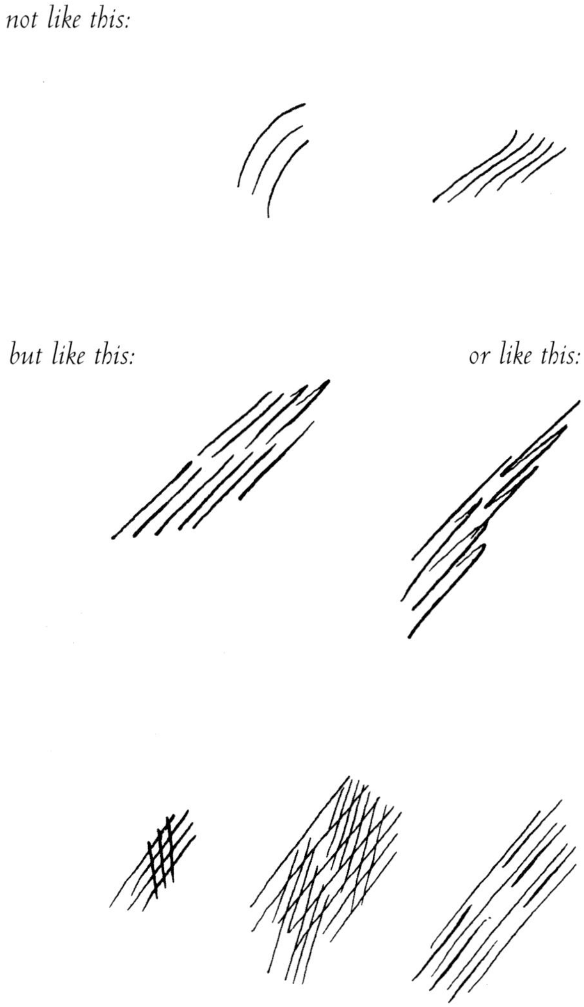

The future depends on these new, consciously acquired instincts won by means of a path of training in the basic elements of art, be it form, color, tone or

---

[51] See the booklet *Rudolf Steiner: Physiognomisches. 12 Karikaturen.* Rudolf Steiner Verlag, Dornach, Switzerland 1971.

word. Pointing the way, a sentence of Goethe's from his "Prose Aphorisms" was often cited by Rudolf Steiner: "He to whom nature begins to unveil her open secret, feels an irresistable yearning for her worthiest interpreter, art." And elsewhere, Goethe says: "The beautiful is a manifestation of secret laws of nature, which, without it, would remain forever hidden." If one seeks to approach nearer the secret laws of nature in light-and-dark, one finds an essential difference between them and the world of color. Colors have the peculiarity of becoming one with forms. One sees this not only with colors that cling to definite forms, as for example, the human incarnadine color, or the green of plants – this tendency of becoming one with, of joining together with the forms and movements one sees also for example in fleeting appearances of the sky. If, on the other hand, one sees an illumined countenance slowly move, it is evident from such a basic observation that light and shadow have nothing in common with the form. Only their effects project into the visible. Though they bring things into appearance, they belong themselves to a world which has nothing to do with form, which does not "accompany" the form.

In approaching these two elements of light and shadow more closely, one finds first of all what is known from the simplest optical experiments: that a light surface has the tendency to expand, to appear larger, while a dark surface has the effect of becoming smaller toward the inside.

In becoming larger, the light surface can be characterized at the same time as tending to evaporate, to become buoyant, to strive upward, to expand – just as the dark surface can be felt as having the opposite tendencies of possessing weight, of clenching itself together, shutting itself off from the above. They bear their own primordial creative tendencies within them, which lead us to the earth-motif and sun-motif, and to the acanthus leaf motif, as described by Rudolf Steiner in *Ways to a New Style in Architecture*. We find this form principle also in the spiral, the meander, in the hexagram, to name only a few examples from the world of original forms.

If one attempts to sense this duality within oneself, to come to terms with it, one can have a feeling-perception which tells one that the left side is related more to the evaporating forces, the right side to the solidifying forces. The inner gesture that establishes a relationship to these two forces (the gesture of a living, mobile equilibrium) results for the human being in the diagonal direction from above left to below right. The stroke directed "from above right to below left" – for the observer – which brings about the alternating play of light and shadow, stands in harmony with the "secret laws of nature," to be the interpreter of which is the task of art. In the central motif of the Goetheanum we find the polarity of light and darkness and its balancing-out represented in the form of actual beings.[52]

Translated from "Erinnerungen an die Anfänge der Hell-Dunkel-Studien" in *Rudolf Steiner: Die Goetheanum-Fenster. Sprache des Lichtes.* (Bibliographie Nr. K 12). Rudolf Steiner Verlag, Dornach, Switzerland 1996.

---

[52] See the photograph of Rudolf Steiner's statue of *The Representative of Humanity* on page 152.

A DRAWING CLASS WITH RUDOLF STEINER

Daniel Johan van Bemmelen
(1899–1982)

In November 1923 Rudolf Steiner visited the Vrije School (Free School) in The Hague for the first time. The school had been founded not long before by a number of Dutch teachers. To begin with, the various classes were taken in by favorably-disposed parents in their private rooms; and so as to have enough light, I had accommodated my class of nine children in a small glass veranda. When Rudolf Steiner visited our Fourth Grade with a few other people, only he could fit in, and the others had to watch through the glass connecting-door.

Roughly half of my children were elementary school children, and our guest was unknown to all of them. A sanguinic boy among them showed off, not able to remain sitting on his bench, he jumped to and fro and made faces. Rudolf Steiner stood up and said, standing in front of the boy: "You must really sit on the bench" and led him amiably back to his place. Astonished, the boy looked at him and laughed, but he then remained sitting still. Another boy of choleric temperament amused those present with his lack of self-control. Rudolf Steiner helped him in writing, and that made him shout with delight in his excitement.

I was keen to show our guest several difficult children, and he gave me pedagogical advice. But he explained to me that it would go better with some children who I brought forward as being difficult, once I had gained enough experience. On the other hand, he had at once directed his attention to a small boy whom I had not presented to him. This boy was very embarrassed and answered my questions only very quietly. Rudolf Steiner recognized the cause of his unhappy condition at once. He had had a severely frightening experience (this was confirmed by our subsequent inquiries). Rudolf Steiner described the organism of the child to us and showed the way to a recovery.

On the next day Rudolf Steiner listened to my lesson in zoology. And since I expected that he would give some further suggestions, I asked him whether there was anything in particular that he would like to see.

"Don't you want to give a drawing lesson?" he asked. I did not understand: "Do you mean a painting class?"

"No, a drawing class," he replied.

I was at a loss as to how I should do this in the Fourth Grade, since in the Free School we had mainly painted. Suddenly Rudolf Steiner got up, in order to give an example himself.

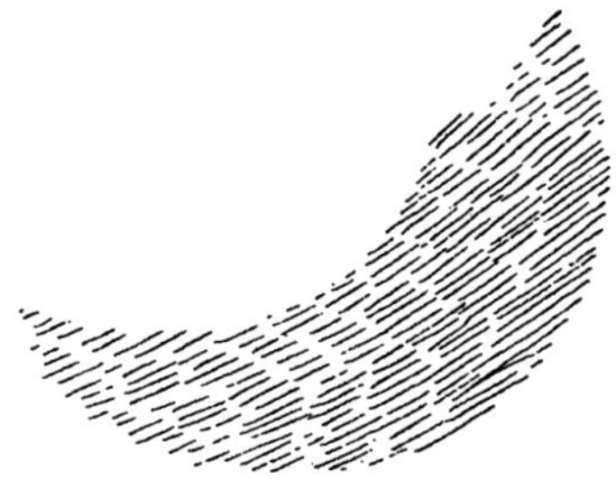

1.

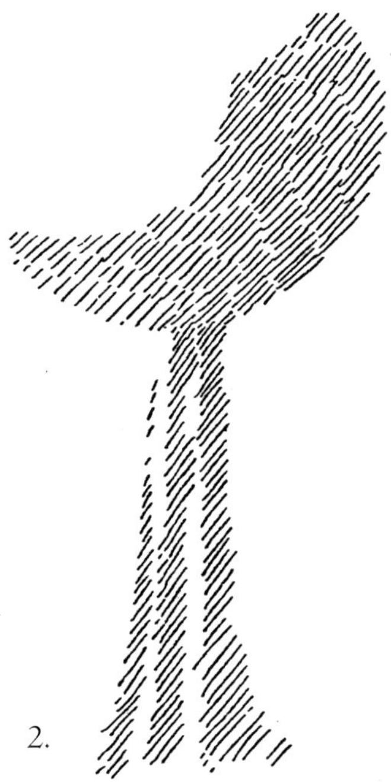

2.

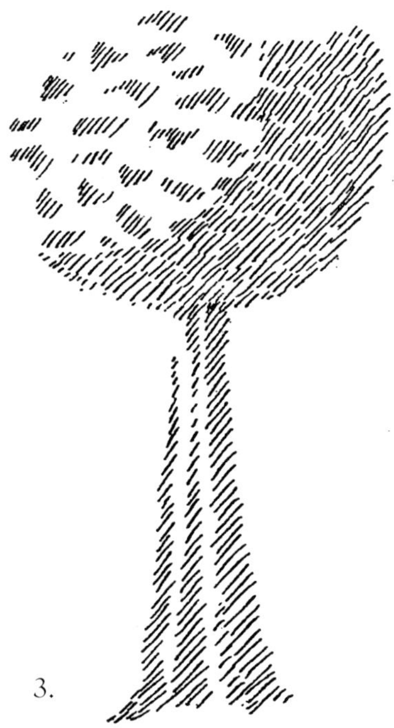

3.

He spoke German, but he made everything clear to the children with such expressive gestures that they understood before I had translated.

He took hold of a teacup and showed it to the children, while at the same time sliding the curtain back and forth.

"Here is a teacup. What do you now see on it?"

The children saw the play of light on the illumined side of the teacup and observed at the same time that the shadow side was now more, now less visible. And after a short time they answered: "Shadow!"

"That's right!" said Rudolf Steiner and drew the shadow on the chalk-board (1).

Then he took a cloth and asked: "And how do the shadows run here?" The children indicated it with their hands: vertically.

"Well!" said Rudolf Steiner and drew brown shadow-streaks (2).

Now he took hold of the sponge and compared it with the teacup. And the children noticed that with the sponge there were separate shadows because of all the sponge-holes. That too he drew on the board. (3).

Finally he explained to the children, how the cup on the table throws an intense shadow (4).

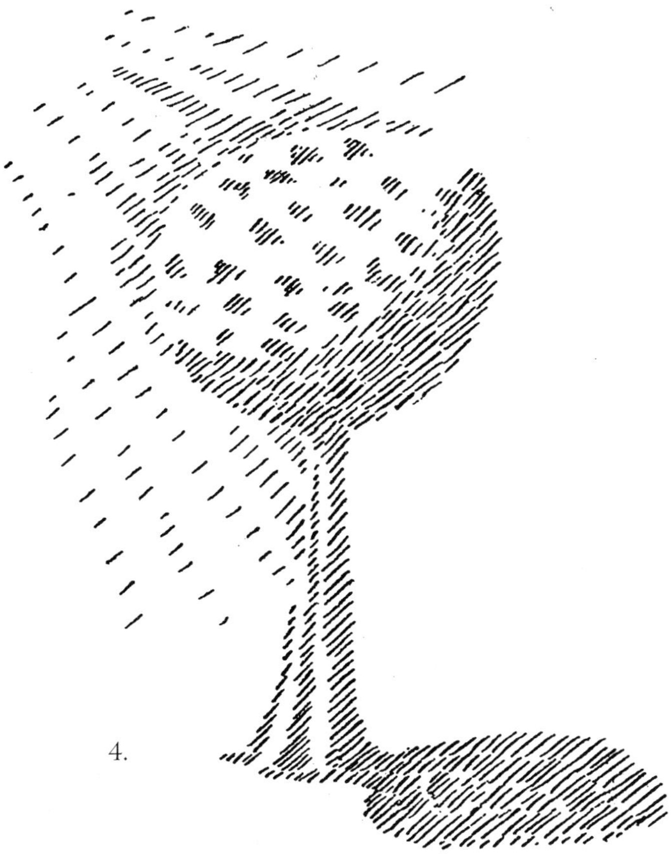

4.

The upper part of the drawing on the chalkboard he colored green, the lower part light-brown, and he let a stream of yellow ray in from the above left. In response to his question: "What is it now?" the children cried enthusiastically: "A tree!"

"That's how you can give a drawing lesson," he said to me smiling, taking his leave warmly, in order to visit another class.

The children were very stimulated by this lesson, and by the friendliness and kindness of our guest. The teacher was grateful, for he had learned, how one can let a drawing arise from the contrast of light and shadow.

This article is an excerpt from a report by the author "Rudolf Steiner in 'De Vrije School'" in the periodical *Menschenschule*. Stuttgart.

About Assya Turgenieff
1890–1966

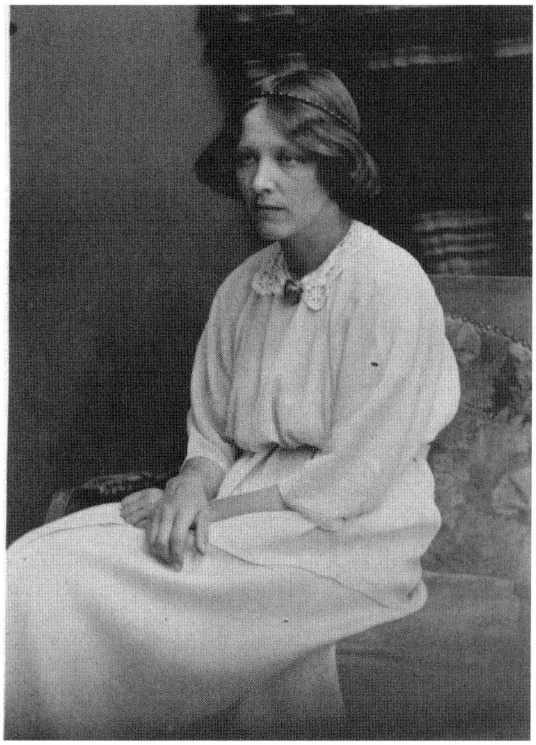

Dokumentation am Goetheanum-Bildarchiv.

Assya Turgenieff was born the grandniece of the Russian writer Ivan Turgenieff on May 12, 1890, on an estate near Moscow. Her sheltered childhood in the country led to a great thirst for knowledge and many questions in her twelfth year. The revolution of 1905 reinforced these questions, causing her to become something of a skeptic. Assya attended anti-religious gatherings and experienced street fighting in Moscow. Since it was deemed too dangerous for her to remain on the estate of her parents, she was sent to Paris together with her sister. The new European surroundings, above all, however, the great works of art in the

Louvre, awakened Assya's artistic energies: She studied drawing and etching in Paris, and soon afterwards in Brussels with the master engraver *Auguste Danse.*

She had already met the Russian poet *Andrei Belyi* (1880–1934) in Paris. Through coming into contact with various esoteric associations, more and more questions ensued regarding her inner orientation. In 1912 Assya Turgenieff and Andrei Belyi met Rudolf Steiner in Cologne. As a result of that meeting they accompanied him on his numerous lecture tours in Germany and abroad.

Two years later, in the spring of 1914, they moved to Dornach, in order to help in the construction of the Goetheanum. Although Assya was originally chosen to grind the glass windows, she first joined in drawing building plans, but was soon assigned to carve on the architraves. Later she carved on the statue of the *Representative of Humanity* under the direction of Edith Maryon. At the same time, she did a eurythmy training.

While the First World War raged in the rest of Europe, people of the most varying social strata from numerous nations worked together at the Goetheanum. The Russians living in Dornach were described by Flossy Leinhas, quoting Rilke: "'Is God there? – Are we here?' These questions ceased for good on meeting people like Assya Turgenieff and her sister, Natasha Pozzo, who were always to be seen together, like a pair of twins. When they first 'made their appearance' in Berlin, there were four of them; they were accompanied, protected and admired by their men, the very tall 'Over-Pozzo' (Alexandr Pozzo) and the delicate Bugayev-Belyi. All of them – as I remember – wore high white fur-hats. In this attire and otherwise 'dressed up' they went around all their lives on this earth. In the midst of this 'here' of ours, they were yet surrounded by a 'there' out of which they were led, as though by a star-power that had guided the Shepherds.... Their real home was not so very much of this world..." (Leinhas 1967, *Mitteilungen aus der anthroposophischen Bewegung,* Nr. 40).

In the winter of 1916–17 Assya Turgenieff suffered a health crisis in consequence of overwork, which led to her neither being permitted to carve nor to do eurythmy for a time. In the meantime she devoted herself to black-and-white drawing and developed, in collaboration with Rudolf Steiner, a new diagonal hatching technique. She soon took up etching once again and received the task from Rudolf Steiner of carrying out all the window-motifs of the first Goetheanum as etchings.

In the middle of the 1920s, her work in eurythmy intensified. Under the direction of Marie Steiner, Assya Turgenieff was active from 1915–1935 in eurythmy performances and tours of the Dornach ensemble.

After the destruction of the Goetheanum by fire, Assya Turgenieff got started on the major task of reshaping all the glass windows of the first Goetheanum, adapting them to the second Goetheanum. Since the forms of the windows were completely different: in the first building broad, with round arches and divided into triptyches, they now had to be transposed onto a tall, narrow format. Motifs that had originally been next to each other were now arranged vertically. Only the Red Window – to be seen today in the west of the Goetheanum – could be carried out in its original form.

The transparency of her being found here the material that corresponded to it: colored glass! Physically, engraving and grinding the glass was hard work. The motifs had to be carved out of the huge surfaces of glass under a continual supply of water.

Only after the end of the Second World War could the last windows be completed. Besides glass-engraving, she did graphic work, especially in the black-and-white hatching technique. Assya Turgenieff illustrated fairy tales, legends, and books for young people, among them a portfolio concerned with the Parsifal saga, probably her most mature work in this field. Over and beyond that, she placed her abilities at the disposal of the publication of Rudolf Steiner's works. Assya Turgenieff was commissioned by Marie Steiner to design all the book covers and to transpose the blackboard drawings of Rudolf Steiner appropriately into black-and-white. She also prepared exhibitions in connection with the art impulse of Rudolf Steiner, conducted guided tours of his artistic work, and communicated her experiences in lectures and courses in Dornach and Bern.

The artistic impulses that had led to the first Goetheanum building were paramount for her – she was prepared to fight for them: When in 1956 the Large Hall of the second Goetheanum was to be redesigned, and she felt the design-conception to be inadequate and not in keeping with Rudolf Steiner's intention for the building, she took a stand and made her views known both in lectures and in writing.[53] However, she achieved no response from those in authority. In spite of this she presented her understanding of the Goetheanum building impulse in a further publication.[54]

As she advanced in years, the circumstances of Assya Turgenieff's life grew more confined,

---

[53] "What Will Happen with the Goetheanum Building? An Appeal." (*Was wird mit dem Goetheanumbau geschehen? Ein Appell.* Published by R. G. Zbinden & Co., Basel, June 1956).

[54] (After the renovation of the Large Hall): "What Has Happened with the Goetheanum Building? Facts and Symptoms." (*Was ist mit dem Goetheanumbau geschehen? Tatsachen und Symptome.* Published by R. G. Zbinden & Co., Basel, April 1957).

conditioned by illness. The matter-of-fact, devoted care of her niece Mascha Pozzo made her home nonetheless a place of human and spiritual exchange. Assya Turgenieff died after a lengthy period of suffering on October 16, 1966, in Arlesheim.

— Jakob Streit / Christiane Haid

From an account of the life of Assya Turgenieff in *Anthroposophie im 20. Jahrhundert,* Verlag am Goetheanum 2003.

AFTERWORD

While studying with the painter *Gerard Wagner* (1906–1999) in Dornach, Switzerland, beginning in the 1970s, the translator became more aware of the work of the pioneer artists brought together here – discovering the sources from which this book is drawn.

In conclusion, it seems appropriate to add a word about Gerard Wagner, who belongs to the generation following the first pioneers and can be seen as the foremost later exponent of Rudolf Steiner's painting impulse. Apart from Henni Geck, with whom Wagner initially studied, no other painter has worked as closely or as extensively with the sketch-motifs of Rudolf Steiner. In unravelling the mysteries of the sketches over a lifetime, Gerard Wagner has given us a detailed artistic method of painting out of the color, indications of which are to be found in the book *The Individuality of Colour* (Rudolf Steiner Press, London 1980). He also left a considerable body of work, consisting of over 3,000 paintings, which are not only masterly in their artistic accomplishment, but full of potentiality.

It will be evident to the reader that we have, on the one hand, the generally acknowledged trends of twentieth-century art, and on the other, the quite different aims and ideals of the artists set forth here.

Neither short-lived, nor subject to changing taste and fashion, these aims and ideals can be recognized as long-term. They concern the very future of art.

– *Peter Stebbing*

SELECTED BIBLIOGRAPHY

Belyi, Andrei / Assya Turgenieff / Margarita Voloschin. *Reminiscences of Rudolf Steiner.* Ghent, N.Y.: Adonis Press, 1987.

Bemmelen, Daniel J. van. *Rudolf Steiner's New Approach to Color on the Ceiling of the First Goetheanum.* Translated by A. W. Mann. Spring Valley, N.Y.: St. George Publications, 1980.

Boos-Hamburger, Hilde. *The Creative Power of Colour.* Edited by John Fletcher. London: Michael Press, 1973.

Goethe, Johann Wolfgang von. *Farbenlehre.* Edited by Gerhard Ott and Heinrich O. Proskauer. Including introduction and commentaries by Rudolf Steiner. 5 vols. Stuttgart: Verlag Freies Geistesleben, 1979, reprinted 1986.

———. *Goethe's Color Theory.* Edited and compiled by Rupprecht Matthaei. New York: Van Nostrand Reinhold, 1971.

———. *Theory of Colours.* Translated by Charles Lock Eastlake. Cambridge, MA: M.I.T. Press, 2000 [1840].

Proskauer, Heinrich O. *The Rediscovery of Color.* Translated by Peter Stebbing. Spring Valley, NY: Anthroposophic Press, 1986.

Raske, Hilde. *The Language of Color in the First Goetheanum.* Dornach, Switzerland: Walter Keller Verlag, 1987.

Schubert, Ilona. *Reminiscences of Rudolf Steiner and Marie Steiner-von Sivers.* Temple Lodge Press, London 1991.

Steiner, Rudolf. *Colour* (GA 291). Translated by John Salter and Pauline Wehrle. Sussex: Rudolf Steiner Press, 1992.

———. *Farbenerkenntnis* (GA 291a). Edited by Hella Wiesberger and Heinrich O. Proskauer. Dornach, Switzerland: Rudolf Steiner Verlag, 1990.

———. *Art as Seen in the Light of Mystery Wisdom.* (GA 275). Sussex: Rudolf Steiner Press, 1996.

________. *The Arts and Their Mission.* (GA 276). Spring Valley, NY: Anthroposophic Press, 1986.

________. *Das Malerische Werk.* (GA K 13-16/52-56). ca. 300 pages. Dornach, Switzerland: Rudolf Steiner Verlag, 2007.

________. *Ein malerischer Schulungsweg. Pastellskizzen und Aquarelle.* Dornach: Rudolf Steiner Verlag, 1986.

________. *Neun Schulungsskizzen für Maler. "Naturstimmungen."* Dornach, Switzerland: Verlag der Rudolf Steiner-Nachlassverwaltung, 1962, 1999.

________. *Die Goetheanum Fenster. Sprache des Lichtes.* Dornach, Switzerland: Rudolf Steiner Verlag, 1996.

Strakosch-Giesler, Maria. *Die erlöste Sphinx.* Freiburg im Breisgau: Novalis-Verlag, 1955.

Turgenieff, Assya. *Erinnerungen an Rudolf Steiner.* Stuttgart: Verlag Freies Geistesleben, 1972; 3rd edition 1993.

Wagner, Gerard, and Elisabeth Koch. *The Individuality of Colour. Contributions to a Methodical Schooling in Experience of Colour.* Translated by Peter Stebbing. London: Rudolf Steiner Press, 1980.

________. Gerard Wagner. *Die Kunst der Farbe.* With contributions by Elisabeth Koch and K. Theodor Willmann. Stuttgart: Verlag Freies Geistesleben, 1980.

Woloschin, Margarita. *Die Grüne Schlange. Lebenserinnerungen.* Stuttgart: Verlag Freies Geistesleben, 1954, 8th edition 1997.

This volume has been assembled mainly from the following sources:

Die Erlöste Sphinx
(The Sphinx Redeemed)
by Maria Strakosch-Giesler
Novalis Verlag, Freiburg im Breisgau 1955

Aus Gesprächen mit Rudolf Steiner über Malerei
und einige Erinnerungen an die Zeit des ersten Goetheanum
(From Conversations with Rudolf Steiner about Painting
And Some Recollections of the Time of the First Goetheanum)
by Hilde Boos-Hamburger
Zbinden Verlag, Basel 1954. Reprinted 1961, 1985

Rudolf Steiner: Ein malerischer Schulungsweg
Pastellskizzen und Aquarelle
(Rudolf Steiner: A Path of Training in Painting
Pastel Sketches and Watercolors)
Rudolf Steiner Verlag, CH-4143 Dornach 1986

Rudolf Steiner: Zwölf Entwürfe für die Malerei der grossen Kuppel
des ersten Goetheanum
(Rudolf Steiner: Twelve Sketches for the Painting of the Large Cupola
of the First Goetheanum)
Edited by Marie Steiner
Philosophisch-anthroposophischer Verlag, Dornach 1930

Rudolf Steiner: Die Goetheanum Fenster
Sprache des Lichtes
(Rudolf Steiner: The Goetheanum Windows
The Language of Light)
Rudolf Steiner Verlag, CH-4143 Dornach 1996

Anthroposophie im 20. Jahrhundert
Ein Kulturimpuls in biografischen Porträts
(Anthroposophy in the Twentiethth Century
A Cultural Impulse in Biographical Portraits)
Edited by Bodo von Plato
Verlag am Goetheanum, CH-4143 Dornach 2003

About Peter Stebbing

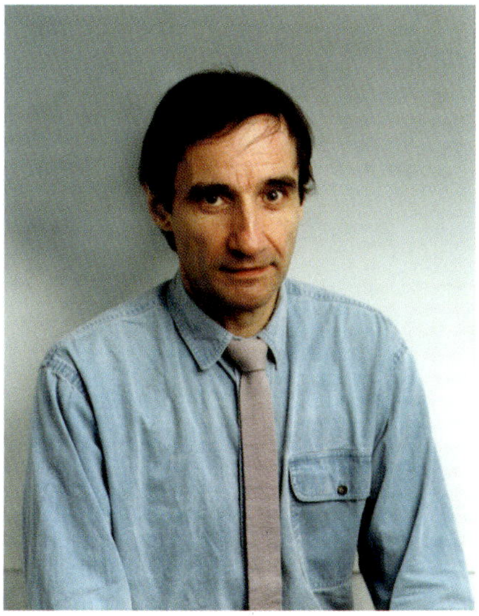

Peter Stebbing, born in Copenhagen, Denmark, in 1941, attended Waldorf Schools in England. Before studying at art schools in Brighton and London, he spent a year as a stagehand and member of the cleaning crew at the Goetheanum. In 1960-61 there was as yet no painting school in Dornach. The training at Brighton College of Arts & Crafts offered a solid foundation with some innovation, whereas the Central School of Art in London had a more abstract direction, with students left largely to their own resources.

After emigrating to America in the summer of 1966, he graduated in 1968 with an M.F.A. degree in painting from Cornell University in Ithaca, N.Y. The two years in the magnificent natural setting of the Finger Lakes afforded the opportunity of getting to know visiting artists of international stature in the art world. Most notable among them was Jim Dine, whose uncompromising artistic ethos made a particular impression. At Cornell, Peter Stebbing's own work reflected something of the minimalist trend of that time.

Following a first teaching stint at the University of Kansas, he was offered a position on the faculty of the City University of New York in 1970, and was asked to teach mainly color courses. He began a practical study of Goethe's color theory with experiments. This scientific preoccupation with color, of immense interest in itself, led increasingly to questions concerning a corresponding artistic approach to color in painting.

After visiting the painting school of Gerard Wagner in Dornach in 1975, he decided on a second course of study. Here he found a true artistic equivalent of Goethe's discoveries regarding "polarity" and "enhancement." Begun in 1976, the training with Wagner on the basis of Rudolf Steiner's sketch-motifs exceeded every expectation. Specific artistic questions were directly and fully entered into that had been as though left aside, indeed sidestepped altogether, in his previous art school studies. While still a student, Peter Stebbing had been asked by Gerard Wagner to teach in the School. At this time he translated the book *The Individuality of Colour* by Elisabeth Koch and Gerard Wagner.

Peter Stebbing later established a painting school at the Threefold Educational Foundation in Spring Valley, N.Y., teaching there from 1983–89.

Over the past thirty years he has given introductory courses in Goethe's color theory with experiments in a variety of centers in England, Germany, Switzerland, and the United States.

Since 1992, Peter Stebbing has been director of the Arteum Painting School in Dornach, Switzerland (www.arteum-malschule.de.vu). He has held a number of exhibitions of his work both in Europe and in America.

Some Examples of Paintings by Peter Stebbing

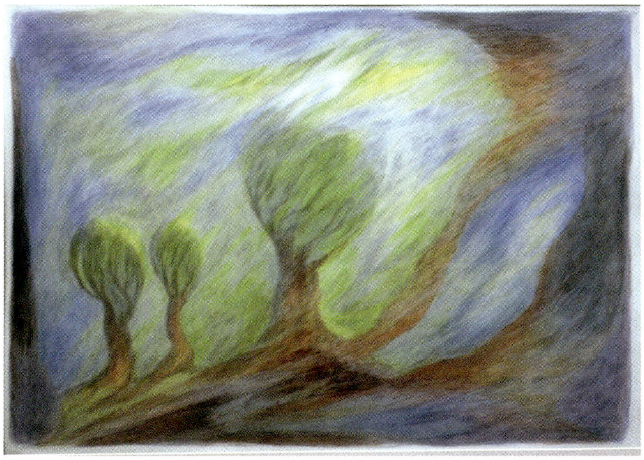

Trees by a Waterfall I. Watercolor. 54 x 76 cm. (1991)

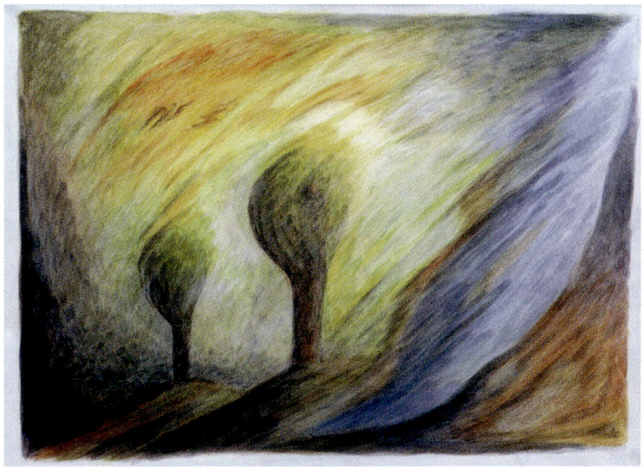

Trees by a Waterfall II. Plant colors. 53 x 73 cm. (1995)

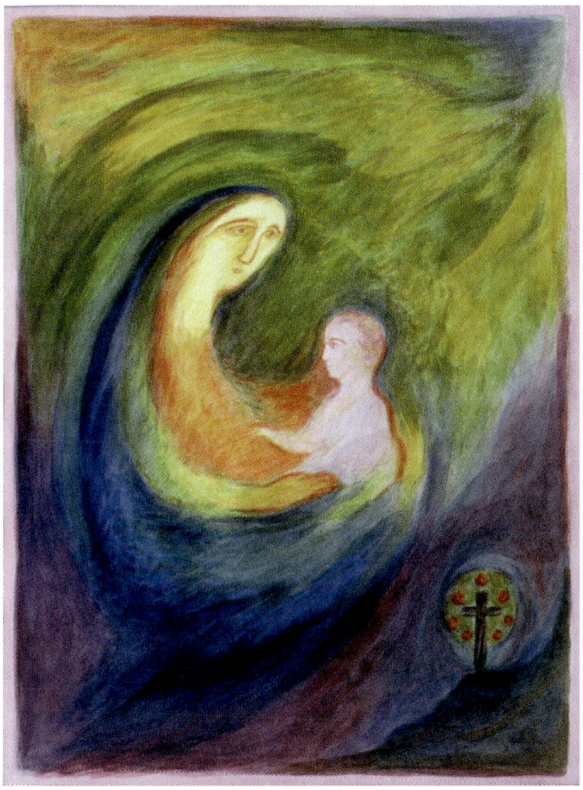

Madonna. Plant colors. 52 x 72 cm. (2003)

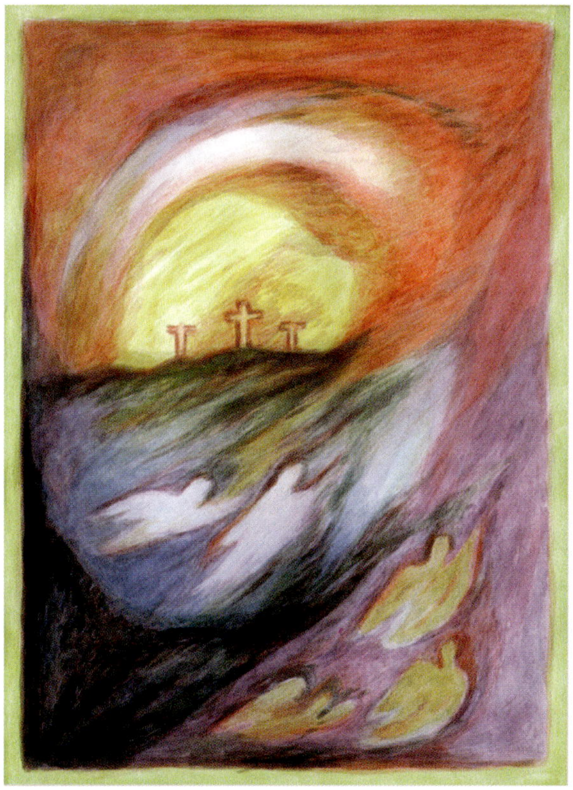

Easter. Plant colors. 53 x 73 cm. (1999)